Dyslexia and Effective Learning in Secondary and Tertiary Education

Dyslexia and Effective Learning in Secondary and Tertiary Education

Edited by

MORAG HUNTER-CARSCH
Lecturer in Education, University of Leicester

and

MARGARET HERRINGTON
Director, Study Support Centre, University of Nottingham

Consultant in Dyslexia
Professor Margaret Snowling
University of York

W
WHURR PUBLISHERS
LONDON AND PHILADELPHIA

First published 2001 by
Whurr Publishers Ltd
19b Compton Terrace, London N1 2UN, England
325 Chestnut Street, Philadelphia PA19106, USA

British Library Cataloguing in Publication Data

A catalogue record for this book is available from the British Library.

ISBN 1 86156 016 8

Printed and bound in the UK by Athenaeum Press Limited, Gateshead, Tyne & Wear.

Contents

Dedication

Morag Hunter-Carsch wishes to dedicate this book to the memory of two educational psychologists who shared a special interest in dyslexia; the late Nettie Brown, a principal educational psychologist, Pollok, Glasgow, and Surbjit Chahall, a trainee teacher at Leicester University.

Margaret Herrington wishes to dedicate this book to the memory of her parents, Edith and James Pey.

Acknowledgements

The editors would like to thank all the contributing writers; also Maureen Hardy, Ted Hartshorn, Fiona Hossack, Aubrey Nicholls and all the speakers and delegates at the 'Sharing Good Practice' conference which inspired the book; all who assisted with the production of the manuscript: Linda Basey, Carole Fitzpatrick, Chac in Lam, Sue Mailley, Judith Schofield; and illustrators Mike Finn and Clare Froggatt of Finn Designs, Nottingham and Paul Stevens; Whurr Publishers and their advisor, Professor Margaret Snowling.

Morag Hunter-Carsch wishes also to acknowledge, with appreciation, the support of Ken Fogelman, Dean of Education, Leicester University; Tom Whiteside, Director of the School of Education; Tim Bunn, Susan O'Brian, Helen Newton (contributing tutors) and the teachers undertaking continuing professional development courses on specific learning difficulties (e.g. dyslexia); all the dyslexic learners and their parents with whom helpful discussions have taken place; and, specially, her husband Henry Carsch.

Margaret Herrington wishes to thank the adult learners in the Leicestershire ABE service; the students with whom she has worked at Leicester and Nottingham universities; colleagues in the School of Continuing Education at Nottingham University; colleagues and friends in the Research and Practice in Adult Literacy Network (RAPAL), in particular, Roz Ivanic, Wendy Moss, Mary Hamilton, David Barton and Gaye Houghton; and, above all, Paul Herrington, Dominic, Kate, Damian, Nancy, her sister and brothers and her extended family.

Contributors

Doreen Chappell Basic Skills Co-ordinator, Leicester College of Adult Education, Leicester

Stella ni Ghallchoir Cottrell Director of Lifelong Learning, University of Luton; adult dyslexia consultant (HE)

Sheila Crossley Co-ordinator, Reading Language and Learning Support Services, Blackburn with Darwen Local Education Authority

Barbara Edgar Recently retired from Manchester Metropolitan University

Nata Goulandris Department of Human Communication Science, University College London

Margaret Herrington Director, Study Support Centre, University of Nottingham

Margaret Hughes Literacy Consultant, Coventry and Warwickshire

Morag Hunter-Carsch School of Education, University of Leicester

Cynthia Klein Teacher Trainer/Consultant, Language and Literacy Unit, South Bank University, London

John Landon Faculty of Education, University of Edinburgh

David McLoughlin Director of Adult Dyslexia and Skills Development Centre, 5 Tavistock Place, London WC1 9SN

Ellen Morgan Co-ordinator, Dyslexia Support Unit, City University

Jenny Murphy Educational Consultant, Learning Curve Associates, Farnham Common

James Palfreman-Kay Additional Learning Needs Advisor, Bournemouth University

Rosemary Sage School of Education, University of Leicester

Margaret Snowling Department of Psychology, University of York

Marion Walker Dyslexia Consultant, 14 Weston Close, Dorridge, Solihull, West Midlands

Dorota Zdzienski Dyslexia Consultant, London

Foreword

I was delighted to be invited to write the foreword to this important book. Both my own work with students with disabilities and/or specific learning difficulties in higher education locally, nationally and internationally, and my links with the schools sector through my role with the National Association of Special Education continue to make clear to me the continuing challenges faced by learners with dyslexia, their families and those who work to support them.

Within higher education, the increased attention given to this growing group of students which has been evident since the introduction of special initiative funding in 1993 led to the setting up of a national working party to carry out a thorough investigation. When its report was published in early 1999, it highlighted a number of major concerns: definitions and terminology, the importance of early identification, the accurate diagnosis of support needs, the procurement and provision of appropriate support, the raising of awareness amongst non-specialists, the availability of opportunities for continuing professional development for specialist staff, the affective aspects of dyslexia and the potential need for counselling and careers advice, and so on. I think that those who work in schools and the further education sectors will not find the list any different from that which they might compile themselves as a result of what they experience in their own daily lives as conscientious, caring professionals.

Let me take this commonality of experience a little further using a small illustration. The scene is the office of the Disabled Students Adviser in the University of Anytown. The telephone rings and then comes the following exchange:

> Hello, my name's X and I'm a tutor in the Department of -ology. I wonder if you can help me. I've got one of your students with me and . . .

This is the kind of conversational opening which will be very familiar to many colleagues working to support students with disabilities and specific learning difficulties in higher education. It will also have some familiarity for SENCOs in schools and learning support staff in further education. On the surface, it seems to be a fairly routine, innocuous comment - and yet it betrays a serious misunderstanding of what the true position ought to be. In reality, SENCOs, learning support or disability services do not 'own' students in the way in which the statement suggests. Certainly, in the case of higher education, students 'belong' to the academic departments and faculties responsible for the programmes they are studying. In replying to this kind of initial approach, perhaps what we should do is to point out that responsibilities are shared - in that sense only can they be described as 'our' students. The emphasis is on learning in an inclusive context with minimal attention drawn to differences.

It is the advocacy of an inclusive approach and for a social-educational model of dyslexia (as opposed to an individual-medical one) which underpins this useful collection of papers. There are other dimensions of 'inclusion' which are features of the book. The editors have tried to include contributions representing every significant aspect of policy and provision for dyslexic students in schools and in post-compulsory education. The background and expertise of the contributors ranges from university-based academics, interested in research on the aetiology and impact of dyslexia, to teachers working in schools, classrooms and local education authority support services trying to find immediate, effective solutions to everyday problems in the teaching, learning and assessment of their pupils. The papers from this group are most welcome since they indicate the high quality of what is happening both in some schools and in some local education authorities in terms of innovative strategies for continuing professional development. Perhaps it will encourage others to publicize and disseminate what they have achieved. The important contributions of parents and of the students themselves are given the recognition they deserve and which have sometimes been overlooked or undervalued.

The intended readership for this book is also 'inclusive' in the sense that the editors state clearly that reading it should develop the knowledge, skills and predispositions of everyone, not just those with a particular interest in dyslexia. After all, our professional skills should be varied and flexible enough to meet the wide range of learning needs we find in our classes in all sectors of education today. Sadly, the old adage that what is good classroom practice for those with additional needs is usually good for everyone seems to have lost some of its impact, although the ideas promoted by contributors to this book suggest that it should still carry weight. To return to the illustrative example used earlier, what is really at issue is striking the right balance between the contribution of specialists and the taking-on of our responsibilities as teachers.

All of our work is set within a context of rapid policy development at national level. Since the election of the Labour government in May 1997 several documents have appeared which are likely to have some influence on educational provision in the first few years of the new millennium and on how we work, no matter whether that is in schools implementing policies set out in 'Excellence for all Children' and 'Meeting the Challenge: A Programme for Action', in further education with 'Learning to Succeed: A New Framework for Post-16 Learning' or higher education and 'Higher Education for the Twenty-first Century' (the response to the report of the Dearing Committee). A major concern for all of these is to ensure that all individual learners have opportunities to receive education of the highest quality in an inclusive setting and to acquire, develop and enhance the knowledge, skills and interests which enable them to participate in and contribute fully to society.

It is against this background that the important contribution of the authors whose work is contained in this book has to be considered. For some, these papers might contain ideas and suggestions which lead to meeting successfully some current challenges. For others, they will prompt and stimulate further thoughts and critical evaluation of their professional practices. Many of us, in our work in schools, further education colleges and universities, have tried to encourage our learners to be informed and inquisitive. Morag Hunter-Carsch and Margaret Herrington, well-supported by their contributors, have tried to pursue this very same strategy with their readers and in this I wish them every success.

Alan Hurst (Professor)
Department of Education Studies
University of Central Lancashire, and
Chair – Skill: National Bureau for
Students with Disabilities 1996–1999.

Preface: Bridging the gap

Morag Hunter-Carsch

Purpose and readership

This book is for teachers in secondary schools, colleges and universities all of whom have amongst their students, some who may be described as 'dyslexic'. It is thus not only for literacy support specialists but for all teachers. It has grown out of cross-sector, multidisciplinary discussions and reflections on research and practice over many years. It brings together research findings and perspectives of professionals and students.

Its point of departure involves the following dual assumption:

- First, that students' learning may be enhanced when the teacher (a) engages their interest in the subject matter, (b) appreciates the individual students' learning strengths and preferences and (c) has awareness and understanding of their learning difficulties.
- Second, that this involves not only the teacher's willingness, skill and ability to assist students to navigate their areas of learning difficulty but also the readiness to assist them to transcend the impact of such difficulties.

The book aims to provide background information to assist in broadening and deepening teachers' relevant areas of appreciation, understanding and skill. It aims to illuminate the connections between diverse factors affecting the efficacy of dyslexic students' learning in the classroom or tutorial context. It sets out to consider matters of continuities and discontinuities across the sectors, attitudes and patterns of communication which may facilitate or impede the intended curricular content learning. The resultant anthology is designed to provide access for readers to selected research reports from diverse traditions, along with reflective discussions with experienced practitioners who share the will to identify and disseminate 'good practice'.

The rationale for selecting certain issues and questions to be addressed in the book

Evidence based on professional experience persuades that for optimal efficacy of the learning experience, dyslexic students require not only early identification and intervention but also the possibility of continuity in learning support. Questions arise, however, with regard to the most effective kinds of support for individual students in each sector:

- To what extent do teachers who are generalists, subject specialists or learning support specialists, share their professional knowledge about dyslexia and effective learning within an institution and across sectors?
- What is the nature and extent of the gap between education sectors' approaches to provision of learning support for dyslexic learners?
- How do dyslexic students experience learning and learning support in each context?

Are there, perhaps, other professionally related questions about 'gaps' to be bridged; for instance, possible gaps between publication of research discoveries, teachers' awareness of their findings and the impact of the findings on classroom practice; elements of theory and practice; the way teachers identify their students' 'learning gaps' and their knowledge about how to bridge these gaps. This book seeks to assist with the process of recognizing the existence of some such gaps and assisting with 'closing them' or 'building bridges' by contributing to the formulation of useful questions about effectiveness of learning, recognition of atypical as well as typical learning patterns, appropriateness of particular teacher responses and the value of different kinds of learning support in secondary and tertiary education.

Origins

The initial conceptualization of the plan for this volume can be traced to a 'meeting of minds' which took place at a multidisciplinary conference on 'Bridging the Gap' between secondary and tertiary education. It took place at Leicester University in 1995 and was one in a continuing series of conferences on literacy and learning. The series, 'Sharing Good Practice', is run jointly between the School of Education's Department of Continuing Professional Development and a group of professional associations. These include the local branches of the British Dyslexia Association (BDA), the UK Reading Association (UKRA) and the National Association for Special Education (NASEN).

It was as a result of Morag Hunter-Carsch's invitation, as conference director, to Margaret Herrington (a tertiary education specialist and member of the Research and Practice in Adult Literacy network) to become co-director of the programme for the 'Bridging the Gap' conference, that the impetus towards this publication began. It is the editors' hope that the work undertaken in writing and research in order to produce this book will disseminate the main messages communicated at the conference by speakers and delegates (who included school teachers, adult educators, tutors in higher education, parents, school governors, educational psychologists, speech and language therapists and medical practitioners), many of whom have contributed to this volume. Their discussions motivated us to attempt to provide a wider contextualization for the work between the secondary and tertiary professionals whose shared aim is to promote effective learning.

Contextualizing the development of this volume

In the past five years, developments in the field of specific learning difficulties have occurred within the wider context of substantial policy changes in education. There was an intensified national focus on literacy standards culminating in the national literacy strategy (McClelland 1997; DfEE 1998), including the 'National Year of Reading' (1998–1999) and the 'Read-on' campaign into the new millennium. This, as part of the larger vision of 'lifelong learning' (i.e. including 'learning beyond the classroom'; Bentley 1998), overlapped with a period of intensification of examination of 'schools' effectiveness' (mainstream and special education; e.g. Thomas 1992; Bowering-Carr and West-Burnham 1997) and of the increasing recognition of the need to engage in a closer examination of learning, the diversity of learning styles (e.g. Gardner 1995; Goleman 1996; Given and Reid 1999; Riding and Rayner 1998), 'meta-affectivity' (Hunter-Carsch 2001c) and of 'emotional literacy' (Sharp 2000).

With reference to dyslexia and the compulsory education sector (primary and secondary schooling), this has been a period of dramatic developments. In 1997, the Teacher Training Agency published in the standards for teacher training, the requirement that initial teacher training include identification of pupils with specific learning difficulties, e.g. dyslexia (TTA 1997). Also plans for the revision of the DfEE's (1994) Code of Practice on Identification and Assessment of Special Educational Needs are well underway with a target for finalization by 2001. In 1999, the OFSTED investigatory Report on Teaching Pupils with Specific Learning Difficulties in mainstream schools provided the findings of government inspection of a sample of schools, and the end of that year also saw the publication of the findings of the British Psychological Society (BPS) working party of the Division of Educational and Child Psychologists (DECP) in the generation of a new 'working definition of dyslexia'. It is as follows:

> Dyslexia is evident when accurate and fluent word reading and/or spelling develops very incompletely or with great difficulty. This focuses on literacy learning at the 'word level' and implies that the problem is severe and persistent despite appropriate learning opportunities. It provides the basis for a staged process of assessment through teaching. (BPS/DECP 1999, 8)

The impact of this new BPS definition of dyslexia on all education sectors remains to be seen.

The tertiary sector, too, has been subject to major policy changes in accessibility and quality and particularly in relation to the support of students with 'special needs' or 'disabilities'. The Further Education Funding Council has driven hard for enhanced access and quality for all students, and the Tomlinson Report, published in 1996, proposed a general, learner-centred 'inclusiveness' for the further education curriculum. These philosophical and funding developments have been encouraging for dyslexic learners.

In higher education, Quality Assurance Agency (QAA) inspections have fuelled the drive for general improvements in quality of teaching and of student support and guidance. In 1999, the QAA also issued quality criteria for the support of disabled students (Section 3 of the Code of Practice for the Assurance of Academic Quality and Standards in Higher Education) and all higher education institutions will be required to draw up plans for implementation. One of the core precepts refers to the staff development requirements of all higher education staff in relation to disability, and this will clearly help dyslexic students if implemented across the sector. In addition, the Higher Education Funding Council has financed a raft of initiatives (1993–2002) aimed at widening access and supporting disabled students, and the report of the National Working Party on Dyslexia (Singleton 1999b) has revealed some of the progress made by many universities in supporting dyslexic learners in higher education.

In adult education the 'lifelong learning' policy initiatives have sought to establish the significance of access to learning opportunities throughout life and that school failure should not mean learning failure for life. These bode well for those dyslexic learners who have found school uncongenial but who have retained their intellectual curiosity and drive.

Throughout this period there has also been a sustained and effective campaign by the BDA to promote wider understanding of the nature of dyslexia and the dyslexic learners' strengths as well as special educational needs (e.g. BDA's annual Handbooks; Salter and Smythe (1997) The International Book of Dyslexia; in 1999, the BDA's first international conference on dyslexia and multilingualism; the summer television season and the Dyslexia Friendly Schools campaign).

It might be suggested, therefore, that there is an increased awareness of the need for learning support for dyslexic students at all levels of education, yet there is still much to be done to bridge the gap between that awareness and the provision of access for all students to effective learning support within and across all education sectors. Some current policy initiatives do suggest a degree of recognition of the need to bridge sectoral gaps: the new Learning Skills Councils (2000) will make important links between school, further education and work; and, in relation to disability, there is a proposal for a new statutory duty to ensure that all school students who have statements of special need will have a needs assessment before moving on to further and higher education (keynote speech, Malcolm Wicks MP, Parliamentary Under Secretary of State, DfEE, Annual SKILL Conference, Milton Keynes, February 2000). However, there remains a relative absence of systematic research related to the monitoring of learning support practices in each sector and of the longer-term impact of changes in policy within and across the sectors. In short, the central messages the editors began to formulate in the wake of the 1995 conference remain pertinent and have now acquired a degree of urgency.

The title and organization of the book

The title of this book centres on 'dyslexia'. It does not, however, represent a single perspective. Rather, the contributors were encouraged to employ their particular modes of approach and terminology. For readers' convenience, chapters are organized into two main parts, relating respectively to secondary and tertiary education. However, since there are themes which run throughout the book, it is hoped that in readers will 'bridge the sectors'. At the same time it will also be evident that in the clustering under one sector of two kinds of educational provision, broadly termed 'higher' and 'further' education, there inheres a risk of obscuring some of the characteristics of each, which may differ in crucial aspects from the other. The aim is to maintain a broad sense of various developments between the phases of adolescence and of adulthood in relation to the diverse factors affecting educational success for dyslexic students in each context. The route through Part I might be regarded in that sense, as providing an introductory framework for reading Part II which extends and develops many of the same themes.

Each part begins with a key chapter relating to the particular education phase. The first part, introduced by Goulandris and Snowling (Chapter 1), sets the scene with the emphasis on longitudinal research investigating matters of identification, diagnosis, stability of definition connecting the primary into secondary phase and highlighting the persistence of dyslexic learning problems, in particular phonological difficulties. The second part begins with a short section exploring adult learning and related issues, including group support and 'empowerment' of dyslexic learners (Herrington, Chapter 8) as well as matters of diagnostic assesssment, counselling and training (McLoughlin, Chapter 9). It is followed by chapters which develop the various themes with regard to further education and to higher education. The themes and chapters are briefly described below.

Chapters in both parts are organized in a conversational pattern perhaps rather like a dialogue which, in successive chapters focuses in turn on mainly 'personal/individual' issues and then on more 'social/institutional-contextual' issues. They pursue specific questions and extend and develop different themes. For example, the research focus in the first chapter shifts from survey research and large-scale case studies, to report smaller scale investigations in Chapter 2 (Hunter-Carsch). These seek to illuminate through interviews with teachers and students, the nature of dyslexic students' learning needs and perspectives on what constitutes effective learning support in practice. The discourse then broadens to include an historical descriptive account of the development of a local education authority's policy for SpLDs, and its impact on practice in teacher training (Crossley, Chapter 3). Subsequently, the direction of the larger argument invites the reader to step sideways to view events from social, cultural and linguistic standpoints with Landon (Chapter 4) who addresses multilingual issues. The ground is thus well prepared for the next theme which involves consideration of communication effectiveness first in terms of the specific focus on linguistic (phonological and orthographic) aspects in English (Chapter 5, 'the spelling chapter' by Hughes and Hunter-Carsch). The theme then moves towards the more general and links with broader dimensions of cognition and semantic factors involved in language and communication in the two chapters which follow. In these, the crucial issues of how to improve thinking are addressed by Edgar in Chapter 6, and understanding further facets of communication by Sage in Chapter 7. Thus, incrementally and cumulatively the chapters seek to contribute to understanding the relationship of language, literacy, thinking and learning for dyslexic students.

In Part II the discussions of matters of diagnosis and the provision of different kinds of learning support are extended. Chappell and Walker (Chapter 10) illuminate teaching and learning from different perspectives in adult education. These contribute to the contextualizing of the subsequently reported case study approach discussed by Murphy (Chapter 11) and the further issues of staff development, social and interpersonal communication raised by Klein (Chapter 12).

The extension of the theme on diagnosis is carried on by Zdzienski (Chapter 13) whose work traverses both further and higher education. She argues strongly for equal opportunities for all students to have access to ICT-based profile assessment of learning preferences and strengths as well as identification of difficulties with language and study skills. The next chapter deals with the reflective case study approach and proceeds to address issues in the development of support in higher education (Herrington, Chapter 14) and is followed by a personal perspective through discussions about spelling (Herrington, Chapter 15) before returning to issues concerning ICT and modes of technical support discussed in Palfreman-Kay (Chapter 16), who contributes research findings from his work with adults and discusses implications for improving institutional provision. This issue and, in particular, the quality of the learning environment, is discussed by Cottrell in Chapter 17, and a further consideration of matters of staff training and professional support is provided by Morgan in Chapter 18. The final words in the last chapter reflect a student-centred approach to learning support.

Emergent key issues

From this anthology there emerge certain issues, distinguished not only in terms of the frequency of their mention by different contributors but also in terms of the urgency to be communicated more widely to the profession. The main message is clearly that there is a need to bridge the secondary–tertiary gap by the provision of access to effective learning support for dyslexic students. The salience of other major themes is perhaps more difficult to evaluate. For example, it is not necessarily the case that the length of chapters on spelling or on ICT should be taken to imply that these are priorities in the view of the contributing editors. There are relatively more diffuse messages which suggest a pervasive need for concern. These include the need for emotional support as a crucial part of facilitating learning and of the importance of recognizing the need for understanding cognitive processing complexities which have a vital impact on thinking and organizational competence.

Thus, in conclusion, the following list of emergent key issues is offered with the caution that the sequence should not be considered as suggesting a hierarchy:

* The dyslexic learners' phonological problems underlying persistent spelling problems require learning support regardless of the phase and context. (See chapters by Goulandris and Snowling; Hughes and Hunter-Carsch.)
- The impact of linguistic experience, cultural contexts and the importance the society attaches to competence in literacy should be taken into account in addressing matters of diagnostic assessment and learning support. (See chapters by Landon; Sage.)
- The wider areas of dyslexic students' patterns of thinking and organizational skills call for skilled learning support. (See chapters by Edgar; Chappell and Walker; Murphy; Herrington.) These also include, for example, mathematical thinking (see also Henderson 2001) and impediments related to visual stress (see Mailley 2001). Furthermore, some

seeming 'memory difficulties' in the learning process may be affected by a range of environmental and health factors as well as teaching and learning strategies.

- The overall picture could reasonably be considered as one of a need for improving the communication skills not only of the dyslexic learners but also of their teachers and tutors. (See chapters by Landon; Sage; Palfreman-Kay; Morgan.) Further sources include: 'Communicating Quality' Smith 1991; Stackhouse and Wells 1997; Snowling 2000). The contributions of speech and language therapists, physiotherapists and occupational therapists are too often seen as 'a luxury'. Perhaps we should more explicitly acknowledge the multidisciplinary facets contributing to the field and the contribution made by therapists to the 'effective communication' dimension in learning support.
- It should be recognized that the identification and acknowledgement of the individuals' preferences in learning can be facilitated or hampered by the 'climate' of the institution (re identification, see chapters by Herrington; McLoughlin; Zdzienski). For further examples of the impact of social and environmental influences see chapters by Hunter-Carsch; Crossley; Murphy; Klein; Cottrell).
- It is not only the provision of appropriate equipment that is required but also of the necessary training in its use. (See chapter by Palfreman-Kay.) Further sources include Singleton (1994), Crombie and Crombie (2001).
- Heightened awareness is required of the ways in which learners' attitudes and approaches to learning support are affected by their prior experience and expectations about transition between phases. (See chapters by Goulandris and Snowling; Hunter-Carsch.)
- The impact of transition from 'childhood' into 'adolescent learning' and then to 'adult learning', and of the different learning contexts on the needs for individuals to 'unlearn' previously learned methods in the event of discontinuities, are matters for sensitive consideration. (See chapters by Hunter-Carsch; Herrington; Chappell and Walker; Murphy; Cottrell; Morgan.)
- Dyslexic learners' attitudes towards their difficulties and the impact of these on motivation should surely be a source of a constant focus in the consideration of promoting an effective learning experience. (Examples may be found throughout the book.)
- It should be recognized that there may be co-existing 'specific' difficulties in any one individual. Their co-occurence contributes to the complexity of both the diagnostic and the teaching challenge. The assumption that there are clearly 'primary' learning problems and that 'secondary' or resultant difficulties can be disentangled, is challenged by evidence from practitioners. It can be a complex matter to trace and track the direction

of cause and effect, especially over time. This may become evident in reading the different emphases which contributors have chosen and which, cumulatively, endorse the importance of recognizing that dyslexia is one amongst several 'specific learning difficulties'.

Finally, it should also be noted that both editors do not, of course, reject the term 'dyslexia'; they value 'specific learning difficulties' as a collective term precisely because it facilitates the study of these complexities and encourages the study of the co-existing learning difficulties which affect all levels of 'general intelligence'. It is the internal consistencies and inconsistencies of learning profiles which, in their view, constitute a basis for identifying and supporting the range of individuals who fall broadly into the cluster currently described as having 'specific learning difficulties'. For further discussion of theoretical models in this field see BPS (1999); Miles T (2001); Pumfrey (2001); Herrington and Hunter-Carsch (2001) and Hunter-Carsch (2001c).

Part I
Learning in the secondary school context

CHAPTER 1

Dyslexia in adolescence: a five-year follow-up study

NATA GOULANDRIS AND MARGARET SNOWLING

Introduction

Educators and other professionals have become increasingly aware in recent years of the problems which may face the child with specific learning difficulties (SpLD), such as under-achievement, school failure and low self-esteem. Consequently, it has been generally accepted that intervention to prevent the reading problems that underlie this downward spiral of events is crucial. Yet, surprisingly there is still a lack of knowledge about the success of remediation and our understanding of the residual problems experienced by dyslexic individuals remains limited. Are we giving specialized help early enough? At what age is it appropriate to identify a child? The danger of labelling a child too early has been well documented, but allowing a child to struggle without adequate provision beyond a certain age has serious repercussions and potentially irreversible consequences. Another crucial question is whether specialist remedial instruction can provide adequate compensatory strategies to enable children with SpLD to attain an academic level commensurate with their ability and interests.

For most individuals dyslexia persists into adulthood (Bruck 1990, 1993; Pennington et al. 1990). Difficulties with phonemic processing and phonemic awareness are present even in highly educated students with a history of dyslexia (Felton et al. 1990; Pennington et al. 1990). Adults with childhood diagnoses of dyslexia have impaired word recognition processing, often performing at the level of reading-age matched control subjects and relying considerably on correspondence rules and context for word recognition (Bruck 1990). Phonemic processing tasks, such as phoneme deletion, phoneme fluency, spoonerisms and memory span for non-words pose greater difficulty for dyslexic undergraduates than for undergraduate control subjects (Snowling et al. 1997). Hanley (1997) reported that poor performance on picture naming and phonological awareness predicts the severity of a dyslexic undergraduate's reading and spelling impairment.

Longitudinal studies are particularly informative because they enable researchers to investigate the developmental changes in cognitive and literacy skills which occur over time and provide information about long-term outcome. Labuda and Defries (1989) followed the evolution of children with learning disabilities for five years. These authors reported that reading retardation increased from one-and-a-half to 3–4 years in the intervening period. The children's progress was related to their full-scale IQ and to the severity of the initial deficit.

Stanovich et al. (1989) compared poor readers with normally developing readers who were initially matched for reading age. The poor readers made progress of one-and-a-half grades, whereas the good readers improved 2.8 grades over a two-year period. However, as no differences were found between the groups on tasks of receptive vocabulary, memory, articulation, rhyming abilities and reading strategies, Stanovich et al. (1989) argued that the dyslexics were delayed in their development.

Manis et al. (1993) found that 21 dyslexics, whose progress they monitored over two years, improved by 2.2 grades in word identification but made little progress on a task requiring non-word reading of stimuli with no orthographic neighbours, phoneme deletion and the spelling of irregular words. These authors concluded that dyslexics have primary phonological processing deficits and secondary deficits in orthographic processing. They also suggested that performance on phonological tasks remained stable, whereas orthographic tasks were less consistent over time. According to this interpretation, children with poor phonological skills at the outset would continue to have persistent difficulties with tasks requiring phonological processing, whereas their ability to encode orthographic information may be less predictable.

Snowling et al. (1996) also tracked the progress of a group of dyslexic children, initially over a two-year period. At the outset of the study the dyslexic children performed worse than their peers on a battery of phonological and literacy tasks despite the fact that their mental ability and visual processing skills were equivalent to those of the control subjects. The dyslexic children were also compared with reading-level control subjects, children who had the same reading age but were younger than those with dyslexia. The dyslexic children did not differ from the reading-level control subjects on any of the cognitive or literacy tasks in the test battery. Two years later, the control subjects, who had originally been matched for reading age, made considerably more than two years' progress and a new set of reading-level control subjects had to be selected. Once again, the dyslexic children performed significantly worse on virtually all the tasks when compared with age-matched control subjects. This time, however, they were also worse than the younger reading-age matched subjects on non-word reading, non-word repetition, and they made fewer non-phonetic spelling errors. The authors argued that the phonological difficulties of the dyslexic children become more pronounced and apparent as individuals grow up and compromise the acquisition of literacy skills.

To summarize, the results of Manis et al. (1993) are compatible with a phonological deficit hypothesis proposing that phonological processing deficits are the primary cause of reading difficulties. Snowling et al. (1996) also conclude that phonological deficits continue to hinder the smooth acquisition of reading and spelling skills, and contribute to dyslexics' increasing reading and spelling retardation. In contrast, the findings of Stanovich et al. (1989) support a developmental lag hypothesis. The longitudinal study reported here will examine these two alternative positions.

Another important issue for practitioners and researchers is stability of classification. Are individuals who are diagnosed as dyslexic consistently classified as dyslexic over time? Various studies have suggested that stability over time is erratic (Jorm et al. 1986; Share and Silva 1986). Wright et al. (1996) compared the reading and spelling development of 17 dyslexics with that of 354 non-dyslexic children aged 8–13 years over a five-year period. These authors subdivided the dyslexic subjects according to the stability of their reading and spelling problems. Only six of the children originally diagnosed as dyslexic were still classified as dyslexic five years later, according to a discrepancy definition using a regression equation which predicted Schonell Reading Age based on chronological age and verbal IQ. Another 15 children who were not previously classified as dyslexic were identified at this point.

This chapter reports the results of a longitudinal study of 18 children followed over a five-and-half-year period. The progress of 18 of the original 20 individuals was monitored approximately five-and-a-half years after their initial assessment (Snowling et al. 1996). Research questions focused on outcome: how had this group of dyslexics fared at school and were their initial cognitive and literacy difficulties still evident? For example, was it possible to distinguish between those children who had overcome their reading and spelling difficulties and attained reasonable success on school examinations and those who were still struggling to acquire functional literacy skills? Were there any individuals who could no longer be considered 'dyslexic'? Finally, what changes had occurred in their cognitive and literacy profiles over the five-year interval?

The progress of dyslexic children over time

The original dyslexic sample was referred by teachers, speech therapists, general practitioners and the British Dyslexia Association. All the participants had verbal and performance intelligence quotients of 85 or above and were monolingual English speakers. Participants had normal vision and hearing and attended school regularly. Children with severe language impairment, neurological or emotional disorders were excluded from the study. At each assessment the dyslexic children were compared with both age- and reading age-matched control subjects.

The average age of the dyslexic children at the outset of the study (T1) was 9;8 (years;months). At the second assessment (T2) their mean age was 12;1. The dyslexic children's reading was below expectation with a mean deficit of 2 years 4 months at the commencement of the study; 3 years 3 months after two years, and 3 years 10 months when assessed after five years. However, spelling was more severely affected. Five years after initial assessment the mean spelling deficit for the dyslexic children was 5 years 3 months.

At the time of the third assessment, the mean age of the dyslexic children was 15;10 (SD 1; 4), mean reading age was 12;0 and mean spelling age was 10;5. The average difference between chronological age and reading age (reading age discrepancy) was 3 years 10 months, whereas the average difference between chronological age and spelling age was 5 years 4 months. There was no significant difference in age between the dyslexic children and the age-matched control subjects nor any significant difference between the reading ages of the dyslexic children and reading age-matched control subjects.

The dyslexic children received a variety of specialist educational provision. Four of 18 children had attended or were attending specialist schools which provided either full-time or part-time remedial tuition. The others received specialist teaching at school or arranged by their parents at home. Only one child in the group did not receive specialist tuition in the interval between T1 and T2. This child actually regressed during that two-year interval and made only marginal progress over the five-year period.

Stability of classification

Stability of classification was evident in this sample when a two-year discrepancy criterion was adopted for either reading or spelling. In line with current thinking, IQ was not taken into account when making judgements (Stanovich 1991; Siegel 1992), although all the children in the sample had average or above-average IQs. At T3 only two of the 17 children were not at least two years behind in reading. Of these two, one highly intelligent young man had a reading age 21 months below his chronological age and would have been identified as dyslexic using a regression equation based on IQ and age. The other child was 4 years, 3 months behind in spelling and consequently was categorized as 'dyslexic' despite his normal reading skills. Two of the 17 children were not delayed by two years in spelling. The highly intelligent young man mentioned above fell into this category, as did another girl whose reading backwardness identified her as dyslexic according to our criteria.

In conclusion, of the 17 dyslexic children followed over a five-year period, only one child could be considered no longer dyslexic using a strict two-year discrepancy criterion, although this child remained highly impaired in reading, despite his high IQ. It is highly unlikely that any practising psychologist would not consider this child as dyslexic. All the other children were still sufficiently retarded in reading and/or spelling to justify a classification of 'dyslexia'. Thus our sample, selected by comparing age with current reading and spelling ages, showed much higher stability than many others reported in the literature, despite the fact that by T3 all the children were receiving specialist remedial instruction.

Calculations of improvement ratios, in which a normally developing child is expected to gain one year's reading age over 12 months, showed that the dyslexic children achieved approximately two-thirds of the expected rate of progress for reading during the first two years and almost four-fifths of the expected rate of progress during the ensuing three years. Spelling, however, progressed at only half the expected rate over both periods. Thus, although the dyslexic children were gradually falling behind their peers in reading, the rate of decline was substantially less marked than for spelling.

The children were assigned to two equal groups according to their rate of reading over the two time periods. At T3, six of the nine children who had previously made the most progress (as measured by a test of single-word reading) shifted to the group making the least progress over the second interval, whereas seven of the nine who had made little progress over the first two years were assigned to the group which showed most improvement at T3. Three others remained in the least-improved group. Of these three, the child who had received the least remedial tuition over the five years remained the most severely impaired of all the dyslexic chldren. In general, the development of literacy skills in these children was marked by stops and starts rather than evenly paced and predictable progress. Correlations between progress made during the intervals between the first and second assessments confirmed this conclusion. No significant correlations emerged between reading and spelling progress at assessments two and three and the first assessment.

Unfortunately, insufficient information was available about the quality and amount of teaching received by the children to take this critical factor into account. However, the unstable pattern described above suggests that the stop and start pattern typified the progress of most of the children's progress over the five years, although children receiving little teaching were likely to have more severe residual difficulties in adolescence.

Despite remediation (in some cases very intensive specialist instruction) and the erratic progress described above, the initial reading age of the dyslexic children was a very good indicator of eventual reading and spelling attainment. Reading age at T1 correlated significantly with both reading and spelling age at T2 and T3. Spelling age at T1 predicted reading age at T1 and spelling age at T2 and T3. Reading age at T3 correlated significantly with reading and spelling at the previous assessments.

Dyslexic children's impairments five years on

Notwithstanding the slow progress of the dyslexic children in the present study over time, it was important to assess their performance, five years after the initial assessment, relative to their peers. The following standardized tests were administered at T3:

- The Block Design of the Wechsler Intelligence Scale for Children—Revised (Wechsler 1992) was administered as a measure of non-verbal IQ.
- The subtests of the Wechsler Objective Reading Dimensions (WORD) (Wechsler 1993) were administered to provide measures of single-word recognition, spelling and reading comprehension.
- The British Picture Vocabulary Scale (Dunn et al. 1982) was used to assess receptive vocabulary.

The following battery of experimental measures was also given: non-word repetition; spoonerisms; picture naming; non-word reading; non-word spelling; and a test of homophone spelling in which frequency of occurrence and regularity were manipulated.

When compared with chronological age-matched control subjects, the dyslexic children did not differ significantly on measures of verbal and non-verbal ability, when requested to repeat non-words or a sentence, or to name objects presented as pictures. However, as expected, the dyslexic children were still worse than their peers on tests of single-word reading and spelling. In addition, they proved significantly worse than reading level-matched control subjects at spelling high-frequency irregular words. This suggests that the dyslexic children found it much more difficult to recall and retrieve correct spellings of words which required precise orthographic information. Interestingly, despite their problems with basic reading skills, the reading comprehension of the dyslexic children was normal. Arguably, the most significant residual impairments of the dyslexic children were in non-word reading, non-word spelling and spoonerisms. The most pervasive and severe deficit was an inability to apply grapheme–phoneme correspondence rules to decode unfamiliar words.

A test of homophone spelling, administered to assess orthographic ability, indicated that the dyslexic children's performance on regular high-frequency, regular low-frequency and irregular low-frequency homophones was comparable to that of reading level-matched control subjects. However, the dyslexic children performed significantly worse on irregular high-frequency words, suggesting that they had difficulties establishing correct orthographic representations of unpredictable spellings compared with the younger control subjects.

Subgroup comparisons

Although, as a group, the dyslexic children were falling behind their peers each year, there were some individuals who were making substantially better progress than others within the group. To contrast the comparatively more successful dyslexic children with those with more persistent difficulties, the group of dyslexic children was subdivided into two subgroups, according to the severity of reading deficit at T3. Significant differences emerged between the two subgroups on several experimental measures (Table 1.1).

Table 1.1. Comparative performance (mean (SD)) of dyslexic average readers and dyslexic poor readers (one SD below mean on the WORD reading test)

Measure	Dyslexic (average) readers	Dyslexic poor readers	p
Spoonerisms	16.58 (3.75)	12.33 (4.18)	*
Picture naming	19.08 (3.94)	22.83 (2.32)	*
Word spelling	82.92 (9.34)	65.33 (6.59)	***
Non-word spelling	13.67 (2.06)	10.67 (3.88)	**
Author recognition	0.39 (0.17)	0.18 (0.21)	*
Title recognition	0.41 (0.08)	0.17 (0.09)	*
Word span	4.35 (0.41)	3.67 (0.63)	*
Homophones, regular high-frequency	13.17 (2.25)	10.17 (1.33)	*
Homophones, irregular low-frequency	4.50 (2.99)	1.83 (1.72)	*

* p = < .05
** p = < .01
*** p = < .001

The subgroup of dyslexic children whose reading scores fell in the average range (≥85 centile on the WORD reading accuracy test) performed significantly better on spoonerisms, spelling, non-word spelling, regular high-frequency homophones and irregular low-frequency homophones. These children were marginally, but not significantly, better on non-word repetition, although the below-average subgroup gained a higher score for picture naming. Thus, better reading scores are associated with higher levels of phonological and, to a lesser extent, orthographic processing ability. The more severe and pervasive the phonological deficits at the outset, the less likely individuals are to acquire age-appropriate literacy skills.

Conclusions

The answers to some of the initial research questions are clearly present in the findings. As a whole, the group of dyslexic childen showed impaired literacy-based skills when compared with children of their own age, despite the fact that most of them received specialist instruction in the intervening period. Moreover, phonological processing deficits (demonstrated by poor non-word reading) persisted throughout the five-year period. Not one of the children had truly overcome their problems or been able to 'catch up' with their peers, despite a positive attitude and their apparent self-assurance.

When compared with reading age-matched control subjects, the dyslexic children showed deficits only at the level of non-word reading and in spelling high-frequency, irregular homophones, skills which draw upon specific orthographic knowledge. These pervasive deficits demonstrate the continuation of severe phonological deficits and an associated depletion of orthographic knowledge. It is interesting to speculate whether the orthographic deficits seen here result simply from earlier difficulties when learning sound–letter mappings which prevented these children from establishing well-specified orthographic specifications of high-frequency words (Brown and Watson 1991) or whether orthographic and phonological abilities are separate and dissociable skills in the developing child (Stanovich and West 1989).

When compared with age-matched control subjects, the dyslexic children – although well-matched on mental ability – were inferior on most of the phonological tasks examined. Considering that many of the dyslexic children studied at T3 were school-leavers, their levels of literacy were woefully in arrears. Contrasting the dyslexic children with much younger reading level-matched control subjects is important when gauging the qualitative nature of their literacy impairments, but care is needed not to underestimate the extent of their difficulties relative to their age. They will, after all, continuously be assessed in relation to their peers and will require educational and emotional support to reach their full potential.

Finally, the poor progress of the dyslexic children in this study (despite the extensive specialist educational input some of them received) should not be regarded as an excuse for not providing adequate specialist tuition. On the contrary, the child who did not receive specialist tuition in the T1–T2 interval was the most handicapped of all the participants in this study. When specialist tuition was provided he began to progress, although the results remained disappointing, and he continued to make poor progress throughout the five years of the study. Although the present study cannot provide any answers about the efficacy and long-term results of remediation, the severe and persistent difficulties seen in this group of dyslexic children indicate clearly that individuals with severe developmental dyslexia require extensive and prolonged educational and moral support.

Acknowledgements

The research report reported in this chapter was supported by a grant from the Wellcome Trust ($436/02680/01). The authors would like to thank St Matthews School, London, and all the children who took part in the study. They would also like to thank Ian Walker for his contribution to the study.

CHAPTER 2

Learning support in the secondary school: needs analysis and provision for dyslexic students

MORAG HUNTER-CARSCH

Introduction

This chapter explores current policy and practices relating to learning support for students with specific learning difficulties (SpLD) e.g. dyslexia, as perceived by experienced teachers and special educational needs co-ordinators (SENCOs) in secondary schools in the English midlands. The following questions are addressed:

- What are the current policies, practices and priorities?
- What is involved in effective learning support?
- What are the priorities for training classroom assistants?
- What are the teachers' needs?
- What are the implications for improving good practice?

A section on the role of classroom assistants and priorities in their training, with reference to supporting the learning of dyslexic students, has been integrated into this chapter. This section was written by Helen Newton, a pioneer in the provision of such training courses and an associate tutor at Leicester University's School of Education. The views expressed in other sections of the chapter are those of the author and three experienced SENCOs, all of whom draw on the voices of their students and teacher colleagues. Among their messages is highlighted the need to provide training for classroom assistants as well as specialist SpLD teachers and, vitally, the need for teachers to listen to their dyslexic students' requests. These messages are derived from a 'needs analysis', involving a series of interviews and reflective discussions, and they reveal the importance of:

- Recognizing the strengths of peer tutoring with trained tutors.
- Involving department heads and all staff in the process of creating and sustaining a positive supportive environment.
- Effective communication with parents as partners.
- Establishing openness with the wider community, characterized by a positive attitude towards life-long learning.

What are the current policies, practices and priorities?

The realities for secondary school teachers in England and Wales are tough. Teachers are required to cope with the tide of changes in examinations in the wake of the introduction of the National Curriculum as well as the Code of Practice for Identification and Assessment of Students with Special Educational Needs (DfEE 1994, 2000a). Despite enormous goodwill - and often heroic efforts - in the face of substantial management changes, severely limited and diminishing financial resources, and the dramatically increasing 'knowledge explosion', the effects of stress on teachers are evident in their cry, 'We simply don't have time to read any more and can't afford to attend courses that are not provided as a part of daily work!'

Teachers' interest in dyslexia may have been aroused by a succession of successful media campaigns and the tireless work of local Dyslexia Association members across the UK. However, there is a fairly sizeable gap between policy and the provision of the essential professional knowledge and skills that are components of effective learning support in every classroom and of effective home-school liaison. This is especially true in multilingual home contexts (see Chapter 4) (Cooke 1998; Hunter-Carsch 1998; Hart and Travers 1999; MacKay 1999; Warwick 1999; Cortazzi and Hunter-Carsch 2000). An additional issue of concern is the increasing gap in multidisciplinary communication of research findings in ways which facilitate their direct effect on the classroom. In short, bridging 'the knowledge and skills gap' may require more than reliance on teachers' sense of obligation to read literature and attend courses. It may require provision, including training, from within existing school management structures and has resource implications for wider access to specialist support. Preliminary questions include:

- Exactly what are the special educational needs of secondary school students with SpLD?
- How might these needs be met most effectively (and most cost effectively)?

In order to answer these questions, or at least to illuminate the relevant issues, a sample of experienced SENCOs (studying towards their MA degrees in Professional Studies in Education at the University of Leicester School of

Education) were interviewed. Their views have been related to the findings of other small-scale investigations and to professional experience and knowledge acquired by the author through working with substantial numbers of teachers in initial and specialist training.

Discussion with colleagues who worked with teachers of different curriculum subject areas, and training classroom assistants, has helped to contextualize issues that relate to the provision of learning support for students with SpLD within a wider framework of support for all students with special literacy and learning needs. These needs may or may not be identified as requiring a Statement of Special Educational Needs (i.e. those with SpLD within the 'Warnock 17%' as well as 'the 2% with SEN statements' (DES 1978)).

What is involved in effective learning support?

What do the students say?

Students' views are unambiguous about the priority for teachers to 'get the feelings right'. The value of positive attitudes and of peer support is evident in Ian's self-report that follows. These values also emerge as significant in the views reported later in this chapter.

Ian was identified as a dyslexic learner during his secondary schooling. Looking back on his school experience, Ian's comments indicate his keen awareness of the importance of – in his words – 'Doing something to help in the classroom'.

> What really worked was when I was allowed to work with my pal and he wrote down what we had to do and he read it for me. I knew the answers but I couldn't keep up with the writing and reading. I could help him too and we made a good team . . . It was the science teacher who let us do that. He was fine. It was OK in PE too. But once I hit the teacher on his head with the ball and I was scared what would happen. And he was great! He said 'Good shot Ian, I couldn't have done it better myself!'

Ian's appreciation of the help of a scribe is evident. Ian's mother, reflecting on his primary school experience, said:

> I knew there was something wrong but no-one would listen to me.

Ian's self-report reflects the tenacity of many dyslexic youngsters. He went on to run the London Marathon and to become a scout leader. Ian weathered the storms of losing one job after another as he was limited in his skills to write and read messages quickly, but he could manage jobs in which he was allowed to have 'a helper', as with his science notes in school:

I could cope in the pub as a barman, as long as the man in charge let my mate help with the messages. But I lost that job when the management changed. So I don't have a job at present.

Getting the whole school environment right

The first need is to ensure the whole school environment reflects a sense of supportiveness for learning. Communicating this requires the right feelings to be shared by all involved in learning and teaching across the whole curriculum. It is not simply a matter of establishing a non-judgemental or even a neutral attitude to special educational needs (SENs), but of having and sharing a positive attitude to the full range of individual differences, including understanding able or gifted students. Getting the conditions right for dyslexic students to achieve effective learning is thus a prerequisite for initiating the learning interactions that are required if the teaching methods outlined in the literature are to come alive.

In practice, teachers may find that once the conditions are right, students themselves are remarkably inventive and, once freed to consider the question of how best they can be assisted, they often have effective solutions. The whole school environment is such an important aspect that without the relevant quality of communication, the work of specialist teachers may be vitiated and individual teachers' positive impact can be so diminished as to be undermined. The resultant loss is all the greater for teachers' professional self-esteem as well as for their dyslexic students' progress.

Special educational needs support in the classroom

Under ideal circumstances it would be the specialist trained SpLD teacher (who may or may not also be the SENCO) who directly provides classroom learning support and/or is responsible for liaison with classroom assistants about the nature and quality of support for students with SpLD. In practice, the classroom assistant is the most immediate source of support in many classrooms. This situation arises because of a lack of trained specialist teachers or because of limited SENs budgets, but may also relate to the assumption that is discussed in the following section by Helen Newton.

What are the priorities for training classroom assistants?

Training SENs classroom assistants: reflections

Helen Newton

There is an assumption in SENs education that once a pupil receives support from another adult his needs will be met (Thomas 1992). SENs classroom assistants (otherwise known as 'learning support assistants' or 'specialist teaching assistants') and SENs ancillaries are a form of support that is increasingly being allocated to children with learning difficulties. This support may be specified on a pupil's Statement or constitutes the result of a management decision to deploy classroom assistants in this way. It may be seen as a means of meeting the needs of pupils identified as having SENs in accordance with the requirements of the Code of Practice (DfEE 1994). Many pupils with SpLD will receive support from classroom assistants (Ainscow 1998).

Increasingly, concern has been voiced about the lack of training of these classroom assistants. A child who has specific difficulty with aspects of reading or writing may not be given the support of a trained, but of an 'untrained' person. Many classroom assistants are excellent. They have 'an intuitive understanding of pupil needs'. But the fact remains that they do not have qualified teacher status.

One solution has been to promote training for classroom assistants (DfEE 1997), the premise being that if classroom assistants are trained their support will be more effective. The University of Leicester provides training for classroom assistants to Foundation and Certificate levels. The DfEE has supported TTA training in higher education institutions. There are also many vocational courses. However, training may not be the answer unless careful consideration is given to the type of training that is provided, its content, format, effectiveness and location.

Training for classroom assistants: what should it entail?

For pupils with SpLD to receive appropriate support there is obviously a need for the classroom assistants to have some understanding of and empathy with the difficulties the pupils are experiencing. They also need to be aware of strategies and methods of alternative recording that pupils may need to use. Classroom assistants need a repertoire of suggestions and strategies that they can employ to support pupils' learning. They need the skills to relate to pupils and to teachers, and to make suggestions, give feedback and to contribute to target setting for individuals. These skills are all really important and many classroom assistants are very able and willing to develop them; and to further their own study and attend training sessions to do so.

Job specifications and role descriptions are also important, as is some knowledge of lesson content and planning. These areas are important for in-school training (Balshaw 1991). Some classroom assistants find liaising with class teachers difficult, possibly because their roles are not clearly defined or because some teachers may feel threatened by classroom assistants who may know more about pupils' difficulties than they do. This can be overcome by role specification and by liaison. Classroom assistants are often familiar with policies and plans because they have photocopied them for teachers!

Thus, important areas for training could be said to be knowledge of the nature of SpLD, strategies that pupils might need, and effective liaison and communication skills. Another skills area - often overlooked yet arguably the most crucial - is that of the training which enables assistants to promote the development of independent, skilled learners who are capable and confident (see Chapters 6 and 7).

By employing classroom assistants to meet learning needs of pupils with SpLD there is a danger that they will meet some needs - the academic ones - but that they will possibly unintentionally create others - the affective ones. Pupils may actually acquire 'learned helplessness' and dependency through the support that they receive.

There are many difficulties inherent in the support model; having someone there to support them may mean that pupils begin to rely on that support (Moyles 1997), they do not listen to the teacher as they trust that someone will explain what was said to them later, they do not relate much to other pupils and, perhaps more worrying, they do not attribute the success that they achieve to themselves (e.g. 'I only did it because Mrs M helped me'.). These difficulties can be exacerbated by the 'feel good factor' - the subject teacher teaches the lesson and delivers the curriculum while the classroom assistant is very busy helping pupils and everyone gets their work done. The teacher feels satisfied and the classroom assistant feels usefully employed, but the pupils may have learned, not necessarily the content of the lesson but that they cannot do without 'Mrs M'. The pupils' access to the curriculum has been through an intermediary - take away the intermediary and they cannot cope. Teachers may also become dependent and their ability to prepare fully for a mixed ability group may not be fully realized.

Priorities and the way forward in training classroom assistants

As part of the training of classroom assistant to provide effective support, learning about the affective areas of learning: independence, self-esteem, attribution of success and learned helplessness, is as important as learning strategies for alternative recording or for supporting spelling. The success criterion for any support must be the learning that the supported pupil achieves. This is not always optimal when the pupils with SpLD have an adult to support them, particularly when that adult is in close proximity. Teachers and classroom assistants both need to consider, as part of their liaison, other forms of organization in the classroom, that meet pupils' learning needs, including their need for independence. Classroom assistants could work with other pupils while teachers give learning support. They may need to step back, observe and advise rather than sit alongside pupils. They could be used to train other pupils to support pupils with SpLD. This is often the most preferable solution for children with SpLD who do not want to be singled out as needing help but who do recognize that they need it in order to access learning.

In conclusion, in-service education for classroom assistants should be concerned with the development of classroom skills and strategies for inclusive education, where adults in the classroom work as a team to meet the needs of all pupils. If training is delivered with a selective emphasis on programmed learning or 'small steps approaches' then support can lead to segregation and dependency within the classroom.

We now return to consideration of other kinds of support which can be provided via the role of the SENCO, Individual Education Plans and the use of Information and Communication Technology (ICT).

What are teachers' needs?

The role of the SENCO

There are several useful publications which deal with the broad picture of the role and responsibilities of the SENCO. These include the excellent small publication by the National Association for Special Educational Needs (NASEN) (Smith 1996a) which sets out guidelines for SENCOs, based on a summary of the Code of Practice (DfEE 1994). This publication concerns the whole of the SENCO's work and, helpfully, includes suggestions about managing responsibilities, time management and stress management. It illustrates Individual Educational Plans (IEPs) for pupils with emotional and behavioural difficulties (EBDs) (p. 35), which category, it notes, is included under the general heading of 'Learning Difficulties' in the Code of Practice. It also refers to other publications on IEPs (Warin 1995) for further examples.

However, it is necessary to look elsewhere (e.g. Peer 1996) to find out about the particular implications for SENCOs' work in relation to dyslexic learners in secondary schools. Most sources on teaching dyslexic students allocate proportionately greater space to information about definitions and characteristics, and about identification and assessment of the condition than to what action to take. The advice in the practical sections of teachers' handbooks on SpLD and dyslexia typically includes sections on study skills and literacy support (access to printed texts and writing support) via ICT, peer reading support, scribes, tape recording and teaching spelling.

Some handbooks (Crombie 1994, 1996; Reid 1996a, 1996b, 1998) also include advice about language teaching, including second or foreign languages, and mathematics teaching. As yet, however, few provide sufficient guidance on ways of managing the range of practical matters and issues that constitute the main points for routine, day-to-day staff communications, and which are the lifeblood of the cross-curricular support required for some dyslexic learners.

In order to investigate more fully practical matters such as SENCOs' perceptions of their role with reference to students with SpLD, discussion with experienced teachers of SpLD, some of whom were SENCOs, and all of whom were students on the MA course, led to agreement on the part of a sample of three SENCOs to engage in further research-based structured interviews. Each interview lasted for approximately 60 minutes and all were spontaneously followed up by further written submissions, including examples of policy and practice notes by the SENCOs. The analysis of their interview responses and open-ended discussions is reported below.

SENCOs' views on policy and practice

The aim of the structured interview was to explore with the SENCOs their views about how schools carry out the obligation to 'differentiate learning' to meet the special educational needs of both students with SEN Statements relating to SpLD (e.g. dyslexia) and those without Statements but who experienced such difficulties. In particular, the SENCOs' views were sought about what they saw as 'good practice' in the field and what they considered to be priorities.

Two of the three SENCOs had studied previous courses on SpLD and all three made strikingly similar comments with reference to their general concerns and their own priorities for dyslexic students. However, the following views may not be taken to be representative of all SENCOs or of any one school or local education authority (LEA). One of the three SENCOs works in a secondary school with approximately 1200 students, another works in an upper (pupils aged 14–19 years) school with similar numbers, and the third works from a specialist learning support service and draws upon extensive experience of advising and teaching in several 'families of schools' (secondaries and their feeder primary schools).

The first impression was one of the impact over the past few years of the enormous increase in paperwork associated with administration, not teaching, responsibilities. Their work in advising colleagues as well as monitoring and counselling them had increased, particularly since the formal introduction of individual educational programmes (IEPs). It included their staff support role relating to assisting colleagues to understand and provide conditions for effective learning for students with SEN Statements (i.e. to implement their IEPs).

The responsibility of writing material for colleagues as well as students had increased and was accompanied by a growing recognition of the limits of effectiveness of written communications, even when they were designed to meet particular expressed needs of those for whom they were written. It was, simply, the repeated problem of not having time to read. Even the circulation of copies of selected published papers no longer seemed to be effective unless introduced in the context of discussions, voluntarily entered and followed up with practical resources or opportunities for feedback.

The SENCOs' concerns included the high incidence of students with literacy and behavioural difficulties. They recognized that, in addition to their responsibility to provide literacy support, study skills support, advice and counselling, their role importantly involved being (in their words) 'a change agent'. Bringing about the desired changes, the SENCOs suggested, required considerable skill in working with colleagues across various departments and areas of curriculum specialism as well as liaising with headteachers, governors and, beyond school, with parents and multidisciplinary agencies in the community. Links not only with primary schools but also with the community, and in particular, liaison with further education colleagues, were promoted as vital in order to facilitate students' adjustments to life after the phase of their compulsory schooling (primary and secondary).

The challenge of responding to the wider requirements of government policy for teachers to differentiate the curriculum loomed large. The question of where and how 'trained SpLD specialist teachers' fitted into the picture was one which prompted reactions such as:

> That's why we came on the course. We don't have any designated SpLD or dyslexia specialists. We want to become better informed.

> We have a part-time teacher who takes the students with SEN Statements. We have several regular voluntary helpers. We can't afford to buy in more specialist teachers. We are training the ancillaries to assist the students without Statements.

The SENCOs endorsed the impression gained from wider discussions that in their LEAs, as in many other LEAs, trained SpLD specialist teachers also support students with a wide range of literacy and communication difficulties and there appears to be a gap in provision of specially trained teachers for students with SpLD/dyslexia.

Wider discussions about other LEAs suggested that prior to the re-drawing of LEA boundaries during 1997–1998, only two LEAs (Lancashire and Lothian) are known to have specially trained SpLD teachers in every school (see Chapter 3 and Reid 2001).

The experience of the sample of SENCOs suggests that the form and organization of learning support varies, even in schools with specialist teachers. In some schools, learning support is solely or mainly offered via withdrawal for one-to-one tutoring for dyslexic students. In others, there are moves toward classroom-based, specialist teacher intervention as well as withdrawal for tutoring. There is, increasingly, a trend towards class teachers becoming involved in developing approaches to learning support which include paired learning (cross-age tutoring: older student with younger and peer-paired learning), use of ICT, scribes, tape recorders, extended time for tasks and adapted materials. Some initiatives have developed through particular interests of an individual teacher; others through a department. Whole-school policy developments were taking place through SENCOs and as a result of LEA initiatives.

SENCOs perspectives on dyslexic learners' difficulties and SENs

The SENCOs spoke about the main problem areas for dyslexic learners as keeping up the pace of work (especially with reading and writing), retaining and retrieving information, and organization, e.g. keeping track of deadlines and homework. Their main points concerning 'factors affecting learning for dyslexic students in secondary schools' are listed below, in order of priority. The same points were echoed, although worded differently, by all three and reflected the findings of wider exploratory discussions with other secondary teachers:

- The 'C' factor; students need to feel 'in control' and to have chosen to work in a particular manner in tutorial sessions or in class. This was linked with the need for support in making informed, realistic career choices, but not underestimating students' potential (Hunter-Carsch 2001b).
- Expectations (of students, teachers and parents) need to be made explicit, understandable and be realistic.
- Students' self-esteem to be recognized as a vital factor and support providers should understand how this relates to motivation.
- Students with SpLD often require support to include social skills and communication.

These views were illustrated by reports of individual students' profiles of achievement and difficulties, and teachers' experiences across the curriculum and secondary age range.

SENCOs' priorities for SpLD (e.g. dyslexia)

Each of the SENCOs stated that they considered that their personal priority in their work was professional support for heads of departments, regarding:

- First, attitude change to overcome fear due to lack of knowledge about SpLD, e.g. dyslexia.
- Second, communicating research, policy and examples of good practice.
- Third, management structure to address the issues via, for example, mission statements, devised in consultation with and relating to the value of teamwork, collaborative work and the use of ICT.

The SENCOs indicated, regarding the second point above, that they felt a need for further training for themselves to increase their own relevant knowledge and skills. Their views about the following aspects are reported briefly under the following headings:

- Dyslexia and effective support.
- Successful initiatives.
- Communicating IEPs.

Dyslexia and effective support

The kinds of support reported by the SENCOs to have been found to be effective in assisting dyslexic students include the following:

- **Systematic screening** of intakes of students to consider achievement profiles in general and for reading speed and comprehension, and spelling; individual interviews with students with 'unusual profiles' or already identified as likely to have special needs.
- **Liaison** with primary, upper school/college or community agencies, facilitating continuity of support.
- **Raising staff awareness** about SpLD in general, concerning: individual profiles of achievement, abilities and difficulties; broadening understanding of the nature of reading and the concept of readability; understanding the developmental stages of spelling (what errors mean and what learning step comes next in normal development); ways of offering support with spelling; having a shared marking policy and consensus on how to improve the quality of work; practical ways of differentiating learning (not solely by 'worksheets'); exploring together, ways of extending involvement of 'trained' auxiliaries; use of the SEN base and special resources; IEPs; putting the onus on students as well as staff to use allocated timed sessions effectively.

Discussion of the above led to the addition of further points regarding:

- Screening for handwriting speed and legibility (see Chapter 5).
- Extending understanding of reading and readability including 'reading the media and social situations' (Hunter-Carsch 1998, 2001a).
- Moving away from selective focus on 'differentiating by worksheets' to implementing creative ways of organizing for learning and of differentiating input, resources and responses (McNamara and Moreton 1995; Visser 1995; Hart 1996a; Hunter-Carsch 1996).
- A shared feeling that there are dangers in withdrawing students from subject areas for support.
- Drop-in 'clinics' and 'surgeries' have proved to be helpful during 'tutorial times' (though it is better to avoid the medical terminology).
- ICT resources (CD-ROM, visual materials and speech-to-text approaches) are used frequently.
- Paired learning (e.g. with spelling partners).
- Widening the 'study skills' approach to building dyslexic students' confidence along with that of others. This was illustrated by suggesting that the 'easiest book' on the topics to be studied should be available to dyslexic students through the school library, 'So they can get a sense of the topic

content before they have to read a more complex book on the subject.'

- Using writing frames (Wray's 1995 Excell Project) and whole-class approaches, which permit individuals to progress at their own speed and teachers to work informally with individuals as a matter of routine coursework (see Binns 1978, 1989, 1990; Watkins and Hunter-Carsch 1995).

When asked about the most effective ways for SENCOs to make contact with colleagues, all agreed on two main avenues: availability in the staffroom at breaktimes and lunchtimes as well as by request; and through notices on staffroom noticeboards, wall display sheets and small leaflet copies for individuals. In addition, it was helpful if notes of summary points from discussions, publications and personal notes about aspects of SpLD were available during and after staff meetings.

All the interviewees pointed out that it was essential for them to budget their time so that they could provide written materials to assist colleagues with their teaching. There was a spontaneous comment by all, generated independently, to the effect that the introduction of IEPs had made the greatest difference and increase in colleagues' interest and understanding of individual differences in learning, but that lack of confidence in implementing IEPs continued to constitute an area of real concern and there was a need for teacher support. The following section provides some examples through selected notes taken from a sample of IEPs provided by the SENCOs.

Selected notes from IEPs

There is no single, agreed format for IEPs across LEAs and schools tend to have preferred formats for internal use. Each IEP is designed to meet an individual student's needs. The following two examples have been selected to illustrate two different aspects of SpLD. The first was devised for a student who was diagnosed as having SpLD (dyslexia) as the major (primary) source of difficulty; practical recommendations are noted in italic type. The second was devised for a student whose difficulties were most evident in attentional and behavioural problems and who responded well to structured teaching approaches.

Individual Educational Plan 1

Name: Tom Sands **Age:** 12 years 11 months **Form Tutor:** Mr Gale
School: Oldtown High School **Year Group:** 8

Learning needs

Tom's reading age is close to his chronological age but his reading rate is slow and he needs to re-read to ensure comprehension. His writing speed is slower and he has a limited spelling repertoire. He can only produce a few lines of writing in a lesson and these are marred by spelling errors and confused structure. Tom's self-organization is also weak – he forgets equipment, homework, messages, etc. His work is at higher level in maths, except where reading interferes. His oral contributions are at a much higher level, especially in topics that relate to his interests, e.g. science. His problems are affecting his motivation in other subjects.

Targets and methods

1. **To read a short story/passage** (chosen with help from learning support staff) each night in order to consolidate reading skills and increase reading speed.

At the start of each practice session, and at the end, try a few brief relaxation exercises. Sharpen focus on the topic by asking Tom to state the purpose/aim of each session. Strategies to develop silent reading may begin with assistance to 'hear himself read' by oral paired reading along with a prepared tape-recorded reading of the passage, to emphasize phrasing and looking ahead to tackle a few words at a time. Gradually try silent visual scanning ahead then reading phrases aloud (e.g. using window markers to reveal a phrase at a time). Then try silent reading, phrase by phrase. Pause at the end of each paragraph and ask Tom to retell the content (check comprehension). (LS staff to organize training, first with Tom and then with peer/parent; Tom 'in charge' of negotiations about agreeing a pattern for practice.) Focus on self-management: recording starting and finishing times for practice sessions and maintaining easy-to-keep records.

2. **To use strategies to increase reading comprehension.**

Explore strategies, such as listening to someone else read the passage aloud, recalling key words or ideas, then find the key words in the printed passage; read the passage silently and attempt to retell the narrative/main content (i.e. 'translate' it into own words). Use range of 'study strategies' (e.g. checking prior knowledge about the subject matter; predicting content; highlighting main ideas; modelling, including verbal mind-mapping/explaining aloud; reporting/dramatizing/making into a visual picture, diagram, flow-chart; creating a question about each paragraph). (See staff materials on study skill strategies.) Tom to report the most effective strategies each session.

3. To complete **agreed amount of written work** per lesson.

Start well within Tom's capability for successful completion and gradually increase, keeping dated records of start and finish (e.g. coloured pen mark in margin/green for 'go' and red for 'stop').

4. With assistance, to identify, devise strategies for and **learn five target words** for spelling each week.

From Tom's written work, select agreed 'most-needed words'. Use strategies which focus on slowing down the phonemic patterns, e.g. singing slowly (aloud then mentally) while (eyes closed) tracing the graphemes indented into a soft surface (e.g. sand); tracing shape on acetate (sliding surface) looking/copying then with eyes shut tracing by memory; writing from memory. Explore ways of adapting Look, Cover Write, Check to suit Tom.

5. To **proofread written work** using a topic and target spelling list plus hand-held spellchecker.

On personal word list accumulate records of successful spelling (e.g. pencil tick - but rub out tick if incorrect and try again, with aim to gain several ticks per word each session). Note when Tom is uncertain about spellings which are actually correct; explore 'rules'/rationale.

6. Use **organizer/Post-It notes** as daily reminders.

Prompt Tom to obtain supplies of Post-It notes, etc. and to use them. Develop the habit. Gradually refine it to a signal and reminder articulated verbally, and then to a mental note (perhaps song/poem triggered by motor action, e.g. leaving home/check at the door, turning around a large Post-It notice (GOT IT?/YES!)); recheck on entering the school gate - deliberately touch gate, trigger mental review count, e.g. '1. Lunch money; 2. homework; 3. PE kit'.

Monitoring progess

1. Mrs F (learning support assistant) to keep record of progress re targets 2, 3, 4, 5, 6.
2. Subject staff to tick/note on weekly record form re targets 2, 3, 4, 5.
3. Mrs B (learning support teacher) to keep record of reading performance and recall of weekly spellings.

Staff support involved

1. Mrs B (LS) 2 × 20 min (tutor time) in groups of five, to work on target spellings, support choice of/discuss reading material.
2. Mrs B (LS) 1 × week × 50 min in withdrawal group from English to model/practise strategies for improving comprehension/writing.
3. Mrs F (LSA) in various subject lessons; to remind of strategies for both comprehension and spelling and to check self-organization.
4. Subject staff to recognize slower reading rate and, where possible, provide time for comprehension. Also to set reasonable targets for amounts of written work, making use of alternatives to extended writing where longer pieces of writing are required (see suggestions in separate guidelines).

Equipment

Hand-held spellchecker, organizer diary and Post-It notes, digital watch.

Parental involvement

1. Fortnightly contact (LS) via note or phone re encouragement/feedback to Tom.
2. To remind Tom about use of organizer diary/Post-It notes.
3. To encourage 15 min reading every evening.
4. To check spellings once weekly.

Review dates: Termly **Completed by:** (SENCO, LS, parents, Tom)

Individual Educational Plan 2

Name: Richard Arthur **Tutor:** Mr Thomas **Year:** 7 **Home language:** English

(a) Difficulties at entry

Richard has been fostered from the age of two years. He is very bright and is intolerant of failure. He has attention deficit disorder (ADD) and is prescribed ritalin for this. He has behavioural difficulties and can refuse to work as directed. He can be disruptive and will lie to get his own way. He has a very poor short-term memory, poor pen grip and writing position, and is left-handed. His writing is a major problem for him. His spelling is also poor. He is highly distractible and will have difficulty in concentrating in some situations. He has attended therapy sessions at child and family clinic since he was five years old.

(b) Progress and achievements

At chronological age 11;2 Richard's test results indicated a general intellectual ability of well above average (WISC IQ 120+) Reading Comprehension 10.6 years, Spelling 10 years but with great difficulty in handwriting. He likes science and mathematics, doing well in both, and studying science in his spare time. He is very good orally in science and loves practical activities, including woodwork and car repairs.

(c) Skills

Richard has exceptional abilities in visual learning without essential motor activity; also in simultaneous processing of information, choosing relevant from irrelevant details and anticipating consequences. He can work well under pressure. He is an able speaker, good kinesthetic learner and a fairly confident, fluent reader.

(d) Current needs

To improve behaviour, motivation, handwriting, homework completion and note-making. Improve peer relationships. Work on handwriting and alternative modes of recording, e.g. use of audiotape recorder. Develop strategies to assist short-term memory.

(e) SEN strategies

I Differentiation – reduce number of written tasks set and let him concentrate longer on the one that is the most divergent and challenging. Share plans/directed learning load /schedules. Monitor peer-paired learning work.
II Reducing distractibility – use 'office' sessions organized in e.g. Room 105. Enclosed space, desk/table surfaces clear, non-cluttered views, clear focus on essential visual materials; time limits, especially for written tasks; structure time for discussions, planning; support information processing.
III Recording observations/discussion points – keep track of consistency/ inconsistencies in patterns of achievement. Try to discern optimal conditions for effective learning. Monitor self-directed learning/shared discussions (with peers and tutor-student).

The above information is summarized and agreed targets, as well as indicators of success, are presented in chart form below.

STUDENT'S DIFFICULTIES	**STUDENT'S STRENGTHS**
ADD high distractibility	Fluent reader
Left-hander	Intelligent and very able
Very poor script	Exceptional visual learner
Poor spelling	Can distinguish essential from non-essential detail
Poor rote learning	Good at seeing 'whole picture'
Poor attention to detail	Good kinaesthetic learner
Disruptive	Works well under pressure
Low motivation, underachieving	Can anticipate consequences
Poor peer relationships	Good at simultaneous processing of information
Short-term auditory memory	
Slow information processing	

AGREED TARGETS

Will be able to, will know/ understand	**Indicator of success**
1. Complete work on a reduced number of tasks; concentrate for longer on the most divergent and challenging tasks in Enquiry, Science, Maths, Mod Lang.	Teacher to facilitate by suitable task differentiation so that better-quality work is produced. Monitored by subject teachers.
2. Reduce distractibility by spending time in class 'office' where written work, planning and verbal information processing can occur without any distraction.	Facilitated by learning support teacher or subject teacher or tutor in real office, or marked office area in class (see guidance notes for advice).

3. Support auditory memory and slow processing speed by working with parent/peer tutor/LS teacher to give instant and periodic verbal feedback on instructions, ideas, aims of learning task. Review regularly.	Parent/peer/ LS teacher to use feedback and review questioning to check understanding. On-task time to be monitored by same personnel.
4. Learn 5–10 spellings per week selected by LS teacher/subject teacher from written classwork. Use Look-Cover-Write-Check method.	98% accuracy in weekly test by LS teacher or parent.
5. Improve pen grip by use of Handhugger pens and paper disc slide to mobilize hand tracking.	Improved handwriting; fluency of letter links; use relaxation finger exercises.
6. Explore alternative methods of recording information, e.g. mind maps, cloze text notes, laptop computer or audio tape.	Improved recording of work. Monitored by LS teacher/subject teacher.
7. All homework to be noted and checked by subject teachers.	Better quality of work; better school-home links.

(See Learning Support File, in Staffroom, for Guidance Notes about methods)

SENCOs' most successful initiatives

Examples of successful initiatives taken by SENCOs include the following:

- Peer tutoring.
- SEN directories and profiles.
- Open Day events.

Peer tutoring

Effective peer tutoring, which was mentioned independently by each SENCO, necessitates appropriate training of peer tutors and is most successful when everyone involved has a shared sense of the meaning and value of the curriculum content being studied and is clear about the purpose of the interactions.

One project initially involved 70 sixth form (age 16+) volunteer peer tutors and, as the programme developed, the numbers increased to a total of 120 volunteers. They undertook to work with first form (11+) secondary students for three lessons each week as part of humanities/English work, including field trips, and on mathematics and language studies. The training of the volunteer tutors involved a basic one-hour session per week, over six weeks. The topics studied in the training course included shared reading, cued spelling and scribing.

Peer tutors were able to support the learners to produce a piece of work with their help. It was not immediately successful as some pairs had to work harder towards establishing trust. However, the value of discussions about the content of the work, not just the words to be learned, moved the pairs towards increasing trust on the part of the younger learners, resulting in a feeling of acceptance and understanding that 'Not everyone managed to get everything correct first time' and that 'It was alright to have some help'. The tutors also benefited from their work towards modelling the strategies and communicating the necessary encouragement to tutees. Staff discovered some striking mismatches between their own low expectations of some students and their actual abilities revealed by peer tutoring, especially in contexts which bridged school and community.

One of the outcomes of the project involved the development of certificated courses for students who would previously not have been expected to cope with GCSE and otherwise had no 'recognized' levels of accredited work. Greater accuracy of matching tasks to learners became evident and teachers worked more effectively in teams. Most strikingly, the student drop-out rate decreased and there was felt to be a positive impact in the reduction of drug-related problems. (For further information on peer tutoring see also Topping 1987, 1995, 1996; McNeil 1995.)

SEN directories and profiles

SEN directories and student profiles were introduced as part of a range of approaches for increasing efficacy of communication between SEN staff and curriculum subject teachers. They were introduced in one school along with a staff training booklet. This included, for example, suggestions for setting homework to support the texts being studied and ways of using set texts with peer support and, for example, highlighted words for special attention. Staff were encouraged to work on making glossaries of special 'subject content words' and given copies of lists of high-frequency words for spelling so that homework policy and parent support could be streamlined for maximum learning support and reinforcement of learning.

Parents' meetings (in groups) were found to be helpful for explaining and discussing ways of assisting with students' workloads. It was suggested that:

> Parents were usually open and interested, ready to discuss literacy and dyslexia issues and generally non-judgemental. They wanted to know what to do to help. They were very interested in talking about learning styles. They understood the problems of accepting that you are dyslexic and how hard it can be to learn how to laugh about it, to get their son/daughter to cope with the stress and to accept help sometimes and to smile.

For all students with SEN Statements, a simplified version of the IEP form presented on a single, coloured page with 'key points' such as the student's profile, learning targets and dates, was introduced for use by student, staff and parents. These easily recognizable, positively stated sets of up to three 'targets' were derived by the SENCO on the basis of individual assessment-interview-discussion with students. The targets were 'generic' rather than subject-specific. The idea was developed and trialled in consultation with heads of departments, all SEN staff, senior managers, counsellors, behaviour support specialists and careers advisers along with representatives of outside agencies and was communicated at departmental meetings to all staff members.

Open days

One of the SENCOs illustrated his approach by describing the provision in his school, of an 'open day' which involved displays of work by particularly able/gifted students and teams of students involved in 'enhanced learning' courses. This event was linked to study skills workshops - for all students and interested parents - and to workshops exploring learning styles. Other workshops for training peer tutors focused on how they could obtain the best responses from tutees, by learning useful approaches to listening, encouraging and cueing, and thence by mastering the art of prompting, facilitating learning, scaffolding and structuring.

These workshops proved particularly helpful - attracting boys and encouraging them to offer assistance to their peers in mathematics, science and design. Larger numbers of girls tended to volunteer as tutors, with emphasis on humanities courses, 'Until . . .,' it was commented, '. . . the practicalities were illustrated to boys as potential tutors working also in other subject areas.'

In addition, part of the event included careers advice, for example Learning Profile explorations. This SENCO reported that dyslexic students tended to need more than average numbers of 'acclimatizing visits' to their future colleges and more discussion time about their future survival skills development - a point endorsed by other, experienced SpLD teachers and tutors. In the SENCO's words, 'They benefit from more time to organize their thoughts in discussions about their future.'

What are the implications for practice?

Differentiation and peer help in developing writing and spelling

One of the strongest messages from the interviews with SENCOs concerns their appreciation of the value of peer tutoring and the strengthening of the shared sense of purpose within the peer-pairs working context. This is endorsed by the author's experience. Peer tutoring is a vital factor in the social support required for dyslexic (and other) students to sustain their efforts to achieve satisfactory work in written tasks (which form a substantial part of the secondary school curriculum for all students). It is particularly important for sensitive adolescents to feel included and supported as a member of their peer group, and not to be singled out for special help.

What is needed is a framework for differentiation which is both wide enough to involve the whole class, yet refined enough to permit inconspicuous individual support from an informed teacher. Just such a framework is provided by Binns' (1978, 1989, 1990, 1991) approach to developing writing through systematic drafting and re-drafting. This may be applied across the curriculum and provides a context within which teachers may be able to support their students, by identifying difficulties and assisting them by 'scaffolding' support over particular 'learning hurdles'.

Binns' approach is particularly helpful for some dyslexic learners who need to see the whole picture emerging clearly in order to be able to develop the parts. Binns' use of space facilitates keeping in mind 'the wood and the trees' when laying out a draft (left-hand) page, where rough notes, ideas or even sketches may be made, and a facing (right-hand) page for re-drafts, which develop only selected points requiring clarification of the writer's intended meaning. Such points are identified by putting brackets around them during re-reading, either silently or aloud.

The re-reading aloud part of the approach can be very helpful, especially when done by a peer who does not know exactly what the writer intended but had to rely on what the writer actually wrote in order to discover the meaning of the content. This is an aspect of peer tutoring whereby the peer helper can be particularly useful as 'the writer as re-reader' often fails to recognize a lack of clarity, since the tendency is for writers to re-read what they intended to put down, not what they actually wrote. Thus, the friendly reading aloud by a good pal or supportive teacher is both encouraging and positive; not 'hunting for errors' but seeking the intended meaning.

When everyone in the classroom is using this approach (which can make for a fairly lively and seemingly noisy class at times!), and the teacher also does this with every individual at some point, this creates a shared sense of engagement with the writing task. It is recognized as a task which really does require clear communication; the sharing of meaning derived from written words becomes a highly motivating factor in improving each writer's communication. Singling out of pupils with difficulties is no longer an issue since everyone benefits from the approach, the range of benefits is respected and no one is ridiculed.

The process is facilitated by the visual emphasis in Binns' use of the overhead projector and acetate copies of students' written drafts (often including a series of three or more re-drafts on more than one overhead projector). Binns prepares for the reading aloud of students' writing, in order to illustrate their intended meaning, by reading aloud their actual written work (which may be less than perfectly formulated and perhaps includes several misspellings) in a fluent rendition, in what Binns terms 'the Ernest Hemingway style'.

The impact on listeners (including the writer) can be significant as the focus is always on hearing the meaning not on correcting surface features. A mood of generally heightened interest in what is actually on the page emerges as the contrast between what is intended and what is actually there becomes sharpened by the quest to communicate - not merely to 'tidy up spelling or handwriting'. It does not take long for students to read aloud accurately their own and their peer partner's actual first (or subsequent) drafts and identify points for possible further clarification. Renditions can be exceedingly funny if the actual spellings and absences of punctuation or errors in punctuation are read aloud! The growth in tolerance as well as shared enjoyment endorses the value of this approach for everyone.

Binns does not 'correct' students' work in the usual sense of correcting surface features, but through his approach, assists them to identify their own difficulties and improve their written work and clarity of thinking. The results are dramatic. After several weeks of employing this approach the increase in confidence to write becomes strikingly evident - the sheer increase in quantity of writing when students are freed from the apprehension of 'mistakes' is substantial and the increase in quality of writing can be seen in students' intensified efforts to refine the precision of the meanings that are communicated. The use of brackets for indicating spelling difficulties can be especially helpful for dyslexic students, some of whom are likely to bracket correctly spelled words as frequently as incorrectly spelled ones (thus readily identifying the severity of their specific spelling difficulties and signalling to the teacher their need for a special kind of assistance).

The extension of this approach to the use of brackets in examination scripts (to signal to examiners that the student is aware of his own spelling problems) can be very helpful. Students who are aware of their tendency to have spelling difficulties and who cannot access spellcheckers during examinations may be recommended to note briefly on their examination papers that they have spelling difficulties, even if not formally diagnosed and with an SEN Statement, and to use brackets to identify words they are uncertain how to spell. When the examiners observe the bracketed words, they are more likely to be sympathetic even if initially puzzled if they find that the student has identified both correctly spelled and incorrectly spelled words in their written papers.

Use of information and communication technology for drafting and re-drafting

The use of ICT for drafting and re-drafting has been found to be very helpful for many (but not all) dyslexic students. Among the advantages are spellcheck facilities and 'cut and paste' features. However, the use of computers/word processors speeds up rather than slows down the process of organizing sequences of letters, words and ideas which are represented on vertical rather than flat surfaces. The different visuo-spatial organization and absence of the 'slowing down process' implicit in the use of handwriting and manipulating pages of drafts, may be less helpful for some, even with the advantage of the printout with easily typed and corrected words. It also seems to be the case that, for some individuals, the motoric involvement of handling pages and being 'in control', of arranging the pages (of an essay, for example) into a different and potentially 'clearer' organization of an argument, provides clarity for the emergent mental (visual) image of the whole paper. The need to make 'blocks of space', representing ideas, visible and 'manageable' in a linear manner differs in mode from the preference for the use of 'mind maps' and diagrams which facilitate, for some, the connecting, organizing and 'moving about' of ideas or potential steps when developing a line of thought. For such 'motoric-visual' learners, even the use of a set of filing cards for manipulating 'chunks' of ideas or components of arguments may not be as helpful as laying out full-sized pages on the floor and viewing them from above ('in control' distance) and walking to and through potential links in order to clarify the thinking (movement - then mental auditorization/verbalization) prior to decisions, possibly numbering and reorganizing the components.

Representations of relationships between audio (thinking/expression in words) and visual representations of words (now facilitated by speech-to-text and vice versa systems) offer further oportunities for refining individual forms of learning support with the aid of technology (Crombie and Crombie 2001; Haase 2001; Haase and Hunter-Carsch 2001).

Further insights into the nature and difficulties of the draft–re-draft process have been gained by observation of students of different abilities and different ages employing the Binns' draft–re-draft approach (1991, 1990) which depends for its efficacy on the identification in the course of re-reading, of points for re-drafting. Many students have been substantially supported through the use of this method (in which the first draft becomes the 'left-hand page' and the next or 're-draft' is developed on 'the right-hand page') thus facilitating the viewing of pages 'in parallel'. This visual layout is, as yet, easier to do on the desk surface with actual pages than on a computer with a split screen and looking directly at the screen. Although the 'decoding' of their 'writing' (typing) from their drafts is perhaps more easily done on a computer in the light of the typed rather than handwritten format and potential 'automatic' spellchecking, for some students, it seems that the re-reading from the computer screen (vertical rather than horizontal or angled on a desk/table) and locating and maintaining attention on a particular point may present its own challenges and difficulties (Haase 2000, Mailley 2001).

Spelling support

For dyslexic students, who may require more specialized support for spelling, teachers can learn (by observation of drafts and listening to students' readings and discussion) where their particular problems lie in the spelling process. The fact that students work either on their own or in pairs, facilitates the organization necessary for observing and listening, as teachers can choose where to move and with which student or pair to share with, at any time within their scheduled sessions.

This is also the case within the Watkins' (Watkins and Hunter-Carsch 1995; Watkins 1996, 1997) Prompt Spelling approach in which the teacher can be the prompter along with trained peers who work with the help of the Franklin spellmaster. In Prompt Spelling, the intervention is directly in the hands of the prompter (a better speller, matched with a weaker speller). The dramatic and sustained progress in spelling made by the experimental groups reported in Watkins' work, may possibly be attributed, at least in part, to the progressive confidence-building effect of the interactions which facilitate the thinking (and, crucially, meta-cognitive awareness-raising) within a meaningful context, on the part of the student with spelling problems (see Chapter 5 in this volume; Lannen et al. 1997 (Chapter 3)).

Parental support and home–school liaison

The SENCOs raised the issue of liaison at transition from primary to secondary school. Increasingly, with the implementation not only of the Code of Practice (DfEE 1994) but also the initial Teacher Training Agency Career entry requirements (TTA 1997), specifying recognition of SpLD at primary stage, baseline assessments at school entry and records of SATs results, there should be more information available from pupils' primary school records about their developmental and achievement profiles.

Currently, it seems that practices at transition vary substantially. In some schools, primary teachers collate extensive records of achievement, with samples of individual pupils' work across the curriculum, and report being disappointed in some cases, when their secondary school colleagues appear to have relatively little interest in the range and detail of this material. It is understandable that secondary schools, drawing upon catchments of several primary schools, wish to establish their own databanks. However, there is much that can be usefully communicated 'across the primary–secondary divide' (see Davidson and Moore 1996; Galton et al. in press).

It is particularly important that primary school students, in transition to secondary school, be alerted to the different features of classroom practice, and to explore continuities and discontinuities of practices in ways which assist students to develop realistic expectations of secondary school and to look forward to the transition. It is no less important for parents to be apprised of aspects which may affect their children's confidence and readiness to respond positively to the scale of the changes which have to be faced by beginners at secondary school.

For dyslexic students and their parents in particular, support at this stage can be greatly facilitated by friendly exchanges from other parents of dyslexic students and links with older dyslexic students through membership of a local dyslexia support group. Such groups, affiliated to the national British Dyslexia Association (BDA), have easy access to the BDA's diverse publications and support services, and often involve local meetings at which professional and lay members can hear informed guest speakers and see new resources. Some groups' activities include workshop teaching and learning sessions for students (with specialist teachers). Most provide good fellowship and opportunities to ventilate problems and frustrations in ways which can lead to constructive local solutions. The Leicestershire Association (in collaboration with the LEA), for example, contributed directly to the production of booklets for teachers and parents. It also provides a regular telephone helpline and access to printouts of pages containing information and practical advice located in the BDA's World Wide Web site: http://www.bda-dyslexia.org.uk/

Additionally, for helpful lists, descriptions and sources of resources for teaching and learning, readers may wish to refer to Lannen et al. (1997), a practical resource book for parents and teachers.

Summary

To return to the original questions addressed in this chapter.

First, with reference to current policies, practices and priorities, the exploratory discussions with SENCOs, SpLD specialist teachers and teacher-trainers highlighted the need for:

- Recognition and resolution of current inequalities in the provision of specialist trained SENCOs, SpLD teachers and SEN classroom assistants.

- Consideration in the training of all teachers, not only SENCOs and specialist SpLD teachers, of the implications of individual differences in learning styles, the specific difficulties experienced by some students who may or may not have a Statement of Special Educational Needs, and their roles and responsibilities in working together in the classroom, not only in tutorial teaching (see the following chapters on secondary education; Reid 2001).

Second, with reference to what is involved in effective learning support, it has been argued that for individual teachers and classroom assistants to be able to provide appropriate learning support, in the first instance they will need to work together with students, listening to and learning from them about the best ways of supporting learning so that the students can become confident and competent, independent learners. The relevant knowledge and skills to support the range of students' learning needs should be extended by professional training.

Third, in relation to teachers' needs, the discussions suggest that despite the difficulties and constraints within the compulsory education sector, there are some interesting and successful approaches emerging for meeting the teachers' needs to provide effective learning support for dyslexic students. Among these approaches are:

- Peer tutoring (with trained tutors).
- Establishing and communicating SEN directories, profiles and IEPs.
- Communicating within the school population and with the wider community through Open Days, including workshops.
- Training classroom assistants, with special reference to support for learners with SpLD.

With reference to the second bullet point above, a website on 'inclusion' on the National Grid for Learning has been developed by the DfEE and the British Education Communication Technology Agency (BECTA) to provide access to the catalogue of online resources to support individual learning needs (see http://inclusion.ngfl.gov.uk). A range of resources for understanding and supporting students with SpLD is presented in close proximity to resources for understanding and supporting those with, for example, physical, emotional and behavioural difficulties. New research questions may be prompted by the opportunities afforded by the wider 'inclusion' policies and the potential for use of this and other websites in the designs of new approaches to professional training.

In practice, the requirement for schools to provide special learning support (gained through SEN Statements for the 'notional 2%') needs to be related not only to individual schools' working definitions of the attitudinal aspects of the wider concept of 'inclusive education' (Norwich 1996; DfEE 1999; Booth et al. 2000; Clough and Corbett 2000) but also to the interpretation in practice by all staff, of the implications of different learning/cognitive styles (Riding and Rayner 1998) and the implications for differentiated learning possibilities and support for all pupils. This is particularly important for 'Warnock's notional 18% of students with SENs without statements' and for all those who are very able learners, bilingual and multilingual students (see Chapter 4; Peer and Reid 2000; Peer 2001).

Finally, the implications of improving good practice have been discussed throughout this chapter. They focus on the importance of the quality of communication between all staff members, students, parents and members of the community. They involve recognizing that individual learners' needs may be affected by context but it is likely that quite specific forms of self-knowledge and support from others can together contribute to equipping dyslexic students in secondary school with the necessary confidence and competence to go on with effective adult, 'life-long learning'. To do this well requires both initial and further training for teachers as well as classroom assistants. In this context, although much remains to be done, it is respectfully acknowledged that during the period of writing and publication of this volume there have been substantial developments at national level (TTA, 1999; OFSTED 1999; Singleton 1999a, b; DfEE 1998, 2000a, 2000b; see also DfEE website http://inclusion.nfgl.gov.uk for 77 sources on SpLD Dyslexia (early 2001)).

Acknowledgements

With appreciation and thanks to the MA students on the SpLD 2 course (1996–1997), in particular, Susan O'Brien, Christine Tozer, Ivan Scales and colleagues at the Cavendish School. Thanks are also due to Helen Newton for her passage on the training of SEN Classroom Assistants, to Richard Binns and Gill Watkins for inspirational discussions about their work relating to peer learning support and to Judith Schofield and Ian for sharing Ian's story.

CHAPTER 3

Shaping policy and practices in secondary schools: support for learning

SHEILA CROSSLEY

Introduction

As teacher training in the field of SpLD progresses, courses are diversified and terminology changes, it is important to be aware of the directions of change and also potential losses as well as gains in relation to the bases for training courses. This chapter provides a description of the rationale, development, content and outcomes of one local education authority's initial Diploma in Professional Development (SpLD), documenting its contribution to the history of such courses. It is believed that this professional development course represented a unique and possibly first 'competence-based' approach; one which integrated coursework with the development of good daily practice in the classsroom.

My account was written in 1997, the Year of Reading in the UK and the time of launching of the National Literacy strategy (McClelland 1997; DfEE 1998). The effect of the campaign - to raise standards of achievement in literacy and, relatedly, to promote recognition of dyslexia through, for example, a series of television programmes, national, regional and local conferences and courses - is beginning to be felt and is still to be researched and evaluated. Also, between 1997 and the time of publication, there have been many changes in local education authorities and patterns of administration. The account presented here thus needs to be contextualized historically as a case study on one initiative in teacher training in one local education authority in Lancashire. It is reported from the point of view of one of the contributing tutors to the teacher training course.

In 1986-1987 I began to work with some of the first pupils 'statemented' for SpLD in one of the eastern districts of Lancashire and also became one of the earliest participants in the modular Postgraduate Diploma (Professional Development, SpLD) which was established in 1992 by the University of

Central Lancashire. Subsequently, I completed my MA Teaching and Training Studies (1995) with the same university, and I am currently involved as both a mentor and moderator for the local education authority in the delivery of the diploma to colleagues.

This chapter addresses the following questions:

- Do local education authorities (LEAs) have policy statements/guidelines about teaching students with specific learning difficulties (SpLD)?
- What training/support is available at local level for teachers of students with SpLD?
- How have whole-school policies affected the learning environment positively and contributed to students' learning?

Do local education authorities have policy statements/guidelines about teaching students with SpLD?

In the years immediately following the 1981 Education Act (the early and mid 1980s) Lancashire Education Authority had very few written policy documents for students with SpLD. There appeared to be no progressive planning of logical steps. Arrangements were made on an ad hoc basis, depending very much on the opinions and priorities of District Education Officers, on educational psychologists' beliefs, and on local arrangements between schools and support services such as the Reading and Language Service. The first pupils statemented for SpLD began to receive additional support from teachers appointed for this purpose. These SpLD teachers were gradually gathered into teams in the districts and were placed under the auspices of the Reading and Language Service for administrative purposes.

During 1987–1988, in-service training for newly formed SpLD teams began to develop rapidly, and with the spread of these teachers into primary and secondary schools, awareness of children's SpLD problems began to spread among teachers in the LEA. The late 1980s and early 1990s were characterized by an enlightened response from some LEA professionals, who recognized the need for a professional qualification for the growing number of SpLD teachers. The LEA was fortunate to be able to work in partnership with the University of Central Lancashire, and in January 1993, the first Postgraduate Diplomas (Professional Development, SpLD) were awarded.

A second strand of LEA development since the 1981 Education Act has been the general development of special educational needs (SEN) policy, as more and more pupils with SEN are educated in mainstream schools. Whole-school policies for dealing with pupils with SEN have evolved, and schools have become more adept at providing their own support teams and strategies for working with them. The role of special educational needs co-ordinators (SENCOs) has become more complex, and involves liaison with a wider range of external support teams, including in-service training for school staff and advice about differentiation of work for pupils.

Gradually, a more coherent LEA policy for pupils with SEN has emerged. During 1993–1994, a guidance handbook, Managing Special Educational Needs in Schools, was issued. This handbook provides a definition of SpLD and points out features of SpLD of which classroom teachers should be aware. It also suggests ways in which teachers can help these pupils.

The third strand of development has emerged since the 1988 Education Reform Act. This legislation gave schools responsibility for their own budgets and all departments (including SEN) have had to be more accountable and justify their use of resources. School governors now have a role to play in SEN policy and provision and, in their bids to attract parents, many schools have formulated policy statements with regard to SEN.

Other factors which have affected the development of SEN policy in general include the appraisal of teachers and inspections of schools by OFSTED staff.

At national level, the Code of Practice on the Identification and Assessment of Special Educational Needs (DfEE 1994) gives a definition of SpLD along with guidance for the LEA and schools on the type of problems encountered by pupils with SpLD and appropriate teaching strategies for them. The Code of Practice places the emphasis for identification and the first stages of dealing with pupils' SpLD problems (or any SEN) firmly in the hands of schoolteachers. In October 1994, Lancashire Education Authority issued a further SEN Handbook to give guidance to schools on the implementation of the Code of Practice. The LEA is attempting to develop 'a comprehensive and common format' and encourages schools 'to contribute to the development of a shared system'. This Handbook has been developed (1996) to include the common format of a Lancashire Pupil Record for all pupils identified as having SEN.

It was not until 1995 that the local education authority produced Criteria for the Assessment and Statementing of Children with Special Educational Needs. This was in response to suggestions in the Code of Practice (DfEE 1994) which encouraged LEAs to set up a moderating group to make consistent decisions about whether to make Statements for all types of SEN. Previous guidance for pupils with SpLD, developed by the Educational Psychology Service, concentrated on children who had low attainment levels and a degree of underachieving. The current criteria place more emphasis on underachievement and correspondingly less emphasis on low attainment levels.

In 1996 the LEA proposed guidelines not only for statementing but also for ceasing to maintain SpLD Statements. The LEA continues to review and restructure its support services (including SpLD) which are available for pupils with SEN.

What training/support is available at local level for teachers of students with SpLD?

A Postgraduate Diploma (Professional Development, SpLD)

In order to ensure that the developing policies were delivered, staff had to be trained appropriately. Hence, a Postgraduate Diploma (Professional Development, SpLD) was planned to start in 1992 for newly appointed and serving SpLD teachers in the Lancashire LEA. This modular course, which would be 'competence-led' and result in the completion of a professional portfolio, was designed to take account of the prior achievement of each participant in the training scheme. It recognized the need for provision of in-service education for the specialist training of learning support teachers working with statemented SpLD students in mainstream primary and secondary schools.

The Diploma is based on a programme of training and work-based accreditation, organized around key specialist areas associated with SpLD. At the heart of the competence-based scheme is the Ability Profile. This is a summary of key competence areas considered essential for effective professional practice, derived from an extensive needs analysis undertaken by the LEA in 1990. There are 48 key competencies (or units of competence) grouped under five main professional functions: relationships and self; assessment; specialist methodology; ensuring curriculum entitlement and access; and case study.

The aims of the Diploma are to:

- Acknowledge existing areas of competency.
- Minimize the need for a large number of centralized courses.
- Allow for a degree of personal choice within the overall framework.
- Have sufficient flexibility to meet individual needs.
- Allow for the complex working arrangements of SpLD teachers.
- Provide an 'open learning' format, allowing students to proceed at their own pace.
- Be seen as valuable by school staff, governing bodies, parents and voluntary agencies.
- Establish links between specific competencies, knowledge and understanding, and key principles in educational practice.
- Offer access to a nationally recognized qualification.

Course delivery

Delivery of the taught components of the Diploma programme has been provided by the LEA Reading and Language Service. A substantial element of the course involves the accountability of practical work. The University of Central Lancashire, working in partnership with Lancashire LEA, has provided assessment, ongoing quality assurance and validation of the Diploma.

Students attend the LEA training programme for SpLD work and construct a portfolio of evidence matched to the standards for the four key roles and the case study. They are each allocated a mentor for the duration of their time on the programme. This support is an integral part of the course delivery, ensuring that professional development is linked to LEA priorities while providing regular guidance and moral support. Students may present their work for assessment as soon as they have completed all the training sessions and put together their portfolio of evidence, and this normally takes about two years. Each module is graded and students are awarded a final overall grade with the prospect of obtaining a pass, merit or distinction.

The portfolios are subject to initial assessment by mentors, followed by internal moderating. A final moderating session involves university tutors and an assessment interview. An external examiner usually samples portfolios, especially case studies, as well as attending some of the assessment interviews.

Course content and processes

The student's portfolio provides a structured means of producing evidence of competence, critical reflection and assessment. Knowledge and understanding are of central importance to any scheme based on accreditation. Demonstration of these should be considered as an integral part of the demonstration of competence as a whole and should inform the way evidence is brought together and interpreted. Appropriate levels of knowledge and understanding can be demonstrated in the ways identified below:

- Involvement with the accreditation process, negotiating and obtaining evidence to demonstrate competence.
- Personal research which has a focus on recent educational developments and innovations.
- Transfer of understanding across functional areas.
- Handling contingencies in relation to changing circumstances and unanticipated events.
- Reference to developments associated with educational policy at regional and national levels.

- Reference to specific issues and concerns which impinge on effective professional practice.

Knowledge and understanding are key aspects of the presentation and interpretation of evidence. Broadly, they refer to students' ability to make judgements for planning, based on observation of their pupils' progress. Evidence of such understanding includes interpretation of diagnostic test results and their use as a basis for constructing an individual learning programme. This might be in relation to reading or a number of other subject areas, such as history, geography or French.

Such knowledge and understanding should be demonstrated in each area of the programme, but should be of an extended form in relation to the case study report. Here, there should be an indication of reading undertaken and a demonstration that learning support is based on key principles derived from the fields of educational psychology, reading and language research, and curriculum theory. Students will also have an opportunity to convey their knowledge and understanding in their final assessment interviews.

Theoretical framework for the course

It is essential to recognize that knowledge and understanding arise from processes of learning and self-development evident in the learning cycle illustrated in Figure 3.1. Observation of pupils' learning difficulties in the classroom leads to informed reflection, analysis of the problem (via diagnostic testing, for example) and application of a learning programme - this to be followed by a further period of observation, reflection, analysis and so on as the cycle is repeated.

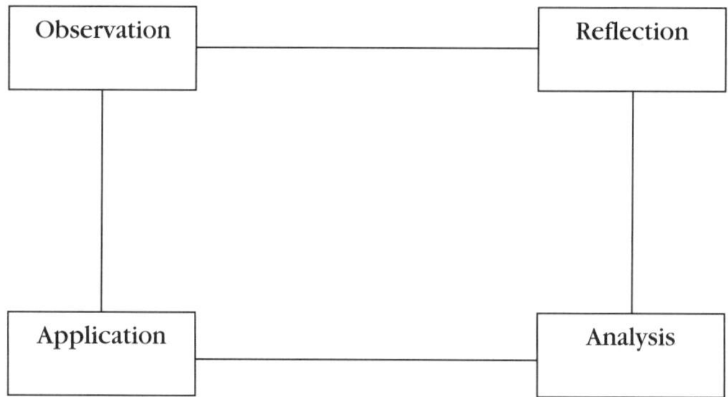

Figure 3.1. Theoretical framework for the course.

Outcome of the course

Between 1992 and January 1997 a total of 123 teachers successfully completed and were awarded the Postgraduate Diploma (Professional Development, SpLD) by the University of Central Lancashire. This is an outstanding achievement for the teachers on the course and for the LEA team of mentors. Standards have been very high, with a considerable amount of exemplary work from children being utlized as well as innovative learning programmes, assessment strategies and critical assessment of methods.

Some successful students have progressed to become mentors for their colleagues, and some continued their studies to MA programmes at the universities of Central Lancashire, Stirling and Bangor. By 1997, seven Diploma students had completed their MA teaching and training studies programmes. Examples of research issues studied include:

- SpLD, statementing and secondary schools.
- Relevance of self-esteem in children with SpLD.
- Approaches to teaching spelling in children with SpLD.
- Friendship patterns and SpLD.
- Dyslexia on trial? (A study of dyslexia as a contributory cause of imprisonment.)
- The effects of simultaneous hemisphere stimulation in learning disabled students.

As news of the successful effects of the training course on the work of SpLD teachers spread, and as it was endorsed by numerous examples of 'good practice' in mainstream schools, it became apparent that there was a demand for more widespread provision of SpLD training. Consequently, a University Certificate (Professional Development, SpLD) has been validated by the University of Central Lancashire in partnership with the LEA.

This course is delivered by LEA tutors and comprises a ten-session programme (30 hours) covering a range of SpLD issues. Its aim is to provide teachers with background knowledge, an understanding of problems of definition and terminology, with knowledge of identification, assessment and teaching/support strategies. The programme is open to a range of serving teachers, including teachers of pupils with SpLD, moderate learning difficulties (MLD), and emotional and behavioural difficulties (EBD), and reading/language specialists. It is proposed to convert this programme into an Advanced Certificate by adding a case study and further extending the provision of tutor support. The first cohort completed this award in June 1996 when 43 candidates were successful.

Sadly, the very successful Postgraduate Diploma (Professional Development) course came to an end in 1997. Its demise can be attributed to a combination of factors, including structural LEA changes, loss of central educational grant funding and declining numbers of potential students. This last factor does not stem from a lack of interest in the course, but occurred because the LEA had tightened the criteria for statementing of pupils with SpLD, and was conscious of the need to 'recycle' resources. It was was not, therefore, appointing SpLD support teachers in the same numbers as it did between 1992 and 1997.

However, the successful partnership between the LEA and the University of Central Lancashire has continued to develop a new generic SEN diploma with the recently validated Certificate (Professional Development, SpLD) as a key component. Such developments take into account Teacher Training Agency (TTA) requirements and advice, especially for expert teachers, subject leaders and SENCOs.

Two examples of good practice

Among the many examples of good practice in teaching pupils with SpLD are the two which are briefly described below.

Example 1: A school's learning support provision

St Michael's – an integrated approach

St Michael's High School, Chorley developed a very successful support system for pupils with an identified difficulty in either literacy or numeracy and who often also experience resultant emotional and behavioural problems. An intensive campaign was mounted to illustrate to class teachers and school governors the difficulties faced by pupils with SpLD. Parents were also involved in various home-school liaison initiatives and the PTA raised extra funds for technology equipment and reading materials. Gradually, the staff realized the need to alter their teaching methods and changes in the way in which pupils with SpLD are viewed by staff have led to more pupils being entered for formal examinations.

Pupils are now offered more independence through the use of technology. Laptop computers, dictaphones, scribing, photocopying of notes, spellchecking and paired reading have all become normal practice among pupils with an SpLD Statement. Letters to GCSE Boards have secured special provision for coursework and the final examinations once 'normal practice', i.e. strategies encouraged daily, was established. Pupils with reading and/or spelling ages some six or more years below their chronological age gained 'C' grades and above in the sciences, history, RE and design. In fact, in 1996 statemented pupils with SpLD achieved 'A' and 'A*' grades - but not without tears and doubts at times.

Many of the strategies put into place for supporting pupils with SpLD have now been offered to other pupils with SEN - both of low ability and also for 'gifted' children. Individual multisensory programmes are available for pupils across stages 1-5 of the Code of Practice. Strategies used to deliver these programmes include:

- One tutorial 'form' period per week – pupils are encouraged to attend private consultation time for their Individual Education Plan (IEP), counselling, coursework help or homework help.
- Throughout breaks and lunchtimes pupils have access to all learning support staff, tuition, social activities, games, computers and equipment in the Learning Support area of the school.
- After-school homework surgeries and specialist tuition is on offer to any pupil, in line with the school's equal opportunities policy.
- Working alongside the experienced, trained SpLD staff is a band of volunteers, including governors, parents, past members of staff, friends of the school, initial teacher training students who register an interest in supporting SEN pupils and Year 11 pupils. This allows more individual attention to be given to pupils without the added cost of staffing such an ambitious programme of support. Pupils do not become too dependent on an individual member of staff, and this allows for more effective in-class support across the curriculum.
- A positive learning support environment has been created throughout the school. The deputy headteacher is actually an in-class support teacher for one-fifth of his time. The headteacher is regularly seen in the Learning Support area and is keen to bring visitors into the department. SpLD/SEN support does not take place 'in the broom-cupboard'.
- Raising self-esteem in pupils with SpLD/SEN is an essential part of their IEP. Pupils who feel that they are failing all too often may 'throw in the towel'. The following strategies are used to enhance motivation, confidence and self-worth: commendations/merits for progress, socially and academically; certificates for attendance, spelling programmes, effort, etc.; colourful stamps on pieces of work; reward charts; treats, e.g. drinks; achievement notice boards; monitoring of effort with individual report booklets; monitor badges for pupils helping with lunchtime activities; and praise – positive comments both orally and written on pupils' work. Pupils are also regularly photographed during their lesson times and breaks, and displays around school show pupils of all abilities mixing, talking and working together.

Example 2: The language skills course at Beardwood School

The language skills course is followed by all pupils in Year 7, who attend one of the six sessions timetabled. Each weekly session lasts for 40 minutes. Pupils are initially divided into groups, based on primary school information relating to literacy skills.

The file

The course is modular and each pupil is issued with a file which is used as a cumulative record of pupil progress during the academic year.

Assessment

All pupils follow an initial assessment module which takes place during the first half of the autumn term. During this period, pupils' reading, spelling, handwriting and listening skills are tested. A record of scores is kept at the front of the file.

Upon completion of the assessment module, staff made recommendations in the report section of the file.

Tailoring the course to meet individual needs

Pupils are regrouped each half term so that their individual needs may be met. The teacher writes a report at the end of each module. Over the course of a year, therefore, pupils follow individually tailored courses to enhance and develop their language skills. The course emphasizes the importance of communication in all its forms.

Working in groups

Group sizes are deliberately kept small to maximize opportunities for pupils to participate in their courses. Group sizes range from 1:1 for exceptionally weak pupils up to 1:12 for the more able. Currently, 17 staff are involved in teaching the course, although not all teach every session.

Course content

All pupils learn and are tested on five curriculum-related words each week. Spelling and vocabulary scores are recorded weekly and prizes awarded for those who achieve 100% during a term. The remainder of the session is spent on working through their particular module. Teachers are issued with lesson plans to follow. There is a total of 17 modules in all, so there is a wide variety to meet pupils' needs. The modules are a mixture of commercial and school produced materials relating to the following topics: basic reading; spelling; handwriting, handwriting and spelling; spirals; library skills; study skills; research skills; reading for pleasure; listening skills; and higher level reading skills.

How have whole-school policies affected the learning environment positively and contributed to students' learning?

Factors which may be identified as central to the examples of 'good practice' illustrated in this chapter include:

- Individually tailored multisensory courses for students.
- Cumulative records of student progress.
- Involving pupils in their learning.
- Regular and easy access to counselling and advice for students.
- Raising students' self-esteem.
- Raising levels of support across the curriculum.
- The importance of information technology as an aid to SpLD students.
- A positive whole-school approach to SEN.
- Raising awareness of SpLD problems.
- Creating a positive learning support environment.

Conclusion

Central to the spread of good practice in secondary schools across the LEA has been the investment in personnel and the resource commitment to fund the training needs of both teaching and non-teaching staff. The LEA Diploma and Certificate have fostered an openness and willingness to share and exchange information about best practice for students with SpLD. The LEA's partnership with the University of Central Lancashire has encouraged critical and reflective debate about good practice with SpLD students. It has also heightened awareness of SpLD developments in the wider research community.

Thus, returning to the questions posed at the beginning of this chapter, it might be suggested that in the course of developing local education authority policies about SpLD, working collaboratively with colleagues in the local university may contribute not only to the development of a policy statement and guidelines but also to the shared creation of a wider framework and deeper research-based training programme for continuing teacher education. This also has a vital impact on the quality of support which can be provided in schools.

Acknowledgements

LEA: Ann England, Rosemary Bacon, Ron Radley and Sandra Farmer. University of Central Lancashire: Professor Alan Hurst, Ken Foster and Dr Gary Heywood-Everett. St Michael's CE High School, Chorley: the headteacher and governors, the learning support curriculum manager, Jan Farrow and Sue Craddock. Beardwood High School, Blackburn: the headteacher and governors, J Sturgess, SENCO, the Special Needs Department and L Cosby for secretarial and technical support.

Chapter 4

Multilingualism and dyslexia

John Landon

Introduction

Studies in England (ILEA 1985) and Scotland (Curnyn et al. 1991) have revealed that bilingual learners from minority linguistic communities are significantly under-represented in provision for SpLD/dyslexia. It is reasonable to assume that this is a 'false negative' (Wright 1991) and that, in fact, there is a failure to diagnose SpLD in bilingual students. Consequently, bilingual learners who have SpLD will not be receiving appropriate support at an early stage, leading to a situation later in their education where progressive lack of academic success is interpreted as a general learning difficulty or as the result of an inability to acquire English as a second language, or both (Hall 1995).

Current theories of dyslexia in native speakers of English concentrate on difficulties with phonological processing (Stanovich 1991; Snowling 1995). As a result, early screening procedures and intervention strategies, such as those recently advocated by central government, have concentrated on phonological awareness, letter recognition, and onset and rhyme. Teachers, therefore, may have become accustomed to interpreting good decoding skills as early predictors of reading success, and poor familiarity with rhyme and phonology as triggers for early intervention approaches (see McMillan and Leslie 1998). Recent research into the acquisition of second language literacy, however, suggests that these assumptions may be misleading as predictors of reading success in English for emergent bilingual learners.

Bilingual learners, phonological awareness and literacy development

A number of studies have indicated that bilingual learners may demonstrate levels of phonological awareness which are comparable, or even superior, to those of monolingual learners. This may be due to the complex processes of recognizing and distinguishing between the sound systems of two or more languages which bilingual learners inevitably face (Bialystock 1988; Campbell and Sais 1995). Alternatively, or additionally, phonological skills which develop in a child's first language through experience at home or in the community may transfer to aid word recognition in the child's second language (Durgunoglu et al. 1993). In this case, the patterns of phonological awareness and their relative dominance at different stages of the development of bilingualism will partly reflect the salient phonological characteristics of the dominant input language (Bruck and Genesee 1995). Thus, on entry to an English middle school, Bengali-speaking children often have good phoneme awareness because of the consistent phoneme–grapheme correspondences in Bengali (Gregory 1996; Frederickson and Frith 1998). As they, or children from other language backgrounds, acquire English they will develop onset–rhyme awareness since the onset–rhyme distinction is highly salient in English (Caravolas and Bruck 1993). Pre-reading verbal play, even in non-literate homes (Gregory 1994; Martin-Jones and Bhatt 1998), and approaches to the teaching of early literacy within a specific language community (Gregory 1996) will also reflect the salient features specific to that language. Thus, sustained practice leading to greater phonological awareness, in whatever language, will lead to effective literacy development in that, or any other, language.

Diagnosing subtle non-dyslexic learning difficulties related to limited oral proficiency and cultural experience in the second language

Students whose first language is not English who undertake a diagnostic reading assessment through English often score well on measures of accuracy (Frederickson and Frith 1998; Landon 1998). They also perform well in terms of accuracy when reading aloud in English. This may well satisfy a teacher who is looking for competent decoding that the learner is progressing well. However, more in-depth analysis of the reading behaviour of bilingual children at this stage reveals that a significant number are experiencing difficulties which are not evident on the surface. These difficulties manifest themselves in the high rate of reading failure which becomes evident among children from minority linguistic and cultural communities by the end of the second year of primary schooling, or after the initial development of decoding skills if the learner has entered the British school system at a later stage. These hidden difficulties may be the result of poor oral proficiency in the second language (Verhoeven 1990) which affects access to utilization of lexical and syntactic cueing systems to make predictions and inferences about meaning. In addition, when the cultural context of the text is inaccessible the learner's difficulties are compounded (Landon 1998).

These shortcomings in development in the majority language and culture only become evident as the focus of the curriculum shifts from an emphasis on decoding to a concern for reading for meaning. At about that time there is also a move in the choice of texts away from those which are well illustrated and use language that is closer to the spoken form, towards novels which observe the characteristics of literary genres. As Cummins (1984) and Thomas and Collier (1997) have shown, bilingual learners can perform well in settings supported by cultural familiarity and clear visual presentation within the first two years of learning a second language, but require much longer to perform adequately on tasks in which access to meaning is mediated through the second language alone.

Poor readers use compensatory strategies to make up for those areas where they are deficient. Whereas poor monolingual readers use their understanding of the cultural context of the text to compensate for their inadequate decoding skills, bilingual learners frequently use their superior decoding skills to mask their inadequate grasp of meaning (Carrell 1988). Indeed, their socialization into the function of literacy, both within their heritage culture and within the early reading regime of the school, may suggest that decoding alone is sufficient to demonstrate reading competence (Gregory 1994). An intervention programme, therefore, which focuses entirely on the raising of phonological awareness will miss the mark for failing bilingual learners. Instead, they require a programme which strengthens command of English syntax and lexis through development of the oral language, and which seeks to develop strategies to facilitate access to the cultural schemata of the text (O'Malley and Chamot 1990).

Bilingual learners, dyslexia and diagnostic errors arising from mistaken causal associations

As well as the bilingual learners, described above, who are experiencing reading difficulties, there will be a small number who fit the classic definition of dyslexia and experience 'problems in phonological coding resulting from segmental language problems' (Stanovich 1996). Current research (Deponio et al. 1999) suggests that their very different problems are being confused with the more general literacy difficulties common among bilingual learners from the second year of schooling onwards. Before that, their poor performance in screening tests is put down to the fact that they are at an early stage of second language development. Teachers and others involved in assessing such children are reluctant to diagnose dyslexia because they cannot exclude, to their satisfaction, other obvious causes of reading failure. This reluctance continues in some cases right through to the start of the GCSE or Standard Grade course, when concern to confirm dyslexia as a cause of reading failure is related more to the need to secure dispensations in the conduct of examinations from examination boards.

A small research study (Landon 1998) recently carried out in two Edinburgh primary schools suggests that early intervention through the medium of a child's first language within the first year of schooling may distinguish between children who can access English language texts once language and cultural difficulties have been mediated through the first language and those who cannot. Those who cannot may more reliably be assumed to have a general and/or specific learning difficulty. This research found that first language intervention was a powerful aid to raising literacy achievement in children who appeared through baseline assessments to be at risk of reading failure.

The discrepancy model and the question of reliability of assessment instruments

There still remains the difficulty of finding reliable instruments to determine whether the cause of reading failure is a severe phonological processing difficulty or whether other intellectual, social or emotional factors are interfering with the learning process. The use of discrepant achievement on performance and verbal subtests of IQ tests such as the WISC-R (Wechsler 1996) is now widely criticized as an indicator of language processing difficulties. Verbal subtests of IQ are particularly unreliable with regard to bilingual learners for two reasons. First, the tests have in almost all cases not been standardized on particular groups with different linguistic and cultural backgrounds resident in the UK (Cline and Reason 1993). Second, discrepant achievement is frequent among learners in the early stages of bilingual development and has more to do with the differential acquisition of contextually embedded and contextually disembedded language (Cummins 1984).

A recent exploratory project with Sylheti Bengali speakers in east London (Frederickson and Frith 1998) has suggested that the *Phonological Assessment Battery* (Frederickson et al. 1997) may be used to assess phonological awareness in monolingual and bilingual students alike. If these findings can be generalized to other linguistic groups, we will have a useful instrument for separating measures of phonological processing from other measures which may affect the reading behaviour of bilingual learners.

In the case of Chinese and, to some extent, Japanese children who come from linguistic backgrounds where non-alphabetic scripts are used, there is some research evidence (Kimura and Bryant 1983; Read et al. 1986;

Goswami and Bryant 1990) which suggests that poor phonological awareness may derive from the non-phonetic nature of the scripts of their first languages. Since ethnically differentiated data is generally not available on the incidence of statementing for SpLD it is impossible to tell whether Chinese learners are particularly at risk of misassessment (Landon 1996). Although it is usually considered that dyslexia, where it exists in bilingual learners, will be evident in literacy difficulties in both or all of their languages (Cummins 1979) there is some research evidence (Wydell and Butterworth 1997) which indicates that where the script of one language is not governed by phoneme-grapheme correspondences, non-reciprocal dyslexia may be possible.

The way forward

Over the last few years research into the literacy development of bilingual learners has gained pace. What we still do not know is what the diagnostic routes are which are being employed by teachers and others as they move from expressions of concern about the literacy development of a bilingual learner, through the assessment and monitoring processes to confirmation or rejection of dyslexia as a reason for literacy failure. However, what is clear is that for every single diagnosis we require far more information than is normally gained about learners' experience of, and achievement in, literacies in languages other than English. We need an interdisciplinary approach to the assessment, monitoring and support of bilingual learners who have reading difficulties. This will involve teachers of English as an additional language, learning support staff, educational psychologists and speech and language therapists. It will also include parents who, in the case of bilingual children, are frequently not kept informed nor involved in the support process (Deponio et al. 1999). We also need reliable means of measuring the early literacy development of bilingual learners which are not based upon monolingual reading behaviour as the sole normative source.

When that is done, we still have the question of how best to support bilingual students who are experiencing difficulties with literacy in English. Support in the first language, involving parents, community members and bilingual teachers, provides an irreplaceable basis. Other support must include the development of oral skills and comprehension strategies in the second language, which stress the social and interactive functions of language in spoken and written forms. Communicating and accessing meaning are the key, particularly for bilingual learners. Approaches which concentrate on levels of language below that of meaning, will open few doors.

Editor's footnote: bridging secondary and tertiary education

With appreciation to John Landon for this discussion which points to the importance of early and appropriate forms of diagnostic assessment, especially in the case of bilingual and multilingual children. I would also like to endorse this point concerning the need for continuing awareness on the part of teachers, taking this beyond the compulsory education phase of primary and secondary schooling into tertiary education. To this end I would like to include in this volume, the following Appendix designed for teachers and students in higher education.

Appendix

Guidelines for teachers and students in higher education**

1. Be aware that academic cultures vary: teaching and learning among culturally diverse groups enable us to see some ways in which this variation works.
2. Be aware that there are cultural aspects of communication and learning: these may affect teachers' and students' understanding of each other's communication and work.
3. Beware of transferring conclusions about cultural variation to representatives of those cultures: the culture is not the person, not every individual conforms to all the cultural trends, cultural generalizations themselves vary in how they are realized according to the context.
4. Try to reflect on how communication for learning is being used by students (and teachers): what presuppositions and cultural styles are involved?
5. Ask students (and teachers) about their expectations of learning; what do they expect about teachers' and students' roles, 'good work', written assignments, seminars, tutorials, etc? Discuss good examples.
6. Observe how students talk and listen to each other (and to teachers): which cultural aspects affect communication? Ask other participants later about any unclear aspects. A list of points to observe: intonation, pausing, silence, turn-taking, ways of asking, ways of showing respect, agreeing and disagreeing, where the main point occurs in discourse, how opinions are shared, attitudes to authority, role of memorization, being creative and original, degrees of explicitness, being critical, and critical evaluation.
7. Praise cultural synergy*; try to understand students' (and teachers') cultures of communication and learning, and other cultures (including

your own). What new teaching (and learning) strategies do you need to develop to take account of their cultural expectations?

* 'Cultural synergy' is defined by Cortazzi and Jin (1997) as 'the mutual effort of both teachers and students to understand each other's academic cultures, cultures of communication and cultures of learning. This would include the effort to understand others' principles of interpretation' (p. 88).

**With acknowledgements to the writers (Martin Cortazzi and Lixian Jin) and to Routledge (original publication pp. 89-90), Figure 5.1 Dyslexia and multilingual issues, in 'Communication for learning across cultures'. In McNamara D and Harris R. Overseas Students in Higher Education: Issues in teaching and learning. London: Routledge, 1997; 77-90.

Chapter 5

Spelling support in secondary education

Margaret Hughes and Morag Hunter-Carsch

Introduction

This chapter concerns spelling policy and practices in secondary schools. First, we put into context issues concerning spelling standards and introduce five premises. Then we review essential knowledge for teachers about spelling development and assessment. Finally, we turn to the development of a whole-school spelling policy.

Issues: standards, characteristics and challenges

Expectations about spelling standards

Secondary schools are obliged to produce school leavers who are competent in spelling in order to meet the expectations of a literate society. This obligation has been translated into the requirements of the National Curriculum in England and Wales (DfEE 1995). The policy document relating to teaching English includes eight 'Writing Level Descriptors' with Level 8 being roughly equivalent to the GCSE public examination level normally undertaken at the end of schooling. For spelling, the Level 7 description indicates that 'Spelling is correct, including that of complex irregular words' (p. 31). Clearly, it is expected that mastery of spelling is achieved prior to Level 8.

A major cause of the continuing difficulty in meeting this requirement is the diversity of spelling policies and practices across education sectors. There is a lack of consistency and continuity between primary, secondary and tertiary phases of education. Organizational patterns may vary across different curricular areas within any school or college and expectations for written coursework, and policy for marking formal examinations, are sometimes inconsistent. Although it seems likely that we are about to enter an era of information technology, offering automatic translation of speech to text and text to speech, the requirement for teachers to assist students to achieve mastery of the mechanics of written English will continue for the foreseeable future.

Dyslexic students frequently show phonological awareness difficulties in the primary phase of schooling and for some these persist into secondary and adult life (see Chapter 1; Snowling 1995). Hanley (1997) refers to two studies of adults who were diagnosed as children as having developmental dyslexia (Felton et al. 1990; Bruck 1990) and reports that:

> The adult dyslexics performed significantly more slowly and less accurately than control subjects on tasks of single-word reading and were significantly impaired in spelling. (p. 22)

However, Hanley and Gard (1995) found three subjects from a sample of 33 dyslexic adults whose profiles differed from the typical developmental phonological dyslexia profile. Hanley (1997) cautions that it is important that

> theories of dyslexia are able to account not only for the performance of the majority but also for those whose performance reliably differs from the typical phonological dyslexic profile. (p. 29)

The authors would add that knowing students' spelling developmental patterns from school records (primary and secondary), including samples of written work, can help to identify whereabouts fuller diagnostic assessment may be helpful in tracking the relative success or otherwise of spelling methods tried in the past.

Before embarking on issues of policy and practice it may be useful to consider briefly the features which constrain and shape spelling work at secondary level.

Characteristics of developing spelling in the secondary school and beyond

The 'archaeological dig'

Secondary school teachers are less likely than primary school teachers to know their pupils' spelling histories. It is, perhaps, not too fanciful to liken the teacher's task of exploring pupils' spelling knowledge initially to an archaeological 'dig'. There are only a few tell-tale signs on the surface to indicate the history beneath. 'Digging' may only unearth fragments from which pictures will have to be built. Here, we offer some suggestions for sources of information about diagnostic assessment and note also the value of liaison with pupils' feeder primary schools about the nature of their policy and practices.

For some years, the approach known as 'emergent writing' has been popular in some primary schools. This approach has much to commend it with reference to promoting children's confidence towards formulating their communications and 'getting them down' on the page or screen. It is not always clear, however, how the introduction of standardized ('correct') spelling is carried out. Nor is there adequate documentation of the effect on individual learners of the transition into use of standard English spelling from emergent writing. So, among the total population of struggling spellers at this stage, there will be some with spelling problems which may be overcome simply through systematic routine teaching - these we might describe as 'poor spellers' - and there will be others who have specific spelling difficulties - the dyslexic learners - for whom more specialist teaching approaches may be required.

'Picking up off the floor'

Many pupils arrive in secondary school with a rock-bottom estimation of their own spelling ability and progress may only be made if they can be supported in picking themselves up from that lowly viewpoint. The need for a fresh start is paramount (Watkins and Hunter-Carsch 1995). Above all, a change of attitude towards their own abilities as learners is the key learning support which those adolescents require. They may need to rebuild their self-esteem while learning how to cope with their individual difficulties in spelling. This need applies to both types of learners, poor spellers (whose problems stem from prior limitations in access to appropriate advice, resources, models, learning support or any combination of circumstances and contributing factors) and dyslexic learners (whose problems relate to the operation of their personal learning processes).

'Dressing lamb as mutton'

Many children will have acquired the ability to spell by the age of nine or ten years. Beyond that age further spelling work for them involves only incidental attention to atypical words. Thus, the learning of spelling may be considered to be primary-phase work. This, of course, exacerbates any disaffection which secondary pupils may already have developed towards spelling and faces secondary teachers with the challenge of engaging their pupils in appropriately mature approaches towards this fundamental building block of literacy.

'101 teachers . . .'

For some pupils entering secondary school, the increase in the number of teachers they meet may be overwhelming. Maintaining continuity and consistency in spelling development in all classes may constitute an additional problem for teachers. Consequently if they are to overcome this problem, schools need a clear, whole-school policy on spelling, all teachers with some knowledge of the teaching of spelling and at least one or two teachers with specialist spelling knowledge.

The aim now is to signal priorities for secondary school staff: what do teachers (both generalists and specialists) need to know about spelling? This question is considered before we address issues related to learning support for students with persistent spelling difficulties and priorities for an effective whole-school spelling policy. The response to the question and related issues is based on five premises:

- It is important to draw upon a wide range of existing research-based information about knowledge of how spelling usually develops and about the characteristics of spelling difficulties.
- It is unlikely that any single approach will successfully meet the needs of all learners.
- It is essential to take into account learners' prior knowledge about spelling, never to assume a tabula rasa.
- It is vital to maintain a sense of learners being 'in control'.
- It is useful to recognize how and when pupils should employ coping strategies.

Essential knowledge about spelling development

Essential knowledge about spelling development for subject teachers and the starting point for specialist teachers of spelling, must surely begin with an appreciation of the range of attitudes to 'correct spelling'. Without entering into the wider discussion about the nature of literacy and what constitutes increments in levels of literacy, dealing solely with matters of attitude to spelling involves recognition that, for some teachers, the assumption that incorrrect spelling is inexcusable still exists. Yet, in January 1996, the Basic Skills Agency estimated that two-thirds of adults, including more than 50% of undergraduates, could not spell *accommodation*, one in three could not spell *receive, sincerely* or *apologize*, whereas more than half the adult population had trouble with *necessary* and *immediate*. A survey of Oxford undergraduates (Ezard 1998), conducted in January 1998, recorded as many as 140 common mistakes, from 'abolishion' to 'skeptickle'. Awareness of the seeming lack of success of schooling in spelling might modify the unhelpfully judgemental attitude displayed by some teachers and perhaps encourage them to explore the reasons for the problems. All teachers (including non-specialists) should be aware that:

- For many learners, spelling is 'caught'; but for very many others it must be taught (Peters 1967, 1985).

- Confidence in spelling frees the writer to concentrate on meaning.
- Spelling can unlock meaning.
- Spelling mistakes are not all equal.
- Some spelling mistakes show greater difficulty with spelling than others (this realization is the starting point for the delivery of individually appropriate help).
- There is a big difference between knowing how to read (decoding) and knowing to spell (encoding), although phonological awareness (awareness of sounds within words and of syllables) is a vital sensitivity which underpins both.
- Spellers may have to relate (and translate) literally heard (spoken) language into words that fit the context.
- The English spelling system involves more than a simple one-to-one correspondence between letters and sounds. (However, there is a system! Teachers and learners need to shed any despairing view that English spelling is impossibly arbitrary and come to understand that there is a system there (Morris 1984, 1993).)
- Teachers who have perceived the essential order become communicators of optimism.
- The teacher's own delight and interest in words will enhance all spelling work.
- In making sense of the system, learners may need some terminology to talk about spelling.

Clearly, teachers' attitudes, knowledge and skills concerning how and when to teach what, constitute interrelated factors which have a crucial effect on learners' access to the right connections in spelling, just as in reading. Debates about how best to relate the whole to the parts, and the parts to the whole, of the language experience (and whether the method should be 'top-down' or 'bottom-up' in direction) have tended to lead to false polarizations. However, the importance for secondary school teachers of appreciating their students' relevant primary school experience of different teaching methods cannot be overstated in cases of persistent spelling difficulties. The effect of prior experiences of learning support for spelling, handwriting and content writing (or its absence), and the accompanying feelings which are recalled, form the basis on which subsequent experiences are to be built (Hunter-Carsch 1990; Chapter 14 in this volume).

For subject teachers, basic knowledge about teaching spelling may be augmented by consultation with specialist literacy teachers and those with special education training who have a more detailed appreciation of how spelling is normally learned and what constitute typical problem areas. The following paragraphs illustrate some of the information in this further tier of knowledge.

How spelling usually develops (and where something might go wrong)

It is useful to consider the acquisition of spelling as comprising three strands. These relate to phonemes, graphemes (requiring visuo-motor memory) and morphemes. The phonological route stems from a fundamental appreciation that writing is a code for spoken language and deals with the written word as composed of symbols which represent the heard word (which represents the referent). In English, graphemes (written letter forms) represent phonemes (sounds). More than one grapheme may be used to represent some phonemes (e.g. *ph, f*). Some phonemes can be represented in various ways (*loud, clown*) and some graphemes can be used for a variety of phonemes (*cat, father; any, was, nation; orange, own, clown*).

The visual-motor memorization route is readily observable in writers' attempts to try out alternative spellings for words in order 'to see which one looks right'. It is the ability to recall visually the patterns of whole words, and of letter strings within words, from which is developed a sense of what letter strings are usual in English. There is also a motor aspect observable in the automaticity of many spellings once handwriting and keyboard skills are developed to the relevant level. 'Spelling is in the fingertips' (Peters 1985).

However, spelling is also 'rooted in thinking' (Ramsden 1993). A reasoning approach is endorsed by the emphasis on investigative activities in the National Literary Strategy. By relating spelling to grammar, writers can deduce correct spelling. This involves awareness of morphemic structure of words (Nunes et al. 1997; Bryant et al. 1999) and also of etymology of words (Miles E 2001).

There is general acceptance that the learning of spelling progresses through characteristic stages, although this is not a concept conveyed with clarity in the English National Curriculum Level descriptions for writing. The limited space available here does not permit full discussion of the anomalies, nor the inclusion of an integrated theoretical model (Hughes, in preparation) drawing on those of several researchers, including Frith (1980), Henderson and Beers (1980), Peters (1985), Read et al. (1986), Czerniewska (1989), Peters and Smith (1993), and designed to resolve some of the problems.

At different developmental stages, one or other of the two routes (phonological or visual-motor memorization) may dominate. For instance, in order to operate at the phonetic stage, learners will have learned all the most frequently occurring phoneme-grapheme correspondences, usually through having been supported by at least some systematic direct tuition. At the later transitional stage, learners will have developed an awareness of visual patterns and common letter strings. Importantly, however, at any developmental stage, and especially for secondary school learners, it is inaccurate (and unhelpful) to regard the two routes as mutually exclusive. Perhaps relating the experiences from both routes may be essential to meeting the range of individual learners' needs. The Leong (1997) research findings were made independently of the Lazo et al. (1997) findings, but both suggest a need for the 'happy compromise of a marriage between current connectionist models of literacy development and stage models' (Leong 1997, p. 102). It is also well recognized that, with reference to diagnosing dyslexia characteristics, there are complexities when attempting to categorize students who show phonological difficulties and those who show morphemic difficulties (with the orthographic system) into discrete subgroups, since mixed subgroups can also be found. It is more likely that there is a continuum for each of the characteristics associated with dyslexia (Maeland 1992, Herrington and Hunter-Carsch 2001).

When addressing questions relating to students with persistent spelling difficulties it may be helpful, in contrast, to sharpen awareness of the characteristics of successful spellers, especially in the relationship of affective to cognitive dimensions of experience. Attitudinal characteristics of successful spellers tend to include the following:

- Motivation to write.
- Confidence to have a go.
- Good self-image as a speller, based on recognition of successful achievement of prior learning goals and knowledge of procedures (e.g. ways of coping - use of charts, dictionaries, spellchecks).
- Carefulness, based on informed awareness of the place of spelling in the writing process and of personal learning strategies.

All of these are closely related to meta-cognitive awareness (being aware of/thinking about the thinking and spelling process itself, not only the communication of the intended message). These attitudinal factors are affected, on the one hand, by the nature and range of learners' access to good models and, on the other, by the opportunities they are given to explore and expand their learning (Hunter-Carsch 2001c).

Attitudinal factors are closely related to cognitive factors which include:

- Verbal ability (vocabulary experience and fluency).
- Articulatory ability (interface between verbal and auditory abilities).
- Auditory abilities (phonemic awareness, auditory discrimination, auditory sequential memory).
- Visual abilities (perceptual skills in differentiating and recognizing letter forms and word forms/being able to 'see' parts of words, e.g. *con* and *science* in *conscience*), visual memory and recall, visual-motor skill in relation to developmental attempts to write.
- Ability to code (understanding the symbol system), memorization of phoneme-grapheme correspondences.

- Ability to generalize.
- Ability to make analogies.
- Ability to form and test hypotheses in relation to emerging awareness of spelling rules.

The ability to generalize both draws upon, and increases, existing spelling knowledge of at least two types. The first is 'word-specific information' which is held in a word store or 'lexicon', and the second is 'orthographic knowledge' which involves stored information and working hypotheses about how the spelling system functions. Ehri (1985) provides three examples of the second type of knowledge. These include:

- Morphemic (meaning-bearing syllable, e.g. *-ing, -ed, un-, -day* (as in *birthday*)).
- Lexical families (words which have the same meaning are spelled in the same way, e.g. *sign/signal, autumn/autumnal, muscle/muscular*).
- Probability (e.g. not many words in English end with *v; q* is usually followed by *u*; *f* is used more frequently than *ph*).

These understandings, and their deliberate deployment in forming analogies and in generalizing (Goswami 1993) are vital tools in the development of spelling. There are, additionally, two 'experiential factors' (hands on experiences) that relate to implementing learned skills. These are 'kinaesthetic memory' (the ability to write swiftly and legibly, i.e. automatically) and 'knowing and accessing resources' (the ability to locate and employ efficiently spelling resources such as dictionaries and spellcheckers). It is thus the analysis of spelling difficulties in terms of the dynamics of such affective, cognitive and experiential factors that becomes essential if effective learning support is to be provided.

Approaches to diagnostic assessment of spelling difficulties (and screening out handwriting difficulties)

Some students' spelling problems may be compounded by handwriting difficulties or obscured by seemingly sloppy writing. A brief screening procedure for a group or whole-class screening for handwriting speed is described by Hunter-Carsch (1991) based on Otto et al. (1973). It is important to differentiate between 'general writing difficulty', including slow writers, and specific problems possibly related to developmental motor difficulties. Specialist assessment and teaching/learning methods for handwriting are described elsewhere (Fernald 1943; Cruickshank 1963; Gordon and McKinlay 1980; Wedell 1982; Alston and Taylor 1990; Alston 1992; Augur and Briggs 1992; Markee 1995; Alston 1995; Sassoon 1995; Chapman 1998).

With reference to the assessment of spelling, as the scope of this chapter prohibits equal depth of discussion on all of the issues relating to spelling policy and practices, readers are referred to other sources for selection of tests of spelling achievement and for diagnosis of difficulties (Peters 1983; Ellis 1989; Klein and Miller 1990; Smith 1994; Alston 1995; Vincent and Claydon 1992; Reid 1996a; Montgomery 1997; Ott 1997; Turner 1997; Vincent and Crumpler 1997). However, it should perhaps be noted that although the concept of 'spelling age', like 'reading age', may be helpful in surveying large groups to ascertain the range of levels of achievement, the spelling age conveys limited information, is not designed to take account of motivational factors and may be based on word lists that may not include words which individual learners either know or wish to know. Furthermore, there may be limited connections between the strategies employed in a test situation and those in a learning interaction with a skilled teacher. In addition, teachers need *in situ* criterion-referenced forms of monitoring learning and retention, i.e. diagnostic profiles based on active learning, which indicate learners' strengths and error/miscue patterns more dynamically, and is able to explore what happens when different approaches to learning spelling are tried (see Chapters 13 and 15; also Peters and Smith 1993; Watkins and Hunter-Carsch 1995; Lannen et al. 1997).

Broadly, the developmental emphasis in the preceding section, and Table 5.1 below, may provide information to support both task analysis and miscue analysis but have not dealt with issues involved in working with learners of English as another language, whose home cultural and literacy expectations and spelling conventions of other languages may need to be taken into account (see Chapter 4).

Teaching and learning support for spelling

Secondary school adolescents are particularly sensitive to the attitudes of their peers, and are likely to dislike appearing to be different. As adult life is approached, they may not welcome offers of in-class adult support and, increasingly, need to set their own agendas about what they write and the nature and extent of their written communications. If secondary pupils are not given effective encouragement and peer acceptance their will to write by choice may be limited. The peer tutoring approach developed by Watkins (1996) and Binns' (1984) systematic drafting and re-drafting provide organizational approaches which permit teachers to observe and offer incidental tutoring while managing the whole class. By the use of information and communication technology (ICT) approaches, it is also possible for teachers to organize individual teaching in a manner which can extend to adapting ICT programmes to meet individual needs (see *STARSPELL 2001* (Fisher-Marriott and Hughes 1999)). Speech-to-text and text-to-speech systems, with suitable adaptations to facilitate slowing of speech, are being developed by

Table 5.1. Some indications of types of spelling difficulties

Areas of difficulty	Typical indications
Articulatory	'tuaffic' for *traffic*, 'juke' for *duke*, 'must of' for *must have.*
Phonological awareness (phonemic awareness, syllable recognition, word boundary)	Phonemic awareness: confusion of vowel sounds, e.g. 'pen' for *pin*, 'are' for *our*, 'except' for *accept*. Confusions of voiced and unvoiced consonant-pairs, e.g. c/g, d/l/th, v/f - 'ufn' for *oven*, 'fin' for *thin*. Syllable recognition: 'organation' for *organization*. Word boundary recognition: 'trade you none' for *trade union*.
Visual	Confusions and reversals of letters, and of whole words, e.g. b/d/p, m/w, n/u, s/z; *was/saw, no/on*. Difficulty in recalling sequence of letters, e.g. 'fihgt' for *fight*, 'paly' for *play*; vowel phonemes with *r* are often mis-sequenced to form an unwanted blend with *r*, e.g. 'gril' for *girl*, 'from' for *form*. Failure to memorize a core of common words, *there/their, because, always,* etc.
Memorization of phoneme-grapheme bonds	'lad' for *loud* because unable to remember how to write the 'ou' sound.
Compensatory tactics	Deliberately poor handwriting to hide spellings. Substitution of easy words for more appropriate but difficult words. Avoidance of writing, producing very short pieces of work.

Haase (2001) for initial reading, spelling and writing training and second language learning; see also *Yak-Yak* (Larsen 1999) which has been developed with, and for, adults.

For those with subtle persistent spelling problems and whose difficulties may be described as SpLD (dyslexia) as defined by the Code of Practice (DfEE 1994) (i.e. employing the 'discrepancy theory' model), it is often helpful to teach spelling within the framework of a structured multisensory approach to literacy. By use of combinations of visual, auditory, tactile and motor experience, learners are able to use their sensory strengths at the same time as developing their weaker sensory processing (Orton 1932; Fernald 1943; Ehri 1980; Brown and Ellis 1994; Frith et al. 1995). However, part of the difficulty for both teachers and pupils when trying to follow the advice to adopt such an approach is that there is such potential for differences in understanding of what is implied by the term 'structured multisensory approach' and, as Cooke (1997) points out, even within one such system (Look-Cover-Write-Check), it is essential to understand exactly how the sequence of steps - involving the use of different sensory processing and the combination of processes - is designed to support the learning of the particular individual.

Kite charts for selecting teaching and learning approaches

The following 'kite charts' (Figures 5.1-5.6) attempt to introduce or remind readers of some of the methods which have proved helpful. Teachers might select from these an approach which is likely to meet the learning needs and style preferences of individual pupils in their particular contexts. The emphasis of each of the approaches is noted briefly. Some charts are followed by a commentary on the characteristics of the approaches. Readers are recommended to go to the original sources for further information.

The writers' experience suggests that pupils' own inventiveness can be a powerful avenue through which to arrive at the most effective approach for developing their own spelling. Different strategies may be employed for different kinds of words according to the students' own systems for classifying degree of difficulty. Spelling recovery can often be facilitated by exaggeratedly slowing down the articulation of the word(s) to be written (spelled) and, preferably, singing them with each syllable and even accompanying the sound (singing) by taking steps forward so that both auditory and kinaesthetic-motor involvement is maximized. Once the components of the word have been experienced separately, it becomes easier to try to isolate the phonemes within the syllables and to begin to identify those, usually by use of a small 'speech mirror' (pocket mirror) to look at the changing position of the mouth, lips and tongue as the phonemes change during spoken articulation and slow singing of the word. (See also speech training and literacy teaching methods currently employed in Finland and in teacher training in Scotland in the 1960s.)

At secondary phase, some sensitivity and good humour may need to attend the use of such an approach, possibly in a one-to-one context and out of sight of students' peers! It usually takes very little practice, however, for students to become confident in 'singing slowly in their heads' (i.e. silently). Comparable sensitivity is required in the use of neurolinguistic programming and some interesting developments of this approach were illustrated by Pool (1993).

In whatever guise, matching individual spelling work to detailed analyses of individual learners' cognitive profiles and their responses to different strategies for learning to spell can lead to greatly improved learning. This is

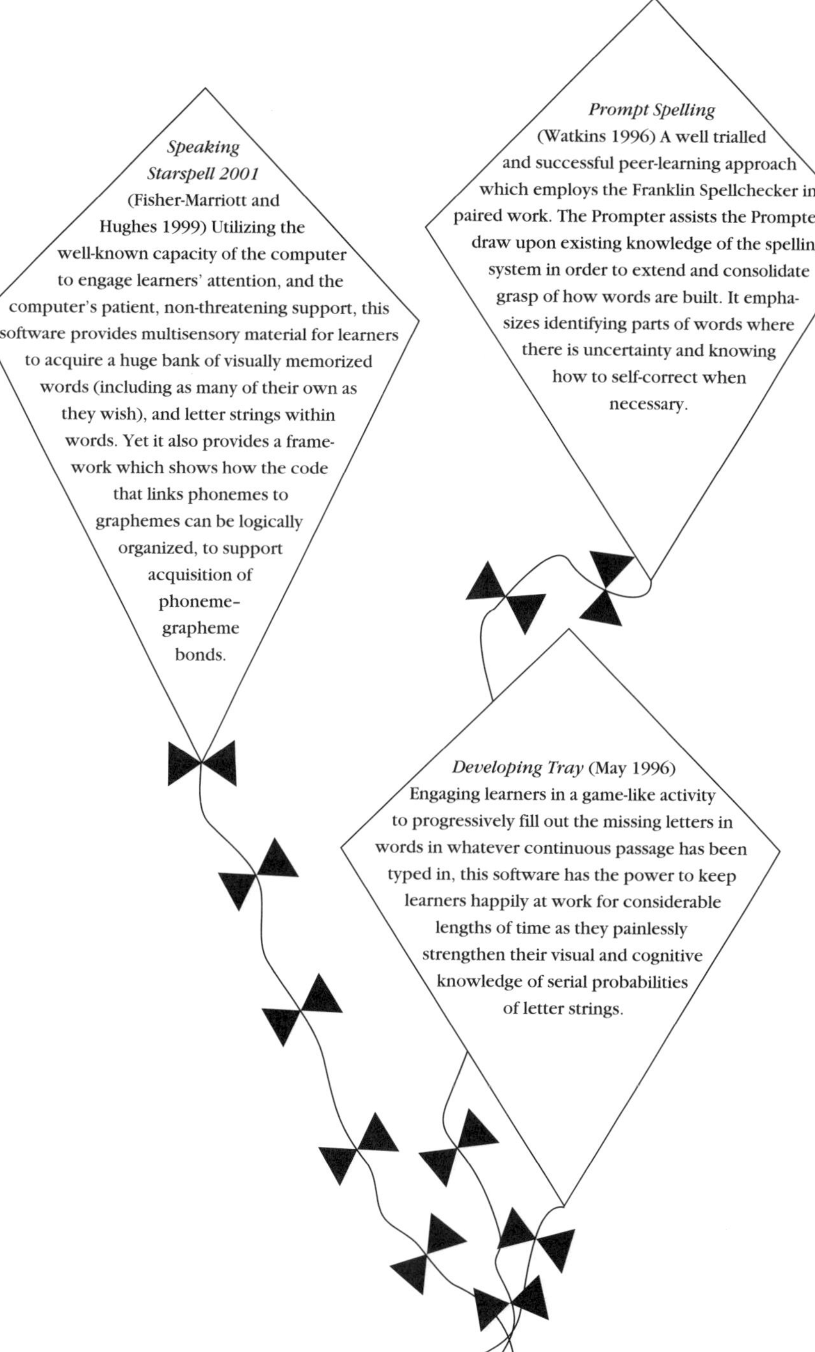

Speaking Starspell 2001 (Fisher-Marriott and Hughes 1999) Utilizing the well-known capacity of the computer to engage learners' attention, and the computer's patient, non-threatening support, this software provides multisensory material for learners to acquire a huge bank of visually memorized words (including as many of their own as they wish), and letter strings within words. Yet it also provides a framework which shows how the code that links phonemes to graphemes can be logically organized, to support acquisition of phoneme-grapheme bonds.
Prompt Spelling (Watkins 1996) A well trialled and successful peer-learning approach which employs the Franklin Spellchecker in paired work. The Prompter assists the Promptee to draw upon existing knowledge of the spelling system in order to extend and consolidate grasp of how words are built. It emphasizes identifying parts of words where there is uncertainty and knowing how to self-correct when necessary.
Developing Tray (May 1996) Engaging learners in a game-like activity to progressively fill out the missing letters in words in whatever continuous passage has been typed in, this software has the power to keep learners happily at work for considerable lengths of time as they painlessly strengthen their visual and cognitive knowledge of serial probabilities of letter strings.

Figure 5.1. Approaches employing ICT.

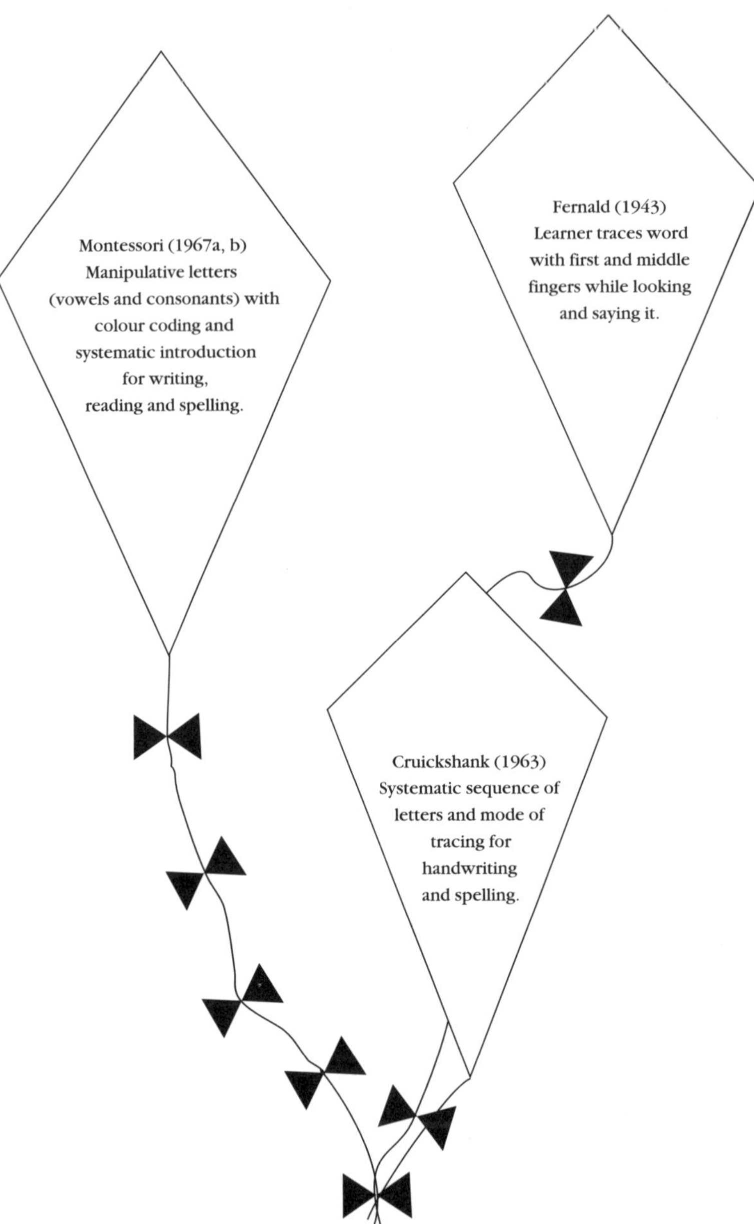

Figure 5.2. Structured multisensory approaches. Extra tactile experience can be added. It can be done quite simply by getting the learner to finger-trace the word letter by letter on the table top before writing it, or strengthened by offering choices of surface - velvet, fine sandpaper, a salt-covered tray or the palm of the hand.

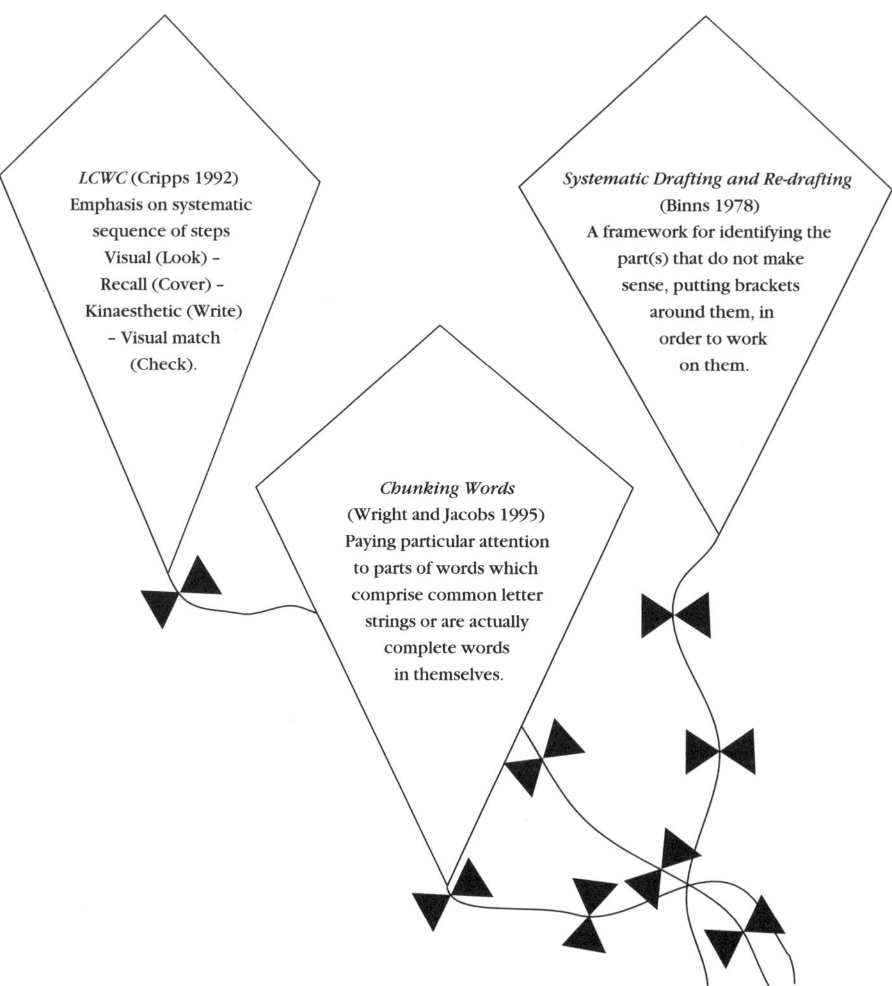

Figure 5.3. Approaches with a strong visual component.

The effectiveness of the Look-Cover-Write-Check routine is greatly strengthened by adding Say-Trace (with finger) between the Look and Cover components. It thus becomes much more 'multisensory'. Pupils usually need training in what to look for, and are helped by advice and tuition in finding 'little words in the big', in identifying morphemes and syllables. Direct the learner's attention to meaning *and* visual elements. They often find it useful to focus on what is, for them, the 'hard spot' and may enjoyably but profitably make up their own mnemonics. They need to be shown that remembering is to do with making links. Peters (1983) summarizes what is necessary when she speaks of the importance of the three *I*s to this routine: *Interest, Intent, Intention*. It is important to train learners to memorize the whole word. They should not copy it bit by bit, but always attempt to hold the whole in mind. In so doing, they may look back at the word as many times as necessary, but never have it in view as they attempt to write it.

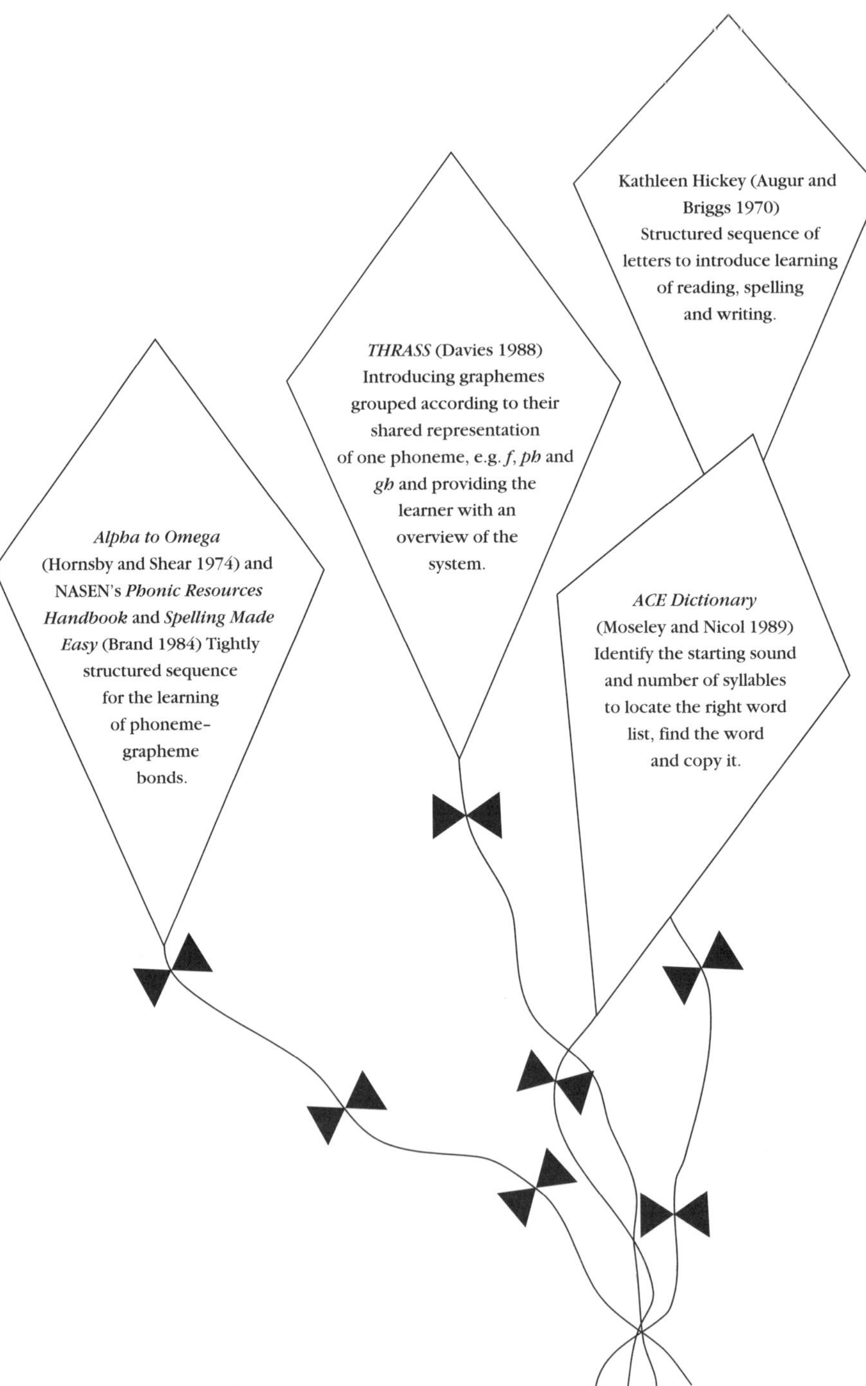

Figure 5.4. Approaches with a strong phonic emphasis.

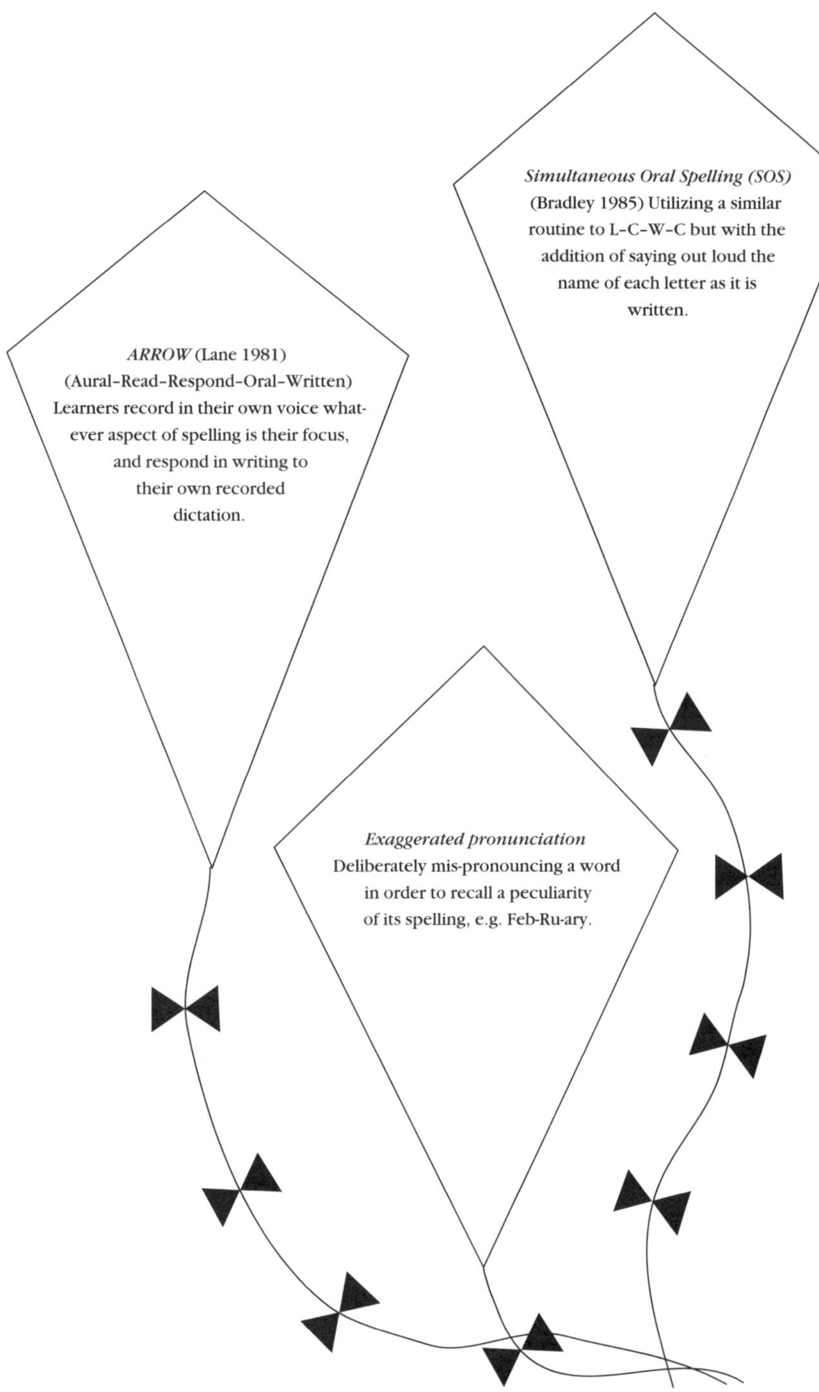

Simultaneous Oral Spelling (SOS)
(Bradley 1985) Utilizing a similar
routine to L-C-W-C but with the
addition of saying out loud the
name of each letter as it is
written.
ARROW (Lane 1981)
(Aural-Read-Respond-Oral-Written)
Learners record in their own voice whatever aspect of spelling is their focus,
and respond in writing to
their own recorded
dictation.
Exaggerated pronunciation
Deliberately mis-pronouncing a word
in order to recall a peculiarity
of its spelling, e.g. Feb-Ru-ary.

Figure 5.5. Approaches with a strong auditory element.

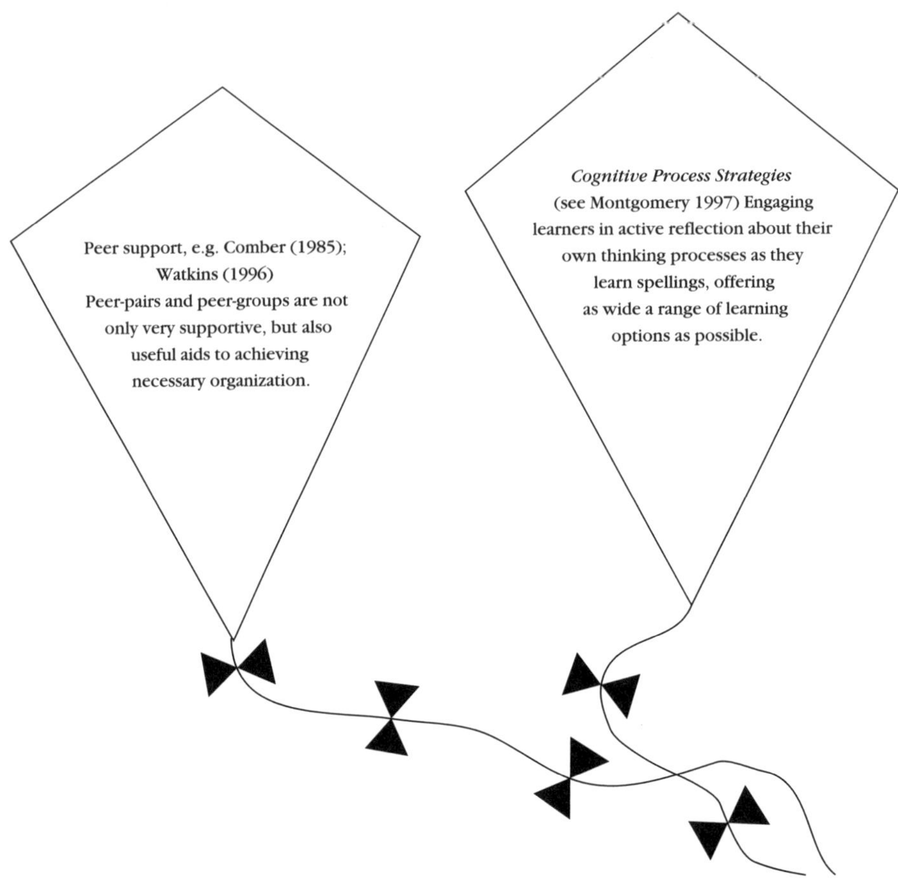

Peer support, e.g. Comber (1985); Watkins (1996)
Peer-pairs and peer-groups are not only very supportive, but also useful aids to achieving necessary organization.
Cognitive Process Strategies
(see Montgomery 1997) Engaging learners in active reflection about their own thinking processes as they learn spellings, offering as wide a range of learning options as possible.

Figure 5.6. Two other approaches.

strongly suggested by a recent study (Brooks and Weeks 1999), which usefully offers a practical and user-friendly format for teachers to conduct their own investigations of their pupils' preferred learning styles.

Developing a whole-school spelling policy

If spelling is to be considered as a formal part of literacy development and that is taken to be a fundamental right for all students' educational entitlement, the knowledge of what to do (how to spell correctly and how to get support when necessary) to achieve this becomes essential information for all staff and students. Gains (1995) provided guidelines for developing a whole-school/college reading policy which we have adapted here for spelling policy. His model guides us to:

- Identify sources of weakness in policy and programmes.
- Focus on particular phases that need further development and strengthening.
- Anticipate staff development programmes.
- Give clearer indication as to the direction in which the school policy might proceed.
- Provide a basis for predicting resource requirements.

In order to begin to take the five steps listed above, a spelling audit should be undertaken.

The policy suggested in the Appendix assumes that supporting the learning of spelling (i.e. teaching spelling) becomes the responsibility of all teachers, even where it may be possible to provide additional advice from specialists for both staff and students. Having an effectively communicated spelling policy, and clarity on the part of all staff and pupils about procedures and support systems, are prerequisites for shared growth in confidence, on the part of individual students, to seek to discuss spelling matters.

Conclusion

Clearly a stronger spelling-development component in initial teacher training is required as is a greater awareness amongst experienced teachers of their role in this field since it constitutes a part of literacy and communication and affects students' learning and achievements in many areas across the curriculum.

The effects of the National Literacy Strategy (McClelland 1997; DfEE 1998, 2000c) are already beginning to suggest that in England and Wales, there is increased teacher awareness of both theoretical and practical aspects of spelling in literacy development. It is not yet clear, however, whether there is increased employment of structured teaching of spelling as a part of primary schools' daily literacy hour practices and to what extent and in what ways children's spelling is affected.

The British Dyslexia Association along with the Teacher Training Agency are working to heighten teachers' awareness of dyslexia in primary and secondary schools, not only by disseminating video materials which illuminate some of the spelling problems discussed here but also by supporting development of a multisensory teaching package to assist teachers to support dyslexic youngsters in individual or group work within the literacy hour in primary schools (Johnson et al. 1999).

In an ideal world, the principles of continuity and progression, and of provision of effective learning support, would be operational in all primary schools and might suggest that a 'fresh start' approach to spelling should not be necessary in secondary schools. But reality includes a range of quality of provision that leaves some spellers struggling at the end of primary school, not all of whom are identified as dyslexic. Thus, some diagnostic challenges remain for secondary school teachers. Reality also includes the fact that students going into secondary school are entering their transition into adulthood that requires, increasingly, independence in learning and secure self-knowledge, as well as self-confidence, in order to refine the literacy skills required within and beyond the secondary curriculum. For these reasons, a different approach from those used in primary school may be needed. In particular, learning support should be experienced positively by the students, whatever the cause of the individual's spelling difficulties.

This chapter has drawn attention to the fact that some of the cognitive skills required for spelling are among those which are characteristically described as areas of SpLD in dyslexic students. Teachers may discover, through dialogue with these students and observation and analysis of their written and recorded work, that they can sometimes 'look through a window on to students' learning processing' and come closer to understanding what their experiences of learning (and, in particular, learning spelling) actually involve and perhaps at what actually constitutes effective teaching (see Chapter 15; Hunter-Carsch 2001c).

Although spelling problems may constitute only one part of the dyslexia constellation, difficulties with literacy skills make it a significant one. The genuinely inclusive quality of our schools' policies and practices may be gauged not only in terms of the successes in increments in spelling test results but in the representations, mental images and affective associations which dyslexic students retain in their memories of both peer and staff support in secondary school.

Appendix

A suggested secondary school spelling policy*

> The main problem is to get the programme put into effect so that the work is not merely spasmodic effort interspersed between long periods of incorrect activities. (Fernald 1943)

1 This policy reflects agreement between the staff about aims.
2 It requires a shared effort by all to convert aims into practice. It recognizes both the ORGANIZATIONAL and the CURRICULUM implications. Senior management agrees the need for: INSET on spelling; agreement on

*Refers to the policy guidelines designed and trialled by Margaret Hughes in teachers' continuing professional development courses in Warwickshire in 1997.

teaching approaches; communication systems between specialist language, SEN teachers and subject teachers (see 9 below); provision and deployment of resources; responsibility for checking the implementation and encouraging the success of the spelling policy.

3 Spelling is the responsibility of all who receive written work from pupils. It is their responsibility to be aware of the stages of development in spelling and of a range of teaching approaches.
4 Resources to support the spelling policy include: staffroom library of informative teacher material and designation/training of spelling specialists; consultation time with the language co-ordinator, SENCO/SpLD specialists.
5 Spelling is part of the whole curriculum and its development requires the following understandings: routine handwriting and spelling screening should take place early each academic year; spelling should not be linked inevitably to testing; pupils with spelling difficulties should be identified and appropriate support, including specialist advice, be provided; pupils should be encouraged to 'have a go'; they should be allowed 'temporary spellings' as holders of meaning, and be able to trust us with their right to be tentative' (Comber 1985); teachers should understand how to deal with these 'temporary' spellings; pupils need time for work on spelling; this should be negotiated where possible, they should not be penalized where this reduces time on other agreed work.
6 Across the curriculum, spelling is taught in the context of routine writing. Subject teachers need to: provide opportunities to write in a variety of genres; encourage pupils to develop positive attitudes to writing; assist them to develop an appropriate view of the place of spelling in writing and communication; point out what is praiseworthy in pupils' attempts (including 'virtuous errors') and show them their work is valued; respond to pupils' work in ways that help them discover more about spelling for themselves; foster a lively interest in words and make spelling enjoyable; identify key vocabulary for each subject and develop approaches which maintain that key vocabulary as a focus for spelling attention; develop methods for providing spellings which avoid pupils simply copying but not effectively learning them; consider any special needs which pupils may have with regard to seating arrangements in class (left-handers, visual and auditory problems, editorial partnerships).
7 Teaching of spelling complementing the integrated cross-curricular work is: an integral part of the school's policy; included in schemes of work across the curriculum; timetabled where necessary (e.g. SEN Code of Practice). It includes: correct letter formation and fluent handwriting, where needed; teaching appropriate to developmental levels and/or specific spelling needs; effective word-study techniques; how to

proofread; how to use spelling resources (personal/class word-bank, graded dictionary and thesaurus, electronic spellcheckers).

8 The school aims to support the teaching of spelling through the provision of adequate resources, including print resources, appropriate ICT and spellcheckers (see para 3.69 SEN Code of Practice (DfEE 1994, 2000a)).

9 Time is to be allocated for co-ordinating a system for communicating about teaching and the specific spelling teaching (e.g. spelling vocabulary from subject areas passed to the 'spelling teacher' with information on pupils' development and needs passed from spelling teacher to subject teachers).

10 A consistent approach should be adopted for dealing with spelling errors. It should include: agreed symbols for marking; expectations of correctness adjusted to match pupils' levels of development; quality not quantity of errors critically evaluated; emphasis on 'corrections' adjusted to focus on priorities in cases of SEN/SpLD.

11 The assessment of spelling, including diagnostic assessment, is fully incorporated into the SEN Code of Practice (DfEE 1994, 2000a).

12 The school aims to ensure that pupils with severe spelling problems are never excluded from writing; strategies may include: peer support; ICT support; in-class tuition; amanuenses.

13 The school aims to ensure that pupils with severe spelling problems are not disadvantaged in public examinations. The Examining Boards have varying requirements and allowances, and specific advice should be sought.

14 The school aims to communicate to parents its policy and practices relating to spelling.

15 The school aims to meet prerequisites for the spelling policy co-ordinator's effectiveness.

CHAPTER 6

Effective learning in the secondary school: teaching students with dyslexia to develop thinking and study skills

BARBARA EDGAR

This chapter is about:

- The importance of analysis in the teaching of study skills.
- The cognitive processes involved.
- The importance of teachers' skills in asking questions.
- Training in inferential thinking and in generalization of learning.
- Focusing on problem solving by scanning and data gathering.

Introduction

Much is already known and practised in relation to study skills for students with specific learning difficulties (SpLD) or dyslexia. Actual use of these skills by students depends on a number of factors, individual learning approaches being one of the most important. Students need to become aware of their own preferred learning style and to acknowledge that they may need to develop a range of strategies to enable them to tackle a range of learning tasks.

This awareness of 'own style' is discussed by Flavell (1976), who maintains that meta-cognition, knowing what we know and how we learn, is a very important skill. He separates this into two separate forms of competence: declarative knowledge, about the cognitive system and its contents, and the effective regulation of that system. Students must be encouraged to focus on the cognitive processes involved in their learning in order to regulate the system.

Sovik et al. (1994) concluded that cognitive functions 'related to and decisive for various strategies' were difficult to determine. They conceded, however, that these strategies play an important role. If teachers can help students to isolate and analyse these strategies, learning may be facilitated. Siegler (1991) identified the 'task-specific' strategies brought to bear in problem solving as vital, whereas Sovik et al. (1994) stressed the importance of 'across-domain' strategies which may be generalizable to many learning situations. In reality, students will benefit from understanding of both. It is often the case that explicit teaching of study skills is essential in terms of enabling students to organize their learning. For this reason, study skills should remain as an important element within the syllabus. In order to develop study skills more effectively it is essential to focus closely on the cognitive processes required to perform certain tasks.

An attempt to isolate cognitive processes and strategies, and to make them accessible to students, has been made in the work of Reuven Feuerstein in the form of Instrumental Enrichment (IE) (Feuerstein et al. 1980) and the Learning Potential Assessment Device (LPAD) (Feuerstein et al. 1979). The LPAD comprises a range of assessments which are used dynamically to endeavour to establish the potential of a child or student to achieve. The belief is that static assessments of intelligence are incomplete and that all children are 'modifiable' and able to change their thinking processes in order to become more efficient learners (this is a simplistic explanation of a complex process). The work on both IE and LPAD has been criticized (Frisby and Braden 1992) and the training for use of the materials is extensive, so that teachers may find it difficult to undertake. The approach is similar to that advocated by De Bono (1986), the difference being that with the latter materials, little training is considered necessary. The approaches recommended, and the structure provided in both programmes can be used effectively with students with SpLD to help them begin to understand the cognitive processes through which they move when tackling a learning task. It is expected, however, that teachers who have undergone some training will use the materials more appropriately.

There are other published resources which are based on the work of Feuerstein. Those easily available in the UK include *Somerset Thinking Skills* (Blagg et al. 1993), *Top Ten Thinking Tactics* (Lake and Needham, undated), *Bright Start* (Hayward et al. 1992) and the materials of John Jensen (Jensen 1993) (some of these aimed at the younger or less experienced student). Many more programmes are available in the USA. The programmes are not, in general, aimed at students with SpLD, but there are elements which, used creatively and adopted into general teaching methods, should prove of benefit to them.

Teacher intervention

Initially, the most important element in this type of work is the teacher. Feuerstein outlines mediated learning experience (MLE) which is based on Vygotsky's (1978) 'zone of proximal development':

> It is the distance between the actual development level as determined by independent problem solving and the level of potential development as determined through problem solving under adult guidance or collaboration with more capable peers. (p. 35)

The initial interventions of teachers in guiding their students' cognitive approaches are seen as crucial to development. Eventually, it is assumed, students will internalize these processes and use them independently. Many students will be confident and competent with the lower levels of thinking. They can often cope with activities which interrogate their knowledge and comprehension of a subject. Difficulties may arise when they are asked to consider higher level activities. These include evaluation, synthesis, analysis and application. It is here that teachers must develop focused questioning techniques. It is necessary to move from the questions which investigate the lower levels of thinking: 'What do we mean by . . .?' and 'Who, what, when, where, how?' type questions to those which focus upon the higher levels of thinking.

Students should be encouraged to consider other examples, to use criteria to judge and assess, to isolate evidence for their understanding and beliefs and to improve upon or re-create arguments from a different standpoint. These may be elicited by the following range of questions (Bloom et al. 1956):

- What other examples are there? (applications)
- What do you think about . . .? (evaluation)
- What is the evidence for . . .? (analysis)
- How could we add to . . .? (synthesis)

The questions can help with the development of many of the skills which students with SpLD often find difficult:

- Classification
- Organization of material
- Sequencing
- Comparison
- Elimination of extraneous material

- Categorization
- Relationships
- Interpretation
- Visualization
- Planning behaviour
- Information processing
- Similarities and differences
- Inferential thought
- Hypothesizing

Many of these skills may be addressed in multisensory programmes such as the Kathleen Hickey (see Augur and Briggs 1992), but they are often addressed in a concrete way. Feuerstein's, and similar programmes, aim to enable students to make the shift from the concrete to the abstract.

Training in inferential thinking

In order to achieve this shift, Blagg et al. (1993) suggest, teachers need to 'develop flexibility and adaptability in the pupils, i.e. teach them to transfer and generalise'. This should be the aim of all thinking skills programmes and it is also stressed in the work of Feuerstein, although he calls it 'bridging' and 'transcending'. De Bono (1986) maintains that 'the ability to tackle easy problems with great fluency and depth seems quite separate from the ability to tackle difficult problems'. Real-life situations are given importance and this reinforces the utility of the programme in the same way as bridging and transcending. The aim for students with SpLD is to enable them to tackle the easy problems easily so that they can develop the structure for further understanding.

If we take just one of these higher level skills and analyse a task which is presented, we will have a clearer picture of what is involved. Inferential thinking, for example, is one area which often causes students difficulties, and lack of perception in this area often means that work produced is flat and lacking in critical analysis.

It is important that this facility is fostered early in a child's education, so that it can be developed fully by the time a student is required to submit essays, etc. for assessment. Tzuriel (undated) has developed some materials in this area for younger children, but they bear looking at for older students as they develop the process in a very structured manner. The materials consist of a book of 'puzzles' which children have to solve, initially with input from their teacher, and they are used as part of dynamic assessment. The interest for students with SpLD is that the later stages deal with greater processing load and transfer of learning. The format, which can be adapted for use as a teaching tool for older students, is presented as follows.

A page is laid out with a series of lines which make a ‘sentence’. The sentences which can be inferred are written underneath each line (Figure 6.1). Students have to collect and eliminate information from each line in order to locate each of the objects on the left of the sentence in the boxes at the top of the page. There is one rule at this stage, an object from the left *must* go into the shaded box.

	Red	**Black**	**Blue**
Line 1 dog mouse	Red	Black	

(From this line, the student can infer that either dog *or* mouse *must enter the blue box)*

Line 2 mouse flower		Black	

(Mouse *and* flower *go in the red and boxes blue)*

Line 3 plane mouse	Red		Blue

(Mouse *must go in the blue box because it occurs in all three lines.* Flower *goes in the red box according to information from line 2. Therefore* plane *must go in the black box as that is the only option in line 3.* Dog *is eliminated.)*

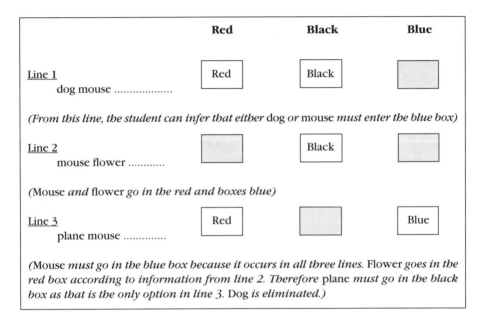

Figure 6.1. Sample of material for training in inferential thinking (adapted from Tzuriel undated).

This task involves many of the skills which students with SpLD find difficult, some of which are listed earlier. It can be undertaken with concrete materials. Tzuriel uses cards with matching pictures which can be placed in the houses at the top as a decision is reached. It is, however, useful with older students, to begin in this concrete manner and slowly to increase the load on short-term memory (STM) by asking students to complete the process in an abstract way and then to sequence the operations verbally. The idea can be used with a wide age range, adapting presentation as appropriate. It is the *process* which is important. The interaction between teacher and student can usefully proceed along the following lines:

T. What do you see on the page?
S. Some words and boxes and some colours.
T. What do you think you are meant to do?

S. *Decide which word goes in which box?*
T. Very good. How do you suppose you might do that
S. *Look at each line and decide which word goes in the box.*
T. Why do you suppose some boxes are shaded?
S. *It could be that you can't use that box.*
T. That's a good idea. What you have done is to try to establish a rule. There is a rule for this page. It is that the shaded box must contain one of the words on that line. So how would you start?
S. *Look at the first line and* dog *goes in the box.* [This is a common response, students react to the first word they see, rather than engaging in reasoning behaviour.]
T. But how do you know that the dog goes in the box? What about the mouse?

Students are thus encouraged at each stage to give reasons for decisions and to consider all possibilities. The teacher focuses on positive reinforcement and always states why a response was good, rather than simply stating that it was good. In this way, students' thought processes are articulated and given greater emphasis and their self-esteem can be raised.

Tzuriel extends the process by introducing new rules. For example, cross-hatched houses on a line mean that none of the objects on that line can enter that house. This requires an adjustment in thinking. The later pages address transfer of learning by giving students the answer and asking that they provide the 'sentences' which will give that answer, using either one or both of the previous rules. The student is required to use visuo-spatial skills throughout the exercises in addition to focusing on information processing. Each new exercise can provide a greater load on STM. Students gain practice in manipulating several pieces of information.

A series of tasks of this nature provide a good introduction to the skills involved in inferential thinking and can be developed further by utilizing these skills when working with texts. One of the problems with transfer is that students are often capable of 'near' transfer, which is what happens in these exercises, but do not make the connection that enables them to make 'far' transfer, i.e. apply what they have learned to different situations (Lidz 1987).

'Far' transfer of inferential thinking skills would be addressed through work with texts. Much has already been written about directed activities related to texts (DARTS) (Lunzer and Gardner 1979) but this has not always been associated with students with SpLD. DARTS activities are designed to encourage students to interact more closely with texts and include Cloze procedure and SQ3, a system for interrogating the text which involves surveying, questioning, reading, recalling and reviewing. The activities are beneficial for students with SpLD, but it is often assumed that once an activity has been explained, students will immediately be able to cope with its application. This is not always the case. Students with SpLD often require plenty of overlearning and reinforcement of a process before they can apply it.

Working with thinking skills in a simpler format often paves the way for them to be able to make applications.

In the case of inferential thinking it is useful to ask students to produce a 'map' for the inferences made from text, as follows:

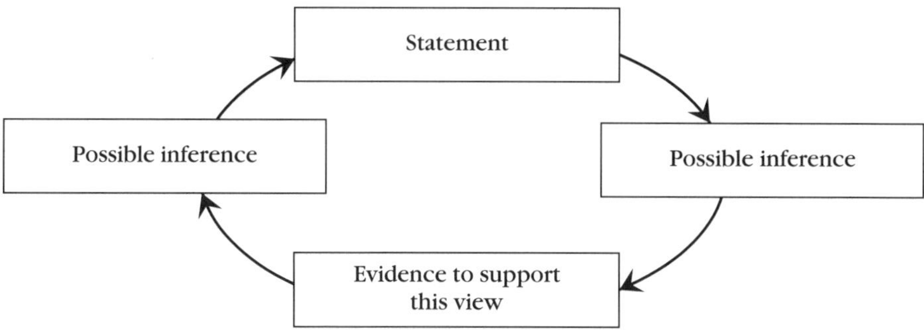

In fact, this method can be used when working on the earlier stages of inferential thinking as well, in order to provide initial support for students. The structure may be withdrawn when students become more adept at the abstract process and reintroduced at the transfer stage or as necessary. A simple example of this in use would be as follows:

Mr and Mrs Elliot could not open the door		
locked, no key	too weak	not their home
	evidence collected from other areas of the text	
they had searched their pockets, looking for something	none, in fact they had young children so unlikely	incorrect, earlier statement confirms that it is

This format can also be used to encourage students to hypothesize about possible reasons and it develops creative thinking in terms of alternatives.

All thinking skills programmes are structured so that the cognitive processes are introduced and explored incrementally. Thus, the strategies which are introduced in the first module are repeated in different formats throughout the course as new ones appear, a very similar format for overlearning to that in acknowledged structured, cumulative, multisensory programmes.

Feuerstein's IE programme consists of 14 'instruments' or modules; Blagg's *Somerset Thinking Skills* programme reduces this to seven:

Instrumental Enrichment (IE)

Organization of dots
Orientation in space 1 and 2
Comparisons
Analytical perception
Illustrations
Categorizations
Temporal relations
Family relations
Numerical progressions
Instructions
Syllogisms
Transitive relations
Representational stencil design

Somerset Thinking Skills

Foundations for problem solving
Analysing and synthesizing
Comparative thinking
Positions in time and space
Understanding analogies
Patterns in time and space
Organizing and memorizing

Programmes such as these, as mentioned earlier, depend to a great degree on skilled teacher input. If they are used, as is often the case, with lack of understanding of their purpose, or by teachers who see them as a set of puzzles which can be used as time-fillers, then their impact will be lost. It is essential that there is discussion at every stage. This involves the students in learning and using new vocabulary to better effect. The programmes are best delivered in a group situation rather than as one-to-one sessions. In this manner, a wider range of situations can be explored.

Supporters of thinking skills programmes stress that listening and speaking are important elements for development. It is not simply a one-way process, however. As teachers, we do not always utilize silence to good effect. If a student does not respond within a short space of time, we often jump in and explain the problem another way round or rephrase the question. Students with processing difficulties may just have reached a conclusion and be about to speak when we change the focus and they have to start again.

As a mediator in teaching thinking skills, silence is a vital tool. Once the student is started in the right direction, using the question formats mentioned earlier, the most useful interventions are often 'Go on . . .' and 'Yes, and . . .?' Students are thus encouraged to make links for themselves and to develop chains of reasoning. It is at this juncture that 'bridging' and 'transcending' are often useful. The main purpose for working on thinking skills tasks is not to be able to solve that single problem but to apply the processes to new learning situations. Feuerstein advocates comparing the task just completed to a task that might occur in real life and thus making the links stronger and easier to recall. Blagg et al. (1993) state that one of the functions of thinking skills programmes is 'to heighten their awareness and control over many cognitive processes that can then be applied spontaneously to many different problems'.

Scanning and data gathering

Two important processes are therefore stressed at the beginning of any problem solving activity. The first is to scan. This does not have the restricted sense of scanning which is used in DARTS. The process is not limited to scanning a book, but to scanning the problem as a whole and isolating the important elements. Students then focus on each of these elements and analyse the task requirements. The framework is thus set for a logical progression through the task.

One of the areas which often causes problems for students with SpLD is that of planning behaviour. This is demonstrated in lack of organization. Thinking skills programmes stress the fact that before any task is tackled, there needs to be a plan. Fisher (1990) outlined the difference between experts and novices in terms of planning behaviour. He claims that experts tend to spend more time planning and divides this into three stages:

- **Stage 1:** Define the problem, what is it that is to be achieved? This is a standard strategy for students with SpLD, they should be asked to rephrase the task that has been set for them. In this way, it is made clear that both teacher and student share the same understanding of the task and it also limits impulsive behaviour. Ideas can often be extended or clarified at this point. If key words are also jotted down, a stronger framework to proceed is provided.
- **Stage 2:** Begin to gather data. Here, again, organization is the key. Many students have no idea of how to make notes, this is one of the skills that many teachers seem to think someone else has taught them. In fact, if students have not been exposed to a study skills course, it is unlikely that anyone has covered this skill with them. Students respond well to different methods: key words are useful; students can also be encouraged to write on alternate lines when making notes so that if anything has been missed when they review their notes (initially with the teacher) then it can be added between the lines without squashing everything in in an illegible manner; pattern notes are useful for still other students who respond to a visual stimulus. The actual pattern created on the page can be a powerful stimulus for both planning and recall. Use of colour for various sections may be an added help.
- The above activities result in **Stage 3:** a visible representation of thought (see Figure 6.2, p. 86).

A major problem for many students with SpLD is often that of low self-esteem or a poor self-image. When students plan efficiently and can justify their chosen approaches or their reasoning in a logical manner, the boost to their confidence, and hence their future work, can be quite outstanding. The main motto throughout Feuerstein's work is 'Just a minute, let me think'. If students are allowed to take that time and plan within structures, they can achieve. Demonstrating to them that they are competent is the first step.

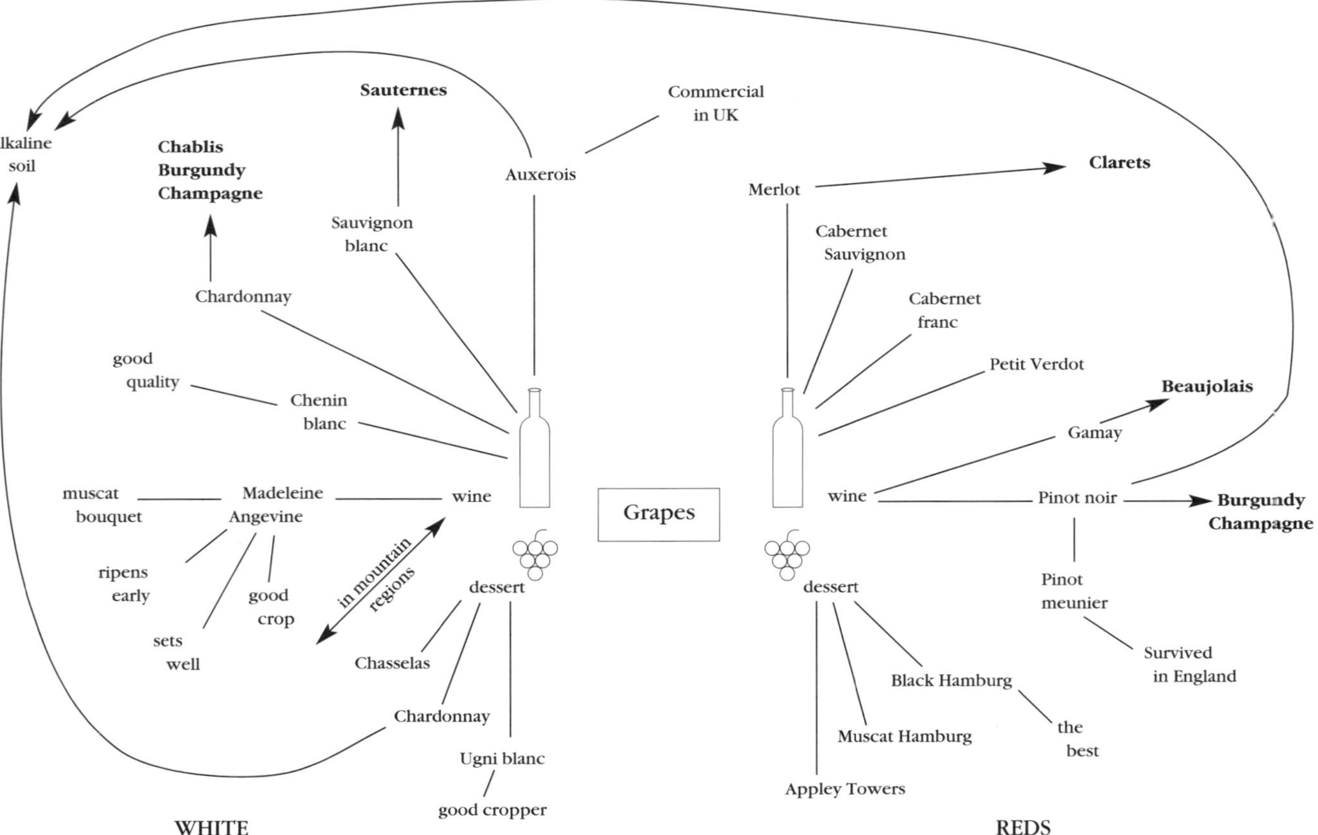

Figure 6.2. Stage 3. A visible representation of thought: possible grape varieties for Northern France.

CHAPTER 7

Supporting communication in education

ROSEMARY SAGE

Introduction

There are students in schools and colleges who have difficulty in processing information presented to them and in producing a coherent response to questions. These communication difficulties go unnoticed as such students usually answer *specific* questions and speak reasonably clearly. They might be considered as having undefined specific learning difficulty(SpLD), which affects their ability to access education through the medium of spoken and written language. The following discussion aims to outline the problems for such students and to examine some of the issues relating to their academic performance.

The pattern

Katy is 12 years old and reads fluently and clearly but cannot retell the content of text as her ideas lose focus and she goes off track. She answers specific questions and gives an impression of knowledge. Her conversation shows a similar scatter performance with irrelevant ideas often expressed. Her teacher describes her as a poor listener with problems in retrieving words as she is inclined to say 'thingy' for the name of something. Observation of Katy among her peers suggests she has difficulties entering a conversation and is often left on the sidelines, saying nothing.

A case history reveals that Katy was slow to speak and benefited from speech and language therapy when she was five. Her mother reports that although her speech became clearer and she was talking in longer sentences she still appeared to have difficulties coping with school work. Her testing at 12 years of age produced the following profile (Table 7.1).

Table 7.1. Assessment profile of Katy at age 12 years

Test	Age level score
Non-verbal intelligence - *Raven's Progressive Matrices* (Raven 1993)	12 years
Comprehension (sentence level) - *Test for Reception of Grammar (TROG)* (Bishop 1989)	12 years
Syntax, semantics, memory - *Clinical Evaluation of Language Fundamentals (CELF)* (Semel et al. 1987)	11 years
Narrative (re-telling a story) - *Sage Assessment of Language and Thinking (SALT)* (Sage 1998)	6 years

This profile shows a clear cut-off between Katy's skills at a primary language level, coping with sounds and sentences, and at secondary level, requiring the ability to build meaning across sentences. This was very evident in the CELF test where Katy scored full marks on the 'listening to paragraphs' subtest. As an extra to this assessment, Katy was asked to re-tell the story. Her response was very different from the text and similar to results on the SALT narrative test.

This example suggests important assessment and management issues that have relevance for learning success. Tests that concentrate on components of language which are assessed in a single-sentence response format do not reveal problems with use of language in chunks of talk or text, as in a discourse situation. For example, if a text comprehension task is given, as in the CELF test, and specific questions are asked and answered, this may not tap overall meaning. Tests of discourse that consider language in a whole context (as in a conversation or story) are not automatically applied, so that this perspective is seldom monitored or considered in case management. A question and answer and story re-telling task, known as the Sage Assessment of Language and Thinking (SALT) (Sage 1998), suitable for use with primary and secondary students, is proving useful in clarifying narrative abilities that underpin spoken and written discourse.

The situation above is common in my experience of helping students who have problems in learning. Such circumstances are supported in the literature (Wallach and Miller 1989; Bell 1991) and by anecdotal evidence of teachers who bemoan the fact that information goes in one ear and eye of their students and out of the other with limited processing in between!

Communication management in education

When students enter school or college they encounter a very different communication style to the unplanned drift of conversation outside.

Classroom discourse is formal and directed to a goal. Frequently, talk is delivered in monologue, with the teacher giving a series of instructions or an amount of information. In a large group, students need to have courage to put up their hands and reveal that they do not understand what is being said.

Classroom communication can, therefore, constitute a challenge for both teachers and learners. The messages that pour out through words, actions and the sense of who and what we are, filter through the minds of others. What finally is understood is likely to be different for each listener or reader, according to how they are able to share meanings with the speaker or writer. The fact that learning takes place through the communicative process makes it a precarious business. One can never be sure that others will be able to take ideas on board. Apart from the message itself, the roles that people have in the situation and their personality, appearance and performance are very influential in deciding how information is received. For example, if someone does not like extrovert, brightly dressed, noisy people who teach in an enthusiastic style, the content of what they say is going to be disregarded. These *affective responses* form an integral part of spoken communication experiences.

Understanding the ways in which students create meanings and providing an environment and curriculum that will refine and expand opportunities for doing so are major concerns. Students need to be able to process large chunks of instruction and explanation and are expected to create a 'Gestalt' and apply this in a variety of ways. The whole 'Gestalt' is the entity from which the interpretative skills of identifying the gist – inferring, predicting, extending, evaluating and concluding – can be processed. Therefore, forming the 'Gestalt' is an integral part of thinking activity.

Roth (1987) reminds us that we know little about the ability to integrate pieces of information into a unified picture. For example, the interaction between people's knowledge of narrative organization (macro-structure) and their syntactic ability (micro-structure) is not well understood. Learning tasks involve deductive (top-down) and inductive (bottom-up) strategies, embracing both macro- and micro-structures. Research by Sage (1986, 1990) demonstrates that students with communication problems often have difficulty in employing both organizing strategies. They do not easily grasp the whole picture, or if they do, cannot flesh out the skeleton with supporting details. Bell (1991) reminds us that we assume students can achieve the whole idea from the bits of information they see, hear, feel and experience. She suggests that many fail to reach a 'Gestalt' and consequently attend inefficiently to classroom discourse and do not make satisfactory academic progress.

Organization of linguistic information takes place at two major levels. At the primary level, sounds are put into words and then arranged in sentences.

At the secondary level, linguistic forms integrate with meaning derived from knowledge of social and cognitive conventions. For example, the sentence 'Take a bow.' only makes sense from the clues of the context which allow us to discover whether the sequence refers to a hair ribbon, body inflection or bow and arrow. Unless one can grasp the whole idea, the sentence is ambiguous and cannot be interpreted accurately.

By the time students have reached senior schools they have generally mastered basic sounds and syntax processes at the primary level of language organization. However, many students display huge problems with deriving and dealing with meaning so that they only grasp isolated details of the lesson content. In helping such students, approaches that go beyond linguistic issues are indicated, and three main areas of support need consideration. These include:

* Teacher/therapist communication styles.
• Interactions of students.
• Resources employed.

All three areas will be considered in turn.

Teacher/therapist communication styles

The research of Miller (1984) suggests that we communicate information according to our own preferred learning style. Therefore, if a teacher or therapist takes in information best by *hearing* it in a 'bottom-up' strategy they are likely to do a great deal of talking and fail to provide an overview of the lesson. This makes it difficult for students with a *visual* preference for learning in a 'top-down' mode to access the information presented. Therefore, those of us involved in giving information to others must be aware of our own communication styles and how we employ them so that adjustments can be made when necessary.

In addition, we need to hone our presentation and performance skills so that our messages are as clearly expressed as possible. We convey meaning primarily with our eyes, facial expressions, gestures and voice so the rest of our visual picture should not detract from this focus. Image, including our appearance, voice dynamics and body language, are important aspects of communication and can affect attitudes and classroom control.

There needs to be strong emphasis on increasing awareness of the limitations of our own learning styles and communication performances in initial professional training. Although communication abilities are implicit in the assessment procedures for therapists and teachers there may be limited *direct* assessment and feedback on these in a range of professional tasks, such as discussion, interviewing, instructing and subject presentation. Since these performance skills require working on to maintain standards, there is a need for a programme of voice and communication workshops so that professionals can refine their skills as communicators. Actors understand this message well and employ a professional coach for each new role they undertake on stage and screen. As professional communicators, teachers and therapists have an obligation to enhance their expertise in conveying clarity of information for the continuing benefit of their students.

Student interactions

Students are organized for work either individually, in pairs or groups in classroom settings. It is important to establish groups that *facilitate* rather than *inhibit*. Sage (1990) looked at students in several classroom situations and found that collaboration and communication were best facilitated with students of similar rather than mixed ability. In mixed-ability groups, students with problems tend to be ignored and are prevented from practising their communication skills. This is an important issue to consider as it may not be beneficial to send students for outside learning support work if there are no opportunities to use their newly acquired skills when interacting with their peers inside the classroom.

Therapists have a valuable role to play in monitoring classroom interactions, and techniques such as sociograms and language discourse analyses can provide helpful descriptions of patterns of communication between students and teachers.

Resources

Students may need work to be differentiated by level, task or output for them to access the curriculum. However, this is rarely enough for those with narrative problems who show difficulties in putting ideas together into a whole and who need teaching which targets thinking and language in a developmental approach. A framework developed by Sage (1986) known as the Communication Opportunity Group Scheme (COGS) has been found useful in developing the macro-structure that facilitates meaning. This is a teaching and assessment scheme that supports National Curriculum and vocational demands, so facilitating what goes on in school, college or work and encouraging independent learning. It can operate in small groups for an hour a week in either the oral English, the personal and social education lesson or through external workshops and training programmes.

Figures 7.1 and 7.2 show data for a student using the COGS approach compared with one who had individual work on vocabulary and spelling. Both students had a similar profile of abilities at the beginning of the academic year, but the COGS produced a greater incremental effect. It has clear tasks at each of the 14 levels which are assessed after about eight weeks' teaching. Students then collect a certificate for their Record of Achievement or curriculum vitae. It, therefore, appears part of the overall education process rather than a supplementary learning approach.

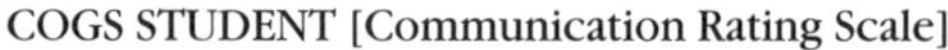

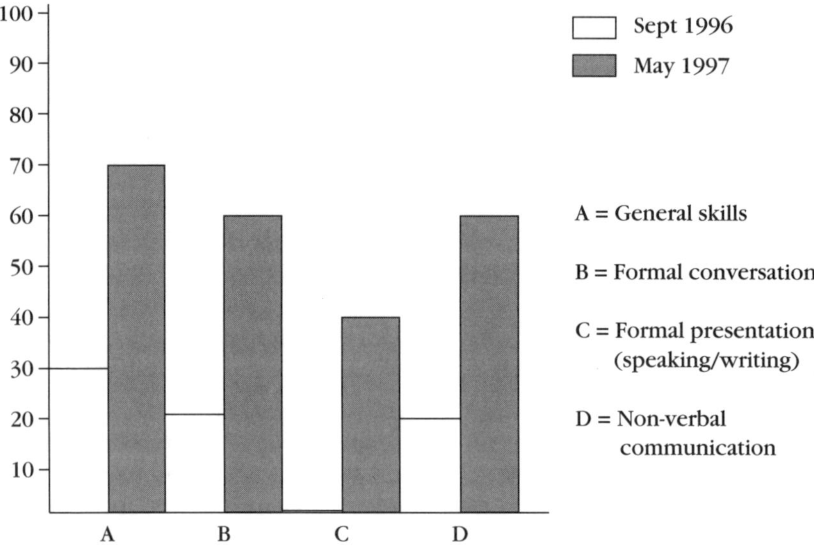

NON-COGS STUDENT [Communication Rating Scale]

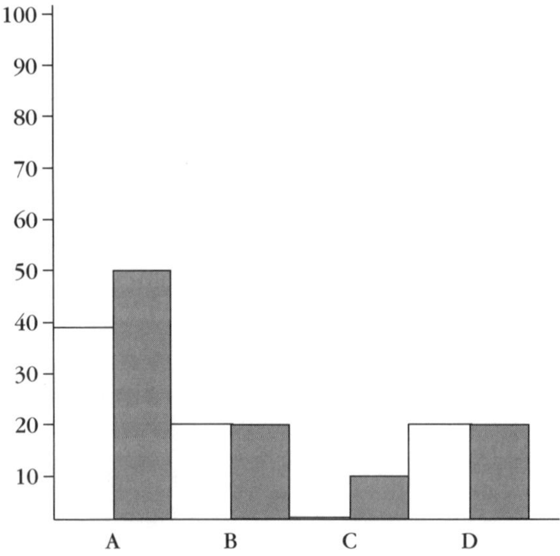

Figure 7.1.

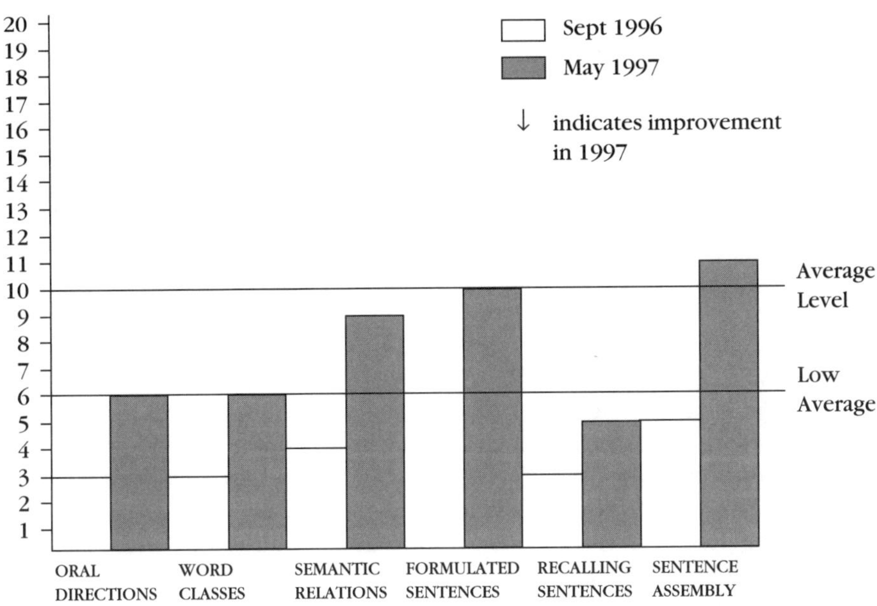

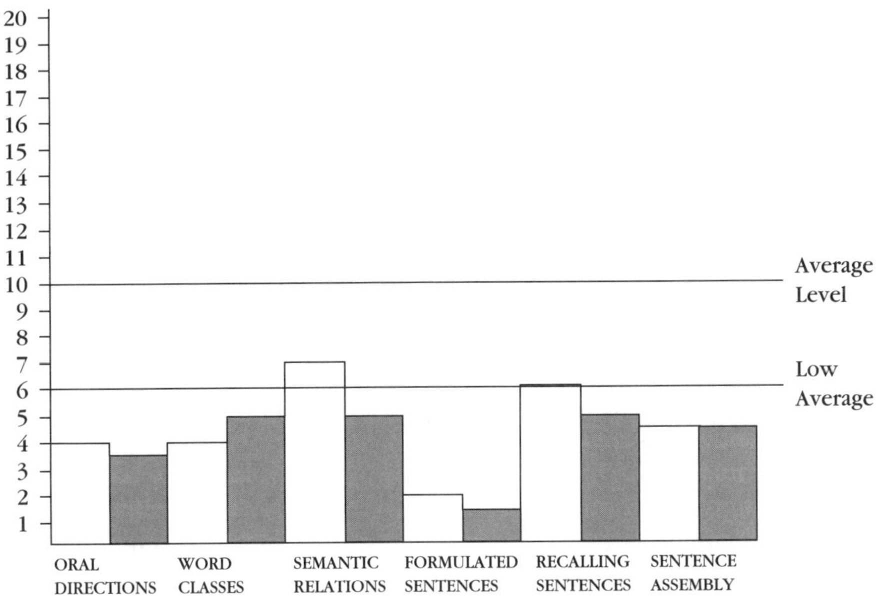

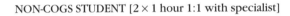

Figure 7.2: The Clinical Evaluation of Language Fundamentals (CELF).

Comment on management

There are many disputes about labelling and service delivery with regard to students who have learning difficulties. Wallach and Liebergott (1984) discussed this with reference to who should be called 'language-impaired' versus those considered 'learning-impaired'. These authors suggest that students who fail to make academic progress may not receive the support they need because their problems are not viewed as communication based, as they do not fall neatly into the 'language-impaired' or 'learning-impaired' categories.

Standardized tests generally fail to differentiate psychometrically between groups of children (Christenson et al. 1982; Mirkin and Potter 1982; Bloome and Theodorou 1985; Otto 1986). Idrisano (1987) argues that the team responsible for diagnosis and support for students needing learning help should include professional knowledge and competence in the area of major academic difficulty. In my experience this nearly always involves two-way problems in communication between teacher and learners.

Similarly, we have difficulties in labelling ourselves as professionals. Statements such as 'speech and language therapists should work on oral language and learning support teachers concentrate on the written' reflect assumptions both about training and the competence of professionals involved, split the communication system arbitrarily and divide services. A recent report (HMI 1996) comments on this being a huge problem in delivering satisfactory support to students. A single service, including a range of professional specialisms, may help to reduce the difficulties arising from different philosophies and practices of separate authorities.

However, support that integrates language, reading and academic perspectives will only evolve if students in training (and professionals during their development) are encouraged to study communication in a manner which stresses an holistic approach to learning. This will be in contradistinction to the traditional methods in which there has been a tendency to rely on discrete skills orientation in support programmes. In the traditional approaches, breakdowns in auditory processing and perception are often viewed as the cause of language and learning difficulties. Intervention might lead to working directly on symptoms, such as auditory discrimination and sequencing, in the belief that these skills are prerequisites for higher level language function (macro-structure).

Recent work in neuroscience, as in the research of Webster (1996) into interhemispheric interference, challenges such notions of discrete training, stressing *affective* issues in effective functioning. Increasingly, models of communication are emerging that integrate information-processing principles with descriptions of social and non-social aspects which acknowledge people and their contexts. The Communication Opportunity Group Scheme has attempted to put this thinking into an assessment and teaching framework that integrates both macro- and micro-structural elements.

Although any communication framework represents abstract and incomplete descriptions of complex behaviours, the greatest failure lies not within the model but with the professionals, some of whom interpret theoretical ideas literally and may not appreciate that selective approaches need to be considered along with holistic notions.

The way ahead

There is a long way to go before the problems of communication in education are solved. However, the future seems encouraging. In 1997, a group of interested professionals from health, education, business and industry came together as Human Communication International (HCI) to start an organization to share knowledge about communication in a new forum. As professionals, teachers, therapists and others tend to move mainly in their own circles and do not always appreciate the wider context in which we all operate. HCI is concerned to support individuals and groups to function better in their learning. In a world which has developed a plethora of detailed information that often overwhelms, we must move ahead to bridge the categories we assess and teach. We cannot possibly instruct students in everything they need to know and must become aware of the principles on which we rely for selection and prioritizing as well as understanding the values that guide and inform clear communication of information to others. This involves understanding and producing what one needs to know and express *situationally*, as well as being clear about the meaning of the intended communication and how to put this across effectively.

Part II
Learning in tertiary education contexts

CHAPTER 8

Adult dyslexia: partners in learning

MARGARET HERRINGTON

Introduction

This chapter offers a retrospective analysis of the development of ideas, understanding and professional practice in relation to dyslexia within parts of the adult basic education service (ABE) in England and Wales from the mid-1970s to the late 1980s. It does not purport to represent attitudes to dyslexia across the entire service during this period, given the patchy and heterogeneous nature of the provision. Rather, it attempts to represent a strand of thinking and practice which was informed in part by the developing 'critical' literacy perspective within ABE. It includes an analysis of why dyslexia was not widely acknowledged until the mid-1980s and provides an account of the work of an adult dyslexia research group, jointly sponsored by the University of Leicester Department of Adult Education and the Leicestershire ABE Scheme, 1987–1989, which generated a deeper conceptualization of dyslexia for work with adults.

The rationale for focusing on this part of the tertiary sector is three-fold. First, there is still a dearth of research evidence about adult dyslexia and what there is, is often highly selective. The experimental research undertaken frequently involves dyslexic students in higher education but is not usually based on random samples drawn from the entire higher education dyslexic population. Adults who seek help from specialist dyslexia organizations or even specialist services within educational institutions may not be representative of dyslexia in the general adult population. Dyslexic adults who are increasingly providing valuable first-hand accounts of their individual patterns are those who have most need to explain dyslexia to the non-dyslexic world and, again, may be atypical.

The dangers of making generalizations on the basis of such selective evidence are rarely acknowledged. There may, for example, be some skewing towards the idea of dyslexia as a distinctive syndrome, largely unchanged by the passage of time. Those who may be left with 'residual dyslexia' after successful 'alternative' strategies or who may be borderline in terms of the population as a whole, may not be fully represented. The research described here is also selective but it describes one of the earliest known attempts to involve working and unemployed dyslexic adults, as co-researchers with non-dyslexic tutors. The limitations of the self-selected sample are acknowledged at the outset.

Second, the research anticipated the powerful individual adult descriptions of dyslexia and the adult dyslexia organizations which have emerged during the 1990s. Adult students revealed themselves as willing to reflect upon and evaluate their own experience of schooling. They articulated valuable insights for teachers; devised their own ways forward; and enlightened a specific learning difficulties (SpLD) research context which was, at the time, heavily child-oriented.

Finally, this discussion reveals that the issues raised and explored within ABE echo to some extent the wider debates between educators and SpLD specialists in all sectors.

Dyslexia: a backward step?

A complaint frequently heard about ABE staff has been that in the course of their literacy work they have remained relatively 'blind' to the nature and significance of dyslexia. Such assertions have never been thoroughly investigated but insofar as they may be valid, the reasons extend beyond sheer ignorance or wilful rejection of evidence. They stemmed, in the first instance, from a sense that the debate about SpLD marked a backward step from the significant progress which literacy educators had made in understanding concepts of literacy and in devising successful methods of teaching. The Adult Literacy Campaign, launched in the UK in the mid-1970s (Street 1997), was in part a response to the growing realization that 11 years of compulsory schooling was an insufficient guarantor of acceptable 'standards' of basic literacy. It was revolutionary in important respects. It operated outside some of the constraints of schooling: tuition was located with the learners in their homes (Herrington 1994) and vast numbers of volunteers who were not trained teachers were 'trained' for the purpose (Elsey and Gibb 1981). The organizers and trainers came from a mix of professional and non-professional backgrounds. Although the distinctive professionalization of ABE developed over the subsequent two decades, and the provision became more institution-based, the professional separation from the school sector was more or less complete for almost 20 years.

However, despite this freedom from the constraints of the school literacy curriculum, the subsequent revolution in the adult literacy curriculum only emerged in some areas after considerable struggle and in other areas over a long period. Alan Tuckett, at the Friends Centre in Brighton, incurred the wrath of a volunteer tutor and a local politician by including current affairs material in literacy sessions (Mace 1979). Yet the initial emphasis in some schemes was on offering 'remedial' methods again (a 'second chance' rather than a rigorous analysis of prior difficulty in learning) but by different types of tutor and in different contexts. The curriculum revolution actually involved the re-working and in some cases the retention of old methods. To claim, as some specialist organizations have, that literacy workers were not aware of phonics and patterns in language (Moorhouse 1977) and did not attempt to teach them is simply untrue; but they did move beyond such a focus and drew inspiration from literacy domains and events in the adult world (Barton 1994).

The adult curriculum: learner-centredness

On the margins of education and with few resources, ABE workers in the UK developed a methodology based on key principles of adult learning (Knowles 1985; Brookfield 1989). There was recognition of the resources the adults brought to the learning experience and their need to have control over this. There was also recognition of the key factors of motivation, of establishing what students were actually interested in and how they wanted to work. Curriculum goals, content and process were now a matter for 'negotiation' and for decision by the adult learners. A 'learner-centredness' developed. Students were to make the decisions about what, how and when they would learn.

This form of tuition was informal, friendly and with great flexibility in terms of time and space. The distance and open learning developments under the auspices of the Adult Literacy and Basic Skills Unit (ALBSU) formalized this flexibility (Herrington 1983). The tutoring role involved a mix of teaching and facilitating the exploration by students of their own learning. Testing with the usual assessment tools was avoided, given the developing critique of such measures. The dominant paradigm was personal 'empowerment', with direct implications for family and vocational settings. Adults who were not supposed to be able to read and write were now proving that they could, given this different teaching and learning methodology. It was not a smooth path of development; critical voices were heard about the developing provision (O'Neill 1974; Jeffrey and Maginn 1979) but for practitioners the effectiveness of this developing approach was clearly evident.

'Critical literacy' dimensions

Meanwhile an even broader and deeper vision emerged on the more radical wing of practice. This was informed by political perspectives which sought equal opportunities for those excluded from educational and training chances by virtue of literacy difficulties. It was also underpinned by a process of fundamental socio/political analysis of the nature and purposes of literacy (Freire 1972; Scribner and Cole 1981; Street 1984; Levine 1985; Schwab and Stone 1986; Freire and Macedo 1987; McLaren 1988). This process was particularly evident in the Research and Practice in Adult Literacy network (RAPAL) established in the UK in 1985. A membership of several hundred UK and overseas literacy workers, students and researchers demonstrated their 'questioning' stance in regular bulletins, conferences and workshops. A summary of their declared interests to the membership secretary in 1986 revealed the depth of their analytical drive:

- The reasons for failure to learn; revisiting the nature of learning and of adult learning; the barriers to developing literacy skills; the relevance of motivation, feelings, relevance and meta-cognition.
- The nature of literacy/illiteracy: ways of conceptualizing literacy/illiteracy; measures of literacy and illiteracy; 'standards'.
- Lessons from the history of language and literacy; the dynamic relationship with the social context.
- Deconstructing literacy and power issues.
- How to teach reading and writing to adults and the deconstructing of spelling: memory, how it worked and why it failed.
- Teaching literacy in multiliteracies and multilingual contexts: awareness of the dominance of school-based literacy in English.
  (Herrington 1996)

Notions of good practice emerged which integrated 'learner centredness' with this acute sense of the social and political realities regarding literacy. It was clear that explicit references to the contextual factors were essential if learners were to reframe their experiences and to understand their own position. If adults had overcome all the barriers to coming to a literacy service then they should have an opportunity to escape a technical, autonomous model of literacy which had been used to establish their failure and to be put in touch with much broader insights into literacy, learning and power. The idea that 'in person' cognitive processing weakness was at the heart of literacy problems thus appeared superficial and unhelpful.

Success?

Such an emphasis did not seem necessary given the apparent success of the new approach. The issue of measuring the success and failure was widely debated if not extensively researched. Charnley and Jones (1979) produced evidence which revealed not only an enhancement of literacy skills but an increase in confidence among learners. However, one of the most obvious indicators of the 'success' of this approach was the outpouring of student writing (Gardener 1999/2000). Adults who had struggled with reading throughout their school days became writers and published authors. Many forms of writing emerged (e.g. autobiography, poetry and short stories) and mechanisms for publication developed at local and national level.

Other measures of success included the involvement of literacy students in research. RAPAL members, for example, began to try to break down some of the old ways of thinking about research:

> Research does not have to be remote, written in mystifying language and published in obscure (expensive) books and journals that few people ever get to see. Research can be something closer to the everyday practice of what we all do as we learn.
>
> It involves asking questions, trying to answer them, asking other people, recording what they say, developing ideas, changing them . . . it's looking at learning in a reflective and critical way.
>
> . . . in particular we need to explore ways of participative research that break down the role of 'researcher' and 'researched'. (*RAPAL Bulletin* 1986 1:1)

RAPAL members believed that those receiving inadequate educational resources during schooling should have an active role in determining research priorities with regard to literacy (Ivanic and Simpson 1988). The organization of research events and weekend workshops revealed that adult students welcomed the opportunity to raise and follow through their hitherto unanswered questions. Though these developments were not uniform across the whole of adult basic education, they nevertheless represented an analytical and power-sharing perspective on this work which produced excellent outcomes.

Measures of failure were more difficult to find. Concerns were expressed about the extent to which adults with literacy difficulties were being reached (Tuckett 1979). Questions about drop-out were asked but very few attempts went beyond retrospective surveys (Herrington 1986). Many questions were not asked: for example, why there was so little public challenge from tutors to the very fundamental ideas about literacy, intelligence and educability, despite a stream of 'evidence' from their students. The fact that most of the students who stayed recorded progress, reassured tutors that the methods were largely effective.

The significance of dyslexia?

However, ABE staff in some areas began to raise questions about the seeming intractability of some literacy difficulties. There appeared little acknowledgement of dyslexia as a possible contributing factor. The likely reasons for this have been summarized elsewhere (see Herrington 1995) and stemmed largely from the confusing nature of the dyslexia debate at the time. Even so, the recognition that dyslexia could be involved emerged in a number of settings at more or less the same time. Dyslexic students within the Leicestershire Distance Learning Scheme in the mid-1980s encouraged a more investigative stance among staff. At the same time, ALBSU financed a special development project (1986–1988; Klein 1989) and in the spring of 1987 a note in the RAPAL *Bulletin* called for work to be done on dyslexia. It asked practitioners to focus closely on students' accounts of their experience in order to develop a clearer view of what was involved. This issue clearly required investigation and the underdeveloped state of the dyslexia debate could not be allowed to prevent this.

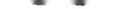

The following section describes the work of a small student/tutor research group established in Leicestershire at the time (Herrington 1998). It shows how ABE methodology, informed by a 'critical literacy' perspective, was used to explore dyslexia. It demonstrates the significance of co-investigation by students and tutors, and the role of the former in unearthing the questions which tutors need to ask.

Exploring dyslexia: the Leicester University/Leicestershire ABE Service Student/Tutor Research Group, 1987–1989

The group was established at the behest of a longstanding ABE student who was concerned at the lack of in-depth analysis of his own literacy difficulties and the apparent and continuing ignorance of many schoolteachers about dyslexia. His letter-writing campaign – to almost every educational institution and political group in the county – provoked a joint response from the Leicestershire ABE service and the Leicester University Department of Adult Education, who offered to set up a research group of students and tutors.

Objectives of the group

The group was formed 'to explore effective methods of working with adults who have acute/persistent difficulties with reading, writing and spelling with reference, in the first instance, to student members of the research group' and to consider the following questions:

- What is dyslexia? What are its causes? How can it be identified?
- Is it distinct from the other literacy difficulties and, if so, how?
- Why is it not recognized by many educationalists, the public etc?
- Are there distinctive methods for helping those with dyslexia – if so, what would they include? Would they differ from standard ABE practice?

- Are methods which are appropriate for children suitable and effective for adults?

Methodology

The intention was to create a framework in which adults, who felt that their difficulties were intractable, could describe and define the nature of their difficulties in their own terms and in which the methods used by the students and tutors would be recorded and evaluated. The general assumptions were that student members would not 'be researched' by the tutors and that the process of asking questions, selecting priorities, collecting evidence, offering interpretation and disseminating findings would be open to all members of the group. The investigative stance of the group would thus be exploratory and enabling. Membership of the group included:

- Two co-organizers (Leicestershire Distance Learning Organizer for ABE and the special needs tutor in the University Department of Adult Education).
- Two experienced tutors, selected for their interest and skills in SpLD.
- Nine students (initially six) who formed a largely self-selected opportunity sample. They were approached via a general invitation to ABE area organizers in Leicestershire and only one had been formally identified as dyslexic.

A two-tier meetings structure was chosen. The first involved the students meeting the two tutors weekly over an 18-month period, in two separate subgroups, with a tutor:student ratio of 1:3. The second involved monthly research review sessions held with the two co-organizers. One of the co-organizers was in close contact with the tutors and students between the monthly sessions. Modest funding was made available by the University and Leicestershire Education Authority.

Recording was undertaken by the tutors keeping individual records and by making audio tapes with the students within the subgroups, when appropriate. Notes were kept from the monthly research group meetings and from all visits and lectures. Students were asked to produce accounts of their own experience both of dyslexia and of the group. Additionally, during the last three months of the project, a colleague from the ABE Service was asked to join the group to study and record the implications of dyslexia for basic maths.

The advantages and the limitations of this qualitative approach were understood at the outset. From the collection of primary and secondary source materials we expected to be able to generate hypotheses about 'dyslexic' difficulties (in the Glaser/Strauss/Mezirow tradition of grounded theory).

Results

The two subgroups worked on the exploration of individual difficulties. The monthly sessions served a variety of purposes: collecting and comparing ideas; raising questions; expressing emotions etc. The actual research process itself was like a moving tapestry in which particular issues were taken up, worked into the picture for a while, put aside and then retrieved. Members were engaged in seeking information simultaneously from their own experience and from the available literature.

Main findings

Three categories were identified:

- The dynamic of the student–tutor research partnership.
- The experience of dyslexia.
- Effective methods.

The dynamic of the student–tutor research partnership

This was a key issue both from a radical and 'empowering' ABE perspective and for the more general question of identifying appropriate mechanisms for releasing adult students' contributions to research about dyslexia. The evidence revealed testing challenges and contests for the group and indicated the importance of analysing precisely the ownership and exercise of different types of power within it.

The challenges came quickly. The first concerned the name of the group. The investigation was into 'acute and persistent' difficulties. Although some found this phrase unrevealing and clumsy, and preferred the term 'dyslexia', others were more concerned to record the evidence than to become unnecessarily embroiled in the controversial issue of when the dyslexia label was most appropriate. Other challenges followed with members having different initial expectations about study/research roles. Some students felt that the tutors were the 'experts', '*You solve this for me, I can't*'. Though tutors felt themselves to have some expertise, they had joined the project to learn more themselves. The idea that all members were there to learn and to share the study/research process had to be experienced before it was fully understood and valued.

Strong differences of opinion also emerged about the priorities of the group and about the relationship between research and policy changes. Some members felt that the crusading fervour which had led to the start of the group should be sustained throughout its life. Other members wanted to assemble the information first. They were conscious of the unique hostility of the dyslexia debate and wanted to avoid the charge that the group was just a pressure group for dyslexics. They also felt that policymakers and resource providers would favour a more even-handed approach.

Underpinning this divide were different views about the nature of 'dyslexic' difficulties. Most (but not all) of the student members felt that it was a clear-cut kind of 'disability' for them and could not really understand the 'boundary' questions raised by some of the tutors. The tutors also varied in their views. These differences could not all be resolved, and the desire for consensus proved to be unhelpful at times. Compromise and 'agreement to disagree' became essential and these differences drove the members to further exploration. Students recorded immense satisfaction as they tackled previously untried tasks and challenges. Table 8.1 summarizes these.

Many lessons were learned about the research process, both in general and in relation to dyslexia. For example, the students recognized the relationship between types of questions posed and types of research method required and learned that 'experts' did not always agree and could not answer many of their questions.

Student members also agreed that much of the group's value lay in the relationships between tutors and students which were unlike traditional student–tutor ones. The tutors and the organizers, meanwhile, felt they had learned so much from the students about 'dyslexic' difficulties that, as an exercise in staff development, it would have been difficult to better.

The RAPAL position on the empowering effects of student research for both students and tutors thus appeared vindicated by this work. The intention had been to 'empower' those members who had experienced discrimination as a result of 'acute and persistent' dyslexic difficulties. The students 'gained power' in the sense of greater understanding, confidence and ability to:

- Articulate their own positions (part 'conscientization' and part self-realization).
- Research the field for themselves.
- Speak to professional audiences.

Further, within the group, both students and tutors became aware of the different types of power-sharing required, i.e. power to decide how research would be conducted and by whom (co-organizers at the start and then all members involved); power to speak out and to determine the ongoing discussion agenda (all members had equal access to this); and power to make final decisions for the group in the case of disagreement (majority of the group or the co-organizers if an urgent decision was necessary). The group members became aware at the micro-level of the interactions between individual empowerment, power sharing within the group, and expressions of external power (funding limits and cultural norms about literacy).

Table 8.1. Summary of the strands of work undertaken by group members

Summary of work	Roles
Ongoing exploration of student members' dyslexic difficulties: individual work*; group discussions (chairing meetings)*	Students record and analyse (their own work/some of each other's) Tutors record and analyse Students and tutors chair the meetings
Visits to other centres	Students and tutors inteviewing authorities in the field
Reading and reviewing some of the literature	Students and tutors as reviewers
Talks to ABE practitioners (locally and regionally), to students, to school-teachers, to the local dyslexia support group	Organizers, tutors and students as speakers
Taking evidence from visitors to the group (other dyslexic students, a cognitive psychologist)	Students welcoming visitors, questioning and supporting them
Alerting various bodies to the difficulties: newspapers*, County Council*	Students writing letters to inform and persuade; organizers and tutors writing letters
Seeking funds from voluntary bodies for members to have their own word processors	Students, tutors and organizers
Survey of local bookshops and libraries	Student as researcher and reporter; student as author
Seeking funds for future provision	Organizer/student
Writing to Exam Boards	Organizer/student/tutor
Writing the final report	Students, tutors and organizers as writers

*As a result of these talks, another group of ABE students in one of the rural Leicestershire areas started to discuss 'dyslexic' issues.

The experience of dyslexia

An emotionally charged debate

The emotional tenor of the debates about dyslexia within the literature was echoed within this particular group. The psychological implications of dyslexia for the members stemmed from the nature of the difficulties themselves (which could be frightening because the effects could not be controlled by the students) and from a sense of bewilderment and/or fury about society's attitude to those with literacy difficulties. All members bar one (a 17-year-old) reported the struggle to retain self-esteem and confidence in a society which valued 'literacy' as a basic and essential adult skill and which viewed it as some measure of intelligence and educability. They had been made to feel 'stupid', 'thick', 'lazy', 'failures'. The school system in particular was implicated in this process. The overall impression was one of schoolteachers who could not seem to understand the kind of struggle the students were having and who seemed also to lack professional curiosity about them. ABE tutors were also reported as having insufficient knowledge and curiosity in this field.

Families and peers were noted for their lack of support. Commenting on their own parents, the students recognized that parents should not be 'blamed' for their children's dyslexia but that they had not been sufficiently well informed about it. Hence, parents were not always in a position to give the consistent help required and in some cases were not particularly suited to the task. One visiting member, however, commented favourably on the confidence her father had maintained in her and how important this had been.

The students were forced to adopt a range of defensive responses to this lack of support: hiding poor literacy, 'cheating' to get out of uncomfortable situations, fear, truancy and, on occasion, violence. They felt vulnerable, expecting to be criticized or undermined at any time. Some developed reasonable coping strategies but for others it would be difficult to exaggerate the destructive effects on the quality of their lives. This variation in response seemed to depend on the particular clusters of characteristics and the degree of difficulty, the personal and social consequences for the individual, and the personality of individuals and their responses to the difficulty/disability. With regard to the last of these, one student felt that his aggression enabled him to keep going but that this antagonized others. Three ways of responding were identified: joking, becoming aggressive and turning inwards. One student felt that the last produced the most long-term psychological damage.

This lack of understanding about dyslexia among educators had led to several members being placed in special schools or 'streams'. Students reported anger and frustration with inappropriate diagnoses and inadequate professional responses. Some became angrier still with the continuing 'non-recognition' by present-day authors and professional groups who appeared to deny the existence of distinctive dyslexic characteristics and who seemed oblivious to their disabling effects. The challenge was an intellectual one: professionals and public alike did not seem to know about and understand these experiences and yet they seemed unwilling and unable to ask the most basic questions about how dyslexia was experienced.

The search for information about dyslexia

Members sought evidence within the literature about the possible causes of dyslexia and about effective teaching methods. Three main collections of evidence were identified:

- **Physiological evidence from medicine, neurology and biology:** members examined evidence about genes; antenatal 'sensitivity to the male hormone testosterone'; mapping of the structures and functions of the brain with regard to language; unusual brain symmetry; the disorganization of the cell layers ('miswiring') in the language-processing sites; anomalies in electrical activity in the brain; use of the right side of the brain for language processing leading to 'overload'; and research findings about acquired dyslexia. Some evidence on hearing difficulties and on visual processing was also examined. Although there was recognition that there could be a physiological basis for dyslexia, members believed that more sophisticated explanations than those currently available would emerge.
- **Evidence from cognitive psychology:** this evidence, too, was far from conclusive. The general paradigm seemed to be one involving single or mutiple faults in the information-processing systems, which were believed to operate within the brain. Snowling's work was placing much emphasis on phonological processing deficits. Students asked questions about these deficits in relation to themselves and also about the nature of the underlying 'models': were there hierarchies of functions? If one organizing and sequencing function was impaired, could this affect the organizing and sequencing of a whole range of tasks, involving literacy and beyond?
- **Evidence from educators:** some educators had long acknowledged these difficulties and had devised methods which they claimed worked for children. The mantra of 'structured multisensory teaching' appeared to be the central message. The theoretical rationale for this was discussed and the question of whether this could be appropriate for adults was pursued.

Alongside the literature search, student members constructed accounts of their own experience of dyslexia. Five of the key points from this evidence are summarized below.

Identification by description and discussion: Given the concerns about definition and assessment noted already, the group avoided formal testing at the outset. Instead, tutors asked 'open-ended' questions, which were refined through discussion. One member said, '*No one ever asks me what I see on the page. Why don't teachers start with that?*' We therefore developed more penetrating questions, such as, 'what happens when you try to read, retrieve or write a word?' The descriptions which resulted were powerful, clear and comprehensible and usually provided the basis on which appropriate methods could be selected or devised:

> The words are blurred on the page - but not all the time. They move about. [visual disturbance]
>
> The words are there in my mind but I just can't get them out. [sense of an expressive language blockage]
>
> I have the word in my head but when I look at the paper I haven't written that. It can even be something completely different to what I was thinking. Sometimes it is just letters in the wrong order. [disjuncture between cognition and motor expression]
>
> I can have the word one minute and the next minute - a complete blank.
>
> I just cannot remember from one minute to the next -and definitely not from one week to the next. I am definitely thick.
>
> It's only words I have trouble with - can't seem to remember them at all. [weak control in relation to memory]

For some students it appeared to feel like a physical problem, involving barriers to both receptive and expressive language:

> There feels as if there's a blockage in my brain - if only I could wash it out.

Some of the most powerful descriptions used analogies:

> My problem is I cannot form letters, so I cannot write. Although this is very extreme I can copy if I see the words but if the words are taken away from me I cannot know where to begin to start to form a letter. To me it seems like having a television set inside my brain with the letter on it and that set is spinning very fast. But to make things even worse there seems to be a curtain in front of the set and I get very fast peeks at the letter. The letter can appear at any angle, at 45° or even backwards. I don't know which is the right way when I try to put it onto paper.
>
> I have to read each night - it's like keeping down the undergrowth on country paths. If I don't keep going through, they get overgrown.
>
> It's as if my mind is a container with very narrow entries.
>
> There definitely seems as though there is a veil over part of my brain . . . my thought pattern is not at all the same.

Descriptions of reading and writing and the particular difficulties when learners were under pressure were recorded:

> I can read and then come back to it and have no sense that I have seen or read it before.

> When I am reading I have to read every word on the page. Although it slows me down I can still get through anywhere from three to five books a week . . .when I am reading it is like having someone inside my head telling me the story.

> All that time I was reading things backwards, and numbers I can read backwards unless I concentrate on them. I can see 47 but I say 74 but I know it's 47.

> I cannot write my name but I can type it.

> [E] . . . can think of a story then her mind goes blank and only something stilted and simple appears on the paper. Even if she tells the story on tape, she is unable to put it on paper as . . . she forgets what she has heard very quickly.

> All the time I am conscious of the fact that I am only using simple words to fill the page still the letters don't mean a thing to me . . . the letters are moving about all over the place and I'm even now having to put my forefinger on each letter that I am putting down . . . the frustration is unbearable . . . my head is really full of words that just won't come out . . .

Speech, too, was implicated:

> Another thing that happens to me when I am talking is that I stop in the middle of what I am saying. It is as though my brain has switched off and I have to wait for it to come back on. To me it seems that my mouth gets too far ahead of my brain and it has to wait for it to catch up with it again. Sometimes I forget what I am saying.

The issue of strengths also emerged. Some literacy strengths became evident: one student wrote a 40 000-word autobiography and another wrote a powerful fictional account of his experience of dyslexia as a child. Writing from the inside was experienced as something very different, and even enjoyable, when personal computers and spellcheckers were available. More general strengths also emerged. Most student members were clearly able. Some were employed in highly skilled, responsible jobs and all had the usual responsibilities of adult lives. Most reported sporting ability of some kind and particular talents with understanding machinery were noted among them.

The group found the above descriptions liberating compared with forms of assessment which involved test scores. Neverthless, methods of testing were discussed in detail. The students expressed several concerns about tests: the psychological impact of testing adults who already felt that they had failed; the effect of the stress on the accuracy of the results; the limited nature of the information provided by some of them; and the confusion about the significance of particular items.

The conclusion seemed to be that with adults, the kind of discussion which focused on the nature of the difficulty, on learners' backgrounds, their learning history and their current situation with regard to all aspects of literacy, memory etc. could produce sufficient evidence of dyslexia without formal testing. By use of language which both students and tutors could understand, and avoiding any undue professional mystique, the students could gain power in articulating their own situation.

Variations in dyslexia:

> I am dyslexic. You are not. [student comment to another student during the first meeting]

Student members started with the idea that they were dyslexic and that their individual characteristics constituted dyslexia in general. Members of the group did not know how to interpret the variations. Although the notion of a 'syndrome' was understood, the differences seemed to raise questions about its coherence and boundaries. These were extended during discussions about the distinction between developmental and acquired dyslexia.

In addition, two types of temporal variation were recorded: individuals who gained in literacy skills over time and individuals who experienced day-to-day variations in performance. Students had gained in literacy skills both as young and older adults. The move into the adult world and the shifts in motivation (already well documented in the ABE service) had led to some members learning to read, largely by their own efforts:

> At 15, I joined the Royal Navy . . . and . . . was told I suffered from word blindness . . . although by this time I could read very well.

This invoked the question of how such learning could be occurring if there were once and for all weaknesses in the processing of certain kinds of information in the brain. Several possibilities were discussed: could the brain be activated to bypass the weaknesses or bring into use some system or channels which were basically designed for some other purpose? Could new channels be created? What was the neurology of compensation?

More puzzling were the day-to-day variations. Seven of the nine members reported 'good day/bad day' variations. For one member, no literacy task was possible on bad days. Other experiences were reported as follows:

- 'Sudden blindness' for words – infrequent and short-lived (for example, a road sign could appear blank).

- 'Seeing' the words on the page but *the intelligence isn't getting through* – short-lived with breaks for an hour or so.
- Long periods when writing is just not possible – *Can't seem to find any words at all* and then good days when a reasonable effort can be made.
- Sudden changes when *nothing comes out in order, all feels jumbled up and upside down and words move on the page.* Regular occurrence but unpredictable.
- Sudden breakdown of writing ability (*even copying becomes impossible*) with an accompanying loss of any sense of direction.

The group considered whether these variations were related to mood swings. The conclusion seemed to be that they occurred irrespective of mood but all agreed that when words disappeared or changed in these ways it could lead to stress, depression and unwillingness to try. Not surprisingly, those with the most frequent and acute swings experienced the most stress. This derived largely from the feeling of lack of control, of never really knowing when it would happen and hence the need to learn to cope without panic.

The group also asked questions about the implications of these variations both for the nature of dyslexia and for teaching purposes. A dynamic paradigm, rather than a view of 'once and for all' blockages or miswirings seemed more convincing. More exploration of individual biochemistry seemed necessary to resolve this.

Clearly, variations could have contributed to schoolteachers feeling that these students had been cheating or not trying. They had probably not realized that on some days the students simply could not perform literacy tasks. In the context of an adult class, the conclusion pointed once again to the need for individual responses: some preferred to press on despite having a 'bad day' and others simply had to stop and not try anything.

Visual issues: Some of the earliest references to dyslexia in the literature had used the expression, 'word blindness', and this is exactly how it felt to some of the students (no picture of the symbols in their minds). However, a range of visual issues emerged early in the discussions. They included general eyesight, perception and processing of print for reading and the apparent visual blanks or reversals when retrieving symbols for writing. Two visual issues recurred on a regular basis: visual disturbance and the effects of colour.

Concerning visual disturbance, various phenomena were described: blurring, text moving in and out of focus, tracking difficulty and the appearance of sudden blanks. One student described the difference between good and bad days in this respect (see Figure 8.1):

Bad day

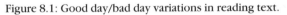

N (line of text seems to rise and fall)
H J
O OHN J (ohn Laf)TON
J (gap appears)

Good day

JOHNJOHNLAFTON (in a gentle wave format)

Figure 8.1: Good day/bad day variations in reading text.

One of the possible explanations for blurring was that of binocular instability: the argument appeared to be that both eyes were not working well together and could not hold the image still. One member went to an optometrist and found that this was the case.

Several students recorded that they had a 'lazy eye' and that they closed one eye when reading:

> It is interesting about the eyes. One eye has a tendency to shut, my left eye when I am reading. It is quite funny really. You don't really notice it shutting and then you think. I've got one eye shut.

Concerning colour, the group found that coloured lenses, overlays and paper had marked effects on their processing of print: by reducing glare, increasing the field of vision in focus, sharpening the focus of the letters and making the words seem larger. Different colours were effective for different people. Different effects were also experienced. For some it was just a reduction in glare whereas for others it was a major difference in the clarity and 'comfortableness' of the text.

It was not clear to the group whether these visual phenomena were intrinsic to dyslexia or whether they were simply co-existing with it for a proportion of the students.

Memory: Several aspects emerged:

- Limited capacity of short-term auditory and visual memory with 'cutting out' when faced with too much information.
- Apparent 'resistance' between short-term and long-term memory when trying to learn.
- Problem of retrieval from long-term memory.
- Inability to forget some sorts of information.

There appeared to be variations within the group with regard to visual and auditory memory but these were not neat categories of strengths and weaknesses. At one extreme was a member who needed 'visual hooks' for learning and retrieving spellings (because it proved impossible for him to learn sounds and patterns of sound). At the other was someone who faced with blanks in retrieval could learn sounds and begin to use these to help the retrieval process. Both of these had sufficient visual memory for reading purposes. Most had some combination of auditory and visual strengths and weaknesses and there seemed to be no other way of proceeding than by a micro-analysis of each individual's experience of memory across a range of language and literacy tasks and situations.

Maths: Each student said initially that they felt that their maths ability was adequate for their own needs in terms of life skills and job requirements. They had developed the required skills through regular practice, such as learning the metric system in order to work in carpentry and measuring hundredths of seconds in order to be a swimming coach.

However, most members felt threatened when asked to do simple mental calculations without the aid of pen and paper. Half of the group found unaided mental calculation almost impossible because they had no visual recall of numbers. All the group specifically drew attention to various connections between their reading difficulties and their maths performance:

> My reading problem was more concentrated . . . the teachers used to concentrate on that . . . everything . . . your science, your maths goes downhill because they used to concentrate on that.

> . . . one of the problems was that you were learning from books and having to read . . . not being too clever at reading it held you back . . . doing maths.

One member reported a short-term delay in his maths learning:

> . . . maths wasn't too big a problem for me . . . I was slow but I eventually caught what was going. It took me approximately twice as long to learn anything in mathematics.

Another member reported the boost in his confidence when he was moved into a higher class for maths away from other poor readers.

Although all the students felt that they could subtract using a pencil and paper, in fact they all made a mistake when asked to complete this operation:

$$\begin{array}{r} 347 \\ -178 \\ \hline \\ \hline \end{array}$$

They made the error in (17–8) and (13–7) and this despite the fact that they had talked through the methods they used and had understood the decomposition method. And all students, except one, could not recite their tables without losing their place.

The discussions produced useful descriptions of how people worked. For example, with subtraction, one student described his approach to the sum 48–19:

> I took the 19, then I took the 40 in half and made 20 – put the one that was left onto that.

and this student had no visual recall of numbers.

This preliminary exploration was limited but valuable. The Miles' dyslexia indicators (Miles 1982) were present for the members of the group but the varied numeracy competence recorded did not seem to have been determined by them. In fact, despite operations errors, members recorded the development of considerable numeracy skill when placed in situations where they had to be competent. This raised questions about the assessment and teaching of numeracy in educational settings. Snapshots of competences are usually taken outside those 'real' situations in which competence is more likely to be evident and to develop. School-based arithmetic results would thus underdescribe real-life competence.

Effective methods

The methods used within the group were not new to ABE but they were new to these students. In general, they focused on building learners' self-confidence, on tutors and learners working together to establish the nature of the difficulties being experienced, on specific teaching about the nature of language, of learning and writing; and drawing on a range of methods (SOS, VAK etc.), as appropriate. Attention was also paid to structuring the sessions carefully to maintain interest and energy for learning.

They led to advances for particular students:

- P could not form the letters to write his name on demand but could copy. This led to the suggestion of a keyboard which would remove the need to form letters for all his writing; he could see them easily in front of him. Tutor observation when he was trying to handwrite his name using his right hand, recorded that he was forming the letters with his left hand in a mirror direction at the same time. P learned that on a good day he could write his name by hand if he made the movements with his left hand before starting with his right hand.
- PM did a considerable amount of work on structure and segmentation of words but he realized that he would have to mask each part visually in

order to control his attempts at retrieval. Hence, when PM spelled *Wed/nes/day*, he wrote *Wed* and then covered it before writing *nes*, and then had to cover that before he could write *day*. If he did not do this the previous syllables blocked his recall.

The group members also identified the two most important elements of effective teaching for them:

- A kind, gentle, exploratory approach.
- The use of computers and, in particular, word processors.

Several advantages of the use of personal computers were identified:

- Computers were essential if letter formation was a problem; they boosted confidence and reduced the drudgery of writing.
- Typing was more comfortable than writing, involving less pressure to remember letter forms, allowing the writer to write more and faster and to use writing in more ways.
- For one student, light letters on a dark background were clearer and less strain on the eyes and errors were more easily identified.
- The spellchecker meant that students could use the words they wanted to use. Games were also enjoyed and encouraged concentration.
- The printer produced a clear, easily read copy that students could feel proud of.

The disadvantages noted by the students were that handwriting did not improve and that spellcheckers did not pick up words which were wrongly used but spelled correctly.

The conclusion about methods was that some general elements were necessary but that the selection of effective ways forward was highly individual and based on an analysis of the difficulty and a logical approach to that. Elements of the structured multisensory approach could be drawn upon but the selection of senses and the creation of meaningful micro-structures for individual curricula seemed most important.

Conclusions

In relation to the initial questions, the group members concluded that they had found ways of describing dyslexic experience that were illuminating and without timed tests. They noted both the commonalities and the variations within the descriptions. There were, however, differences of view and uncertainties about whether this constituted a separate condition or whether it described one end of many continua embracing the whole population. And it was not possible to answer the question about whether the literacy difficulties associated with dyslexia differed from those experienced by other members of literacy schemes.

All considered it likely that there were physiological bases for the phenomena but current evidence was not sufficiently illuminating to clarify the precise nature of these, nor the relationships with the literacy and information processing experience of students.

Although identification of dyslexia (for the purpose of devising appropriate individual teaching) seemed to have been resolved in a way which was consistent with the holistic approach of best ABE practice, it was recognized that if the purpose of an assessment was to decide who should or should not be excluded from the dyslexia syndrome for funding purposes, more work would be necessary on establishing boundaries (of degree and kind) for students with less clear-cut clusters of characteristics. It was also clear that the expertise of other disciplines was necessary for full investigations, and alternative therapies could perhaps also be explored. However, attention would have to be paid to enabling the adult students concerned to stay in overall control of this 'investigative' process.

The messages for educators were clear. It was clearly unacceptable, professionally, to remain in ignorance about learning difficulties and to display hostility to learners whose difficulties they did not understand. The examples of particular teachers who 'showed an interest' quoted by the students demonstrated the appropriate professional stance (for example, the report from one member of her child's primary school headteacher who had successfully instigated work with the whole school about 'difference' and 'inclusion'). The group felt that all schoolteachers required dyslexia awareness as part of their basic and INSET training. Some members felt that specialist teachers would be needed in each school to work outside the classroom on an individual basis and to counsel and teach parents how to help. It was clear that all public examination boards should ensure that additional arrangements were made to take account of dyslexia.

The message for adult basic education tutors was also clear. The original question about distinctive methods for dyslexic learners proved difficult to answer. The group identified most of the very processes which were already central to good ABE practice. It was clear therefore that best practice was simply not available across the schemes and that the essential elements required re-emphasizing in tutor training. The tutors also felt that some 're-tooling' in relation to the key dyslexic parameters would also be required. This work suggested that to incorporate a research and practice stance within their everyday practice would help this process.

Change was also necessary among other sections of the community. Parents would require help if their support role was to be delivered adequately; and teachers should be prepared to discuss such matters with parents. The general public also required far more information about dyslexia if the continuing discrimination was to stop. It was important for employers to realize first that some of their recruitment procedures were unnecessarily excluding and that though particular weaknesses in literacy and numeracy may be recorded on tests, adults learned what they needed to learn for their jobs.

Implications

This piece of work revealed that adult learners 'researching' their own situations and using their intellectual strengths rather than focusing on literacy weaknesses had not only started to analyse their own situations in depth but had surveyed considerable sections of the broader debates. They had actively sought answers to their questions and proved a willingness to disseminate findings. They had also started to produce illuminating descriptions of the experience of dyslexia. This was not too surprising to those versed in the research and practice traditions within ABE, but it was clear that not all ABE staff had been able to tap into the investigative power of the adult learners.

At the time, this process also seemed relatively new in relation to the experience of adult dyslexia. Although Cynthia Klein had started to develop a pioneering programme of adult teaching and training in relation to dyslexia which encouraged much closer assessment of processing strengths and weaknesses, the explicit power-sharing research focus had not really been tried before in this way.

Finally this work suggested that the exploration of dyslexia could no longer be considered a step backwards for adult literacy and numeracy educators. Rather, it involved taking some deeper steps to explore and acknowledge the 'in person' processing experiences and to re-integrate this knowledge with the existing depth of vision. The new knowledge did not undermine or invalidate the 'critical literacy' position. Dyslexic adults were actually articulating their need both for some acknowledgement of the extent of their difficulties with existing forms of literacy and about the need to challenge dominant ideas about literacy and intelligence. In effect, they shared common ground with some aspects of the 'critical literacy' approach.

CHAPTER 9

Adult dyslexia: assessment, counselling and training

DAVID MCLOUGHLIN

Introduction

Recognition that specific learning difficulties (SpLD), such as dyslexia, persist throughout the life span, and that adults who have dyslexia are not simply children with a learning disability 'grown up' (Patton and Polloway 1996) has many implications for good practice. In particular, the model of disability adopted by organizations providing for dyslexic people, as well as practitioners, must change from 'dyslexic as victim' to one of empowerment, specifically self-empowerment; that is, organizations must foster the process of enabling dyslexic people to become increasingly in control of their own lives, and thus increasingly independent (Fenton and Hughes 1989).

Research that has focused on analysing the *successes* of dyslexic people rather than their failures has demonstrated that self-understanding is one of the key factors in this (Gerber et al. 1992; Spekman et al. 1992)*. Awareness and understanding allow deliberate skills and strategy development which can lead to greater control. Interventions, whether they be assessment, counselling or training, should foster self-understanding and control. In particular, interventions should address the questions uppermost in the mind of a dyslexic person seeking help, which are 'Why are certain tasks difficult for me?' and 'What can I do about it?'

> Paul sought advice at the suggestion of his employer. He had experienced some difficulties with reading and spelling during his school years, but this had not prevented him from going to university and gaining a degree. A screening assessment during his time at college had suggested that he was dyslexic, but he had

*The authors of these studies use the generic term 'learning disabilities' preferred in the USA. It is evident from the descriptions of the population samples that both include people who are dyslexic.

thought this only affected his spelling. At 35, he held an administrative position but his supervisor had complained about the following:

- a very messy desk
- being late for meetings
- forgetting to attend meetings
- slowness in producing reports
- spelling errors such as minor letter omission and confusion of homophones
- failing to pick up errors when proofreading.

Assessment

There are many reasons for conducting diagnostic assessments. These include identification for the purpose of ensuring that dyslexic people are able to secure entitlements such as grants, special arrangements on courses of study and protection from discrimination. The main focus of any assessment, however, should be to identify strengths and weaknesses and to facilitate self-understanding.

Diagnostic assessment should begin with measures of cognitive functioning. There has been much debate about the relevance of intelligence testing as part of the assessment process. This has focused on the relationship between IQ and the development of written language skills. IQ is not important and, given that the characteristic profile of a dyslexic person on cognitive tests will reveal strengths and weaknesses, can be quite misleading. Identifying particular abilities, notably language skills such as vocabulary, verbal reasoning and comprehension, is important as these underlie the development of reading and writing skills. Without an adequate vocabulary, for example, skills such as reading comprehension will be impaired.

The overwhelming reason for the continued use of the *Wechsler Adult Intelligence Scale* (WAIS) is that it is a neuropsychological test which identifies strengths and weaknesses. There is increasing evidence for a neurological difference between dyslexic and non-dyslexic people, one of the sources being neuropsychological testing. Further, the neurological differences that characterize dyslexia persist throughout the life span (Bigler 1992). Studies have demonstrated that similar profiles are evident when the WAIS is administered to both dyslexic children and adults (Katz et al. 1993).

The evaluation of literacy skills is essential to assessment, but this must be relevant to adults. The most important aspect of reading skill in the adult years is comprehension. A measure of the ability to assimilate and retain material is essential. Similarly, spelling in context is more important than being able to perform well on a single-word spelling test. It is often the reporting of test findings which causes more concern than the tests used.

Both reading and spelling skills can be rated according to occupational level rather than age levels or percentiles and these are more meaningful to adults:

> Paul's performance on the WAIS showed considerable variation among his abilities. He achieved very high scores on verbal reasoning, vocabulary and comprehension. It is verbal ability which is the best predictor of attainments in reading and writing and Paul is someone who could be expected to have very well-developed skills in these areas. He also achieved excellent scores on most of the non-verbal tests. Paul scored less well on mental arithmetic, auditory memory and copying symbols and he had difficulty with items which involved the labeling process, such as identifying geographical directions on a test of general knowledge. These lower scores rendered the profile of Paul's subtest scores typical of that of a dyslexic person. Assessment of his reading skills showed that Paul read accurately at the professional level, the highest level of reading. His comprehension was also at the professional level but this was at the expense of fluency. He read very slowly so as to enhance comprehension. He also wrote slowly and made the kind of spelling errors reported by his employers.

Counselling

Barton and Fuhrmann (1994) suggest that there are four main problems which can be addressed through counselling. These are:

- Stress and anxiety resulting from being overwhelmed by the complexity of life's demands.
- Low self-esteem and feeling of incompetence.
- Unresolved grief.
- Helplessness resulting from limited understanding of learning abilities and disabilities.

In the case of Paul described here it was the last of these which was judged to be the main issue. The client was stressed but this was a response to his employer's rather than his own concerns.

Although Paul had been given a label he had never been given an explanation about what being dyslexic means. The model outlined by McLoughlin et al. (1994), where dyslexia is described as an *inefficiency in working memory*, was used to improve his understanding.

Most major information-processing models of skill acquisition and learning include the component of working memory (Swanson 1994). It is the system responsible for:

- Short-term storage of auditory, visual and motor input.

- Facilitating the encoding of information for effective storage and retrieval in long-term memory.
- Enabling the recall of learned material from long-term memory.
- The automatic control of a previously learned skill while other incoming or recalled information is processed simultaneously (Chasty and Friel 1991).

An inefficient working memory system will clearly undermine skill acquisition and learning. Describing dyslexia in this way can help explain both the persisting written language difficulties as well as the broader problems experienced by adults; the notion of dual processing being central. Reading comprehension, for example, requires simultaneous word recognition and assimilation of information; note-taking involves listening and writing, whereas organization can be described as multi-tasking. It can also provide a way of interpreting the characteristic dyslexic profile revealed by the administration of the Wechsler scale. Mental arithmetic is one of the simplest examples of the working memory system in operation as it involves dual processing. Coding and Digit Span both involve dual processing and Information requires automatic retrieval of material from long-term memory.

In practice it has been found to be a model with which dyslexic people can identify. It is helpful, therefore, in promoting self-understanding. One young man interpreted it as follows:

> The main effect of my dyslexia in the examination setting has been that I read and write more slowly as my word recognition and retrieval are not automatic. I find it takes me longer to assimilate longer questions. To use a computing analogy, if the mind is like a computer running Windows™, the working memory is like RAM where the processing is done and the long-term memory is like the hard disk. If a computer has more data to process than can be stored in RAM, it stores it temporarily on the hard disk in 'virtual memory' and has to refer to it constantly. This is comparatively much slower than holding it in RAM, thus the task is accomplished, but takes longer than would be achieved by a computer with more RAM. Being dyslexic is like a computer with insufficient RAM, you can accomplish as much as other people but it takes longer.

Training

Promoting self-understanding can lead to successful strategy development and skill acquisition. Although adults with dyslexia who are seeking help are presenting with problems they wish to address, they will already have developed their own way of learning and dealing with tasks. Encouraging them to engage in meta-cognition, that is, think about the *way* they think, can enable them to be more efficient in the way they learn and work. It is particularly important to encourage them to consider things they do well and endeavour to analyse what they are doing. If they can apply the same processes to tasks they find difficult they will often find solutions. Guiding them by suggesting they adopt three simple principles that derive logically from the working memory model can be helpful. The principles, described as the 'three Ms', are:

- **Make it manageable**: reduce the load on working memory; avoid dual processing wherever possible.
- **Make it multisensory**: increase the power of the encoding by use of a variety of stimuli.
- **Make use of memory aids**: to facilitate recall.

These principles can be applied to personal, learning and work settings. Dyslexic people are asked to consider a task and ask themselves: 'How can I make this manageable?' 'How can I make this multisensory?' 'What memory aids can I use?'

Examples

The above principles were explained to Paul and it was suggested that he apply them in the following ways:

Problem: Organization
Solution: Make it **Manageable** by:
Being very organized
A tidy desk
Planning

Make it **Multisensory** by:
Making lists
Using wall planners
Colour coding

Make use of **Memory aids**:
Diaries
Post-It notes
Electronic aids

Problem: Reading slowly to enhance comprehension
Solution: Making a list of questions before reading makes it **Manageable**
Reading the answers aloud makes it **Multisensory**
Highlighting the answers provides **Memory aids**

Problem: Proofreading
Solution: Looking at presentation, spelling and punctuation individually makes it **Manageable**

Reading aloud makes it **Multisensory**
Marking errors provides **Memory aids**

Problem: Report writing
Solution: Make it **Manageable** by planning
Make it **Multisensory** by dictating onto tape and writing from the tape
Make use of **Memory aids**, such as mnemonics as a way of checking content

Problem: Spelling
Solution: Make it **Manageable** by using technology
Make it **Multisensory** by keeping a list of words to hand
Make use of **Memory aids**, such as mnemonics and visual imagery

Outcome

Paul's response to the assessment/counselling session was very positive. He indicated that he understood much more about the nature of his difficulties and had gained insights into what he might do. A report was prepared for his employers and they were very supportive in helping him implement the suggestions which had been made. It enabled him to become more efficient and maintain his position, whereas previously he had been threatened with demotion.

Chapter 10

Effective support for adult learners

Doreen Chappell and Marion Walker

Introduction

This chapter is composed of two parts written by tertiary education specialists. The first is by Doreen Chappell. The second is by Marion Walker. Both discuss dyslexia and forms of support for adult learners.

Part I

Adult dyslexic learners as researchers: developing an accreditation framework

This descriptive account is based on two assumptions:

- Dyslexic adults are willing and able to pose research questions, evaluate practice and in general to work as co-researchers with tutors.
- It is important to find means of accrediting student research work whenever possible.

Background

Between 1987 and 1989, I took part (as a tutor) in a research project on adult dyslexia which was carried out at the University of Leicester (see Chapter 8). The project involved adult dyslexic students and their tutors investigating and exploring both their own dyslexia and dyslexia in general. Over a two-year period, students and tutors discussed, experimented, gave talks and read widely. Students gained in confidence and skills but received no 'paper' qualification for what was often in-depth research.

I also knew of other students attending 'Link into Learning' groups (the name for the Adult Basic Education (ABE) service groups) who were often engaged in the same processes: exploring and investigating their difficulties with various basic skills; teasing out their history of failures and successes and discovering more about the subject in general as they gained confidence from the knowledge that they were dyslexic and not stupid. I felt strongly that there should be a way of accrediting the students' work, which was, after all, informing tutors as well as the students themselves.

Developing accreditation

The establishment of the Leicestershire Open College Network in 1990 offered me an opportunity to put this idea into practice by writing the programme 'Investigating and Coping with Dyslexia'. When I started to draft the programme, there were four important criteria:

- The modules should include tasks and processes that I knew had already been carried out by dyslexic students, so that I was not expecting the impossible.
- Methods of recording information, other than students' own writing, should be deemed valid.
- The programme should be offered at a variety of levels, since a difficulty with spelling or writing does not imply that thinking is at a correspondingly basic level.
- The programme must be flexible, enabling students working either in groups or in individual situations to take part.

In January 1997 the programme consisted of six modules and additional modules are always possible - as tutor and student knowledge grows, so will the recognition of accreditation in different areas. Of the existing modules, more than one can be worked on at once if desired and at different levels. Some modules naturally overlap; some are tackled separately.

Records of students' work can be presented on cassette, written by students, scribed by tutors or another assistant, typed or produced on a wordprocessor, or even videotaped. The choice is the student's. Nominal time for completion of each module is 30 hours, which includes tutor contact and self-study. As students attempt the higher levels, independent learning becomes more important. There is no time limit for completion. The modules are described below.

Case study

A personal case study is compiled which relates students' experiences of dyslexia. This is often a natural and necessary process when working with dyslexic adults. It can be cathartic and can enable students to break down the barriers to learning. As students undertake the higher levels, greater analysis of difficulties and comparison with the case studies of others are a necessary aspect of assessment criteria.

Reading about dyslexia

Students study published writing about the subject. This might include articles from newspapers or journals, whole books or selected chapters or passages; in fact, any written material which broadens the knowledge and understanding of the student concerned. A book or reading list may be compiled for the use of other students and tutors or a report will be made to tutor or group.

Researching information

In this module students examine the media for references to dyslexia; this may involve listening to and discussing radio programmes and references; newspaper and magazine articles; television documentaries and chat shows on the subject; or controversial references in comedy and cartoon. Assessment criteria are covered by the compilation of a folder of references, recording of discussions, reviews and sharing of opinion.

Ways of working

Students set a target or targets to be achieved, based on the skills and knowledge which they see as being most important to their current needs. With a tutor, methods are investigated and devised to cope with difficulties in English, mathematics or organization caused by students' dyslexia. Moving through the levels, students are able to share effective methods with other people, reviewing, compiling a help leaflet or cassette and assessing progress made. A review and report back on technology and other useful aids to learning can be a significant part of this module, especially for students considering support needs for other courses.

Specific topics

For tackling this module, students choose a topic in which they have a particular interest, for example, children and dyslexia; the workplace and dyslexia; mathematical problems. The choice must be the students' and research and reporting must be carried out in depth. Students will need to contact other organizations and devise a hypothesis which can be examined.

The public and dyslexia

Students choose to inform other people about dyslexia, either in a small way or in an organized presentation to a group. This can be a daunting aspect of the programme and requires tutor support. However, many students see this as being most essential as many of them will have suffered from negative public opinion in the past.

Evaluation

So far, the programme has attracted small numbers of students, several of whom have achieved accreditation. For these students, the programme has succeeded: it has enabled dyslexic adults to take on the research and analysis of their own difficulties and of the subject in general. They have shown that they can achieve at a higher level than their written skills might reveal; they have gained confidence in their own worth as givers and seekers of information; and they have used the opportunity and impetus to continue to develop.

Part II

A three-strand approach to specific learning difficulties in adults

Introduction

A research programme was set up in 1990 (Walker 1994) to find appropriate ways of helping and teaching adults with dyslexia. The impetus came from an unexpectedly high response by adults to an awareness campaign organized jointly by the British Dyslexia Association and the Dyslexia Institute in the spring of 1990.

The South Birmingham Dyslexia Association (now Birmingham Dyslexia Associations) decided to offer help on an experimental basis, a 'drop-in' session for adults who had contacted their help line. These monthly meetings provided an opportunity for adults to talk and share experiences. One topic of conversation was the lack of understanding in ABE classes, at that time, of the nature of dyslexia. They had heard of the effective structured, cumulative, multisensory tuition which children were able to receive from some specially trained teachers and asked if a class could be started for adults that would use the same methods:

> Why don't they teach us how they teach my son? (S)

The first model

It was decided to explore the possibility of running such a group. Criteria were established regarding:

- Management, including funding/location of classes.
- Assessment/selection of students.

- Format of the sessions - one-to-one/groups.
- Design and content of the tuition and resources.

Management

Various management options, including the ABE service, private funding, the Dyslexia Institute and the Community Education programme of the local Further Education college, were explored. In consultation with the dyslexic adults the last option was chosen. The class was included in the evening class provision of the local Further Education college. The college agreed to provide one paid tutor and promised the use of its large Access Centre with its bank of computers. The local Lions' Club gave a grant for the initial outlay of expenses.

Assessment and selection of students

The dyslexic adults in the drop-in group were unanimous that the class should be restricted to adults with dyslexia. This raised the question about assessment and whether a student's difficulties were due to a specific learning difficulty (SpLD) or some other cause. To insist on an educational psychologist's assessment was not practicable, so the author devised an assessment based on tests of visual and auditory memory, sequencing, reasoning, and reading and spelling ability. This, coupled with an essential informal initial interview, constituted an informal screening of prospective students. The class was not advertised in the college brochure. Referrals were initially from the local Dyslexia Association and others got to know by word of mouth.

Format of the sessions

To make the group financially viable it was only possible to fund one paid tutor. However, all the dyslexic adults were insistent that one-to-one tuition was essential. Prospective students were asked what they deemed most important in a tutor. All said:

> Someone who understands dyslexia. (D)
> Someone who won't make me feel as if I'm back at school. (D)
> A good listener (P)
> Someone who will be able to help me with my spelling - they won't have to mind if I forget. (B)

It was therefore decided to use trained volunteer tutors - teaching skills are teachable; empathy with dyslexia is more difficult to learn. Volunteer tutors were selected by personal approach. A team of six tutors was assembled, who undertook a course of six two-hour training sessions. This training consisted of awareness of the nature of dyslexic difficultics, their effects on self-esteem and strategies that might have been developed, as well as training in the structured language programme.

The dyslexic adults were insistent on individual tuition. The variety and degree of severity of the symptoms of dyslexia would make group tuition a frustrating experience for both students and tutors. However, the social interaction of a group might have great advantages in terms of mutual support and encouragement. To try to reap the advantages of both methods of support, and minimize the disadvantages, it was decided:

- To use trained volunteer tutors for a 50-minute session.
- To run alongside this, a small group session led by one tutor.

An additional advantage would be that each tutor would have the time to teach two students individually during the two-hour session.

Design and content of the tuition and resources

Although there was, at that time, a good variety of material for use with adults with literacy difficulties, none of it fitted the needs of a structured, cumulative scheme. The materials that were used in structured schemes were designed for children and were not suitable, either in format or vocabulary, for use with adults. Therefore it was decided that a framework of worksheets which supported a new structured cumulative language programme should be devised. Multisensory teaching techniques would be used in their implementation. This pack of resources was trialled over the succeeding four years and suggestions and improvements incorporated (Walker 2000). In addition, books and other resources were purchased to supplement this resource.

The first group started in October 1990 with ten dyslexic adults and six volunteer tutors. After 16 weeks an evaluation and review took place. All original dyslexic adults were still enrolled and a long waiting list had developed. Two more volunteer tutors were enlisted, but it was decided that in order to accommodate the long waiting list, another group would have to be started. As four of the dyslexic adults travelled the 12 miles from Coventry to attend the group, the local Futher Education college there was approached. The college was happy to include the group in its Community Education programme on the same basis and six local volunteer tutors were found and trained. This process was repeated twice over the next four years.

Evaluation and development

The formal evaluations at the end of each term and the informal comments from students and tutors enabled continual refinement and development of the programme.

The one-to-one tuition sessions were vital. The structured cumulative programme enabled students to see patterns and conventions in the English language that could be generalized. The multisensory teaching techniques allowed the adults to discover their own preferred learning styles. What had seemed a vague chaotic muddle of words that had to be learned individually - and forgotten - gradually took shape and the adults were able to feel in control of words for reading and spelling. The worksheets built up into students' personal indexed volumes that could be used for reference and revision (Walker 2000):

> If you don't get it the first time, you know where to go back to. (Student A)

In the one-to-one tuition situation, literacy needs that were uniquely relevant to students could be undertaken. These needs could range from writing an absence note for school to planning an essay. This individual session also provided an opportunity for a bond of trust and respect to develop between the dyslexic adult and the volunteer tutor. The pairing was constant and tutors did not 'fill in' for other tutors. The attendance rate from both volunteer tutors and students was 80% overall:

> Knowing B is waiting for me makes me turn out. (Student R)
> I couldn't let him down. (Tutor J)
> I wouldn't have come if I hadn't got a tutor to myself. (Student D)

The small group sessions, however, took a long time to become useful. Word processing was offered, but was not successful owing to the constant breakdown of the machines. Group discussions and 'information' sessions were tried, but the adults were very wary of each other. One evening the tutor could not be present for the group session and the adults were left to themselves. The noise level gradually rose and by the end of the session, all were talking and laughing together. It had been found by default that the key to the group work was less input from the tutor. The more relaxed atmosphere from then on provided an increasingly helpful and supportive environment.

Emergence of a three-strand approach

Research revealed that what had started out as an attempt at finding an appropriate literacy programme for dyslexic adults had gradually developed into a more complete supportive environment.

The understanding of dyslexia and its effects and the empathy of the tutors was a powerful factor in the establishment of mutual respect and trust between tutors and students. Literacy difficulties are only one symptom of dyslexia. McLoughlin et al. (1994) refer to 'general working memory difficulties, such as forgetting sequences of instructions, an inability to keep track of what is said in a conversation, or following what is presented in a lecture' (p. 17). These bewildering and often frightening and frustrating difficulties could be expressed and talked through in a confidential and supportive atmosphere. The realization that these difficulties could also be symptoms of dyslexia was reassuring and liberating. One student had seriously thought that he was suffering early onset of Alzheimer's disease.

The reaction of adults to this provision of literacy help coupled with understanding of dyslexia seemed to follow a pattern. At first there was relief that the problem was at last being taken seriously and appropriate help was being offered. After this 'honeymoon' period, deeper feelings, often long suppressed, of anger, frustration, guilt and rejection started to surface. The 'safe' environment of the individual tutor/student sessions and the session with a small group of people who may have similar experiences enabled the feelings to be acknowledged and shared. The acknowledgement and resolution of these feelings and experiences enabled students to go forward and begin to take control of their dyslexia. This process has been described by Wilsher (1986). He likens it to resolving any major trauma - a period of denial, a search for understanding, a separation of self from the trauma and a resolution, either by confrontation or by developing viable alternatives.

Gerber et al. (1992) in their study of successful adults with dyslexia also describe this process, which they call 're-framing'. Re-framing allows the dyslexic person to gain control of his or her difficulties. Control represents recognition, acceptance and understanding, leading to action - moving towards a specific individual goal:

> Control meant making conscious decisions to take charge of one's life (internal decisions), and adapting and shaping oneself in order to move ahead (external manifestations) . . . Control was the fuel that fired their success. (p. 479)

McLoughlin et al. (1994) describe the levels of awareness and compensation that must be experienced before this 'control' can take place:

- **Level 1**: not aware of weaknesses and have developed no strategies to overcome them.
- **Level 2**: aware of weaknesses but have not developed strategies to overcome them.
- **Level 3**: aware of weaknesses and have unconsciously developed compensating strategies.
- **Level 4**: aware of weaknesses and have consciously developed compensating strategies.

The group was being offered compensating strategies that were appropriate to their level of awareness. These strategies included:

- Literacy tuition that was cumulative, multisensory and structured.
- Skills that were essential to the adult's everyday needs.
- The re-discovery of self-confidence and self-esteem.

The three strands were all essential for the adult to achieve effective control of dyslexia (Figure 10.1).

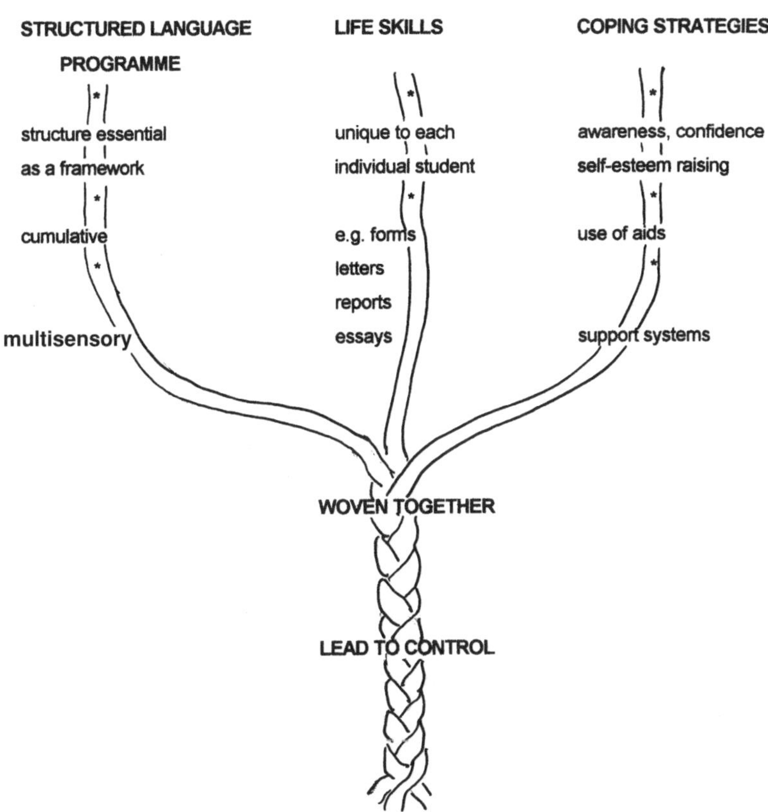

Figure 10.1. Help for adults with dyslexia.

Chapter 11

Effective support in further education: a case study

Jenny Murphy

Introduction

Further education is a unique educational sector because of its diversity and its size. It is larger than both the school and the higher education sector combined. Currently, its student range includes post-16 students from school, day- or block-release students from employment, and mature students wishing to return to education or wishing to gain accreditation for vocational skills. It also provides for a large category of students on courses especially tailored to the needs of the community - of local industry and commerce or wherever there is a market. Full- and part-time courses are offered in modules, as open learning, distance learning or practical workshops, as well as in more traditional ways. This chapter explores the question of how dyslexic students can be supported effectively in such a diverse learning environment, with specific reference to a successful model of support developed in one of the largest further education colleges in England: East Berkshire College (with approximately 25 000 students) during the 1990s. The support described here covers college provision up to and including 1998.

The learning support section is part of a cross-college support services division and aims to provide whatever support is required to enable students with learning difficulties or disabilities to access the curriculum, albeit within financial constraints. In further education, the money to support students with a learning difficulty or disability is attached to individual students. However, this funding is paid based on an estimate of the amount needed, which is made some months before students enrol.

Although the Further Education Funding Council has ensured adequate funding is available for the students who need it, it is one of the tragedies of this area of work that, nationally, many colleges have failed to avail themselves of this money. Some do not follow the guidelines and make the claims for funding; most fail to delegate budgets to provide the means for the learning support staff to deliver support. East Berkshire College is an exception to this pattern in that the additional funding claimed to support students is used exclusively for that purpose. This undoubtedly contributed to the achievement of a Grade One (the highest) in a recent inspection. A high reputation provides scope for external funding from local universities, schools and other bodies.

Dyslexic students at East Berkshire College will make contact with learning support in a variety of ways. If these students have had an assessment at school and know that they are dyslexic, this will be indicated on their application form. Alternatively, if students are aware of needing some additional support, this can also be indicated on their application forms. In both cases, students will be given a confidential interview to discuss their support needs before the start of the course. Other students requiring support would usually be identified within the first few weeks at college, from a cross-college screening test of reading, comprehension, numeracy and free writing. Throughout the academic year, dyslexic students might be referred by their course tutors or refer themselves if they experience difficulties with their course.

All referred students are interviewed individually and their support needs ascertained by discussion and consideration of their preference for how they want to be supported. Negotiation is of paramount importance; students will only use the support offered if it is what they want and what they feel they need.

Dyslexic students are given the opportunity to be supported on a one-to-one basis by trained dyslexia tutors. It is in this respect that East Berkshire College can claim its success. It is a huge operation to interview students, hire staff and support approximately 300 dyslexic students in this way, but the conviction that *individual* tuition is the most successful method of working with dyslexic students enables it to happen. This model of support is the same as that recommended by Klein (1995).

Teaching methodology

Support is arranged outside students' timetables and teaching is within the context of the course that students are taking. There are two strands to the rationale for this method. The first is pragmatic: students are often only in the college for one year and their priority is to complete the course successfully and so time is limited. This often means that the support will be to give students strategies to enable them to cope, and to acquire independence as learners as quickly as possible, rather than to attempt to remediate a long-term difficulty. The second strand of this methodological rationale is to do with the psychology of the learner. There is a need for learners to 'make personal links between their own future lives and the traditional stuff of learning' Salmon (1995, with reference to Kohl, 1971).

'The psycho-logic of learning draws its own lines of demarcation. Knowledge is not free standing or disembodied' Salmon (1995). This point is particularly salient for dyslexic learners, to whom meaning and therefore relevance is all-important. The application of rules to reading and writing, although possible to teach through long and tedious drill and practice, does not suit the learning style of dyslexic students:

> Students need to be able to internalize learning within the context of their actual assignments. The use of exercise sheets or rules are nearly always ineffective because dyslexic students do not spontaneously generalize learning or transfer it to other contexts. Klein (1995)

For this reason, support tutors deal directly with difficulties which arise from course work. The content of the support sessions is discussed between tutor and student in a desire to give the students as much autonomy and independence as possible. It is in working with students in this way that support tutors become aware of the injustice of an education system which, with its dependence on literacy-based methods of assessment, can militate so unfairly against dyslexic students who frequently outperform their peers in terms of what they know and how they perform, but who are often faced with the possibility of failure because of the reading/writing barrier.

> . . . there was hostility ... towards a system bent on proving how inept he was. O'Shea and Dalton (1994)

Whether or not the neurological evidence concerning hemispherical preference is considered conclusive (Galaburda 1993), dyslexia tutors have often observed that their students respond and relate well to creative and *visual* styles of teaching and learning held by many (Springer and Deutsch 1993; Klein 1995) to be indicative of right hemispherical preference. Some adults, however, having experience only of the essentially 'left brain'-biased British education system may have failed to develop or ignored their visual and creative abilities, not realizing their possible relevance in the learning process. Tutors using pictures, metaphor, fantasy and visualization, as outlined by writers such as Williams (1986) or indeed the mind mapping technique espoused by Buzan (1993) have enabled some students to organize their learning visually with great success.

Some dyslexic students find that when material is presented auditorily, they are better able to process and remember it than when it is presented visually. Many of these students use dictaphones to good effect, playing and replaying key lectures and key information.

Klein (1994), whose experience is based on adult dyslexic learners, and whose courses and methods have been undertaken by many of the dyslexia tutors at East Berkshire College, bases her suggestions for teaching methods on a diagnosis of the strengths and weaknesses of dyslexic students and the subsequent teaching of students to their *strengths*. The crux of the argument is that if students have visual perceptual weakness, they will require auditory and/or kinaesthetic strategies. The necessity to establish learning styles concurs with Gardner (1984) and Lawrence (1983). The latter suggests that the *order* in which material is presented is crucial and an analysis of students' learning style in terms of personal mental types, based on Briggs Myers' work (1980) determines this.

Adult further education students have usually already learned to read and write to some extent. Many have compensated for early literacy difficulties, although they will still have problems coping with a further education curriculum. These ongoing difficulties are well documented (Finucci et al. 1985; Lefly and Pennington 1991). Because these students have compensated for early difficulties, many of the teaching and learning methods used for children are inappropriate for them.

Multisensory methods which, historically, have been combined with a structured programme of remediating reading and spelling difficulties should not be considered inappropriate for adults, although the structured programme is undoubtedly inappropriate for the further education student who just needs to be able to produce the next written assignment - due in tomorrow! There is also an argument that these structured programmes are tedious and of doubtful value because of the inability of dyslexic students to generalize, as has been mentioned earlier. It is important not to throw the baby out with the bath water, however, since multisensory methods using the major auditory, visual and tactile-kinaesthetic learning modalities can be of great value to any learner but of particular value to dyslexic students.

Kinaesthetic and tactile learning is perhaps the least used of these 'channels' but for many dyslexic students who have problems with verbal expression, this can provide a method of externalizing thought which has numerous advantages, not least of which is making the learning process an enjoyable one: a novel experience for some dyslexic students!

An intrinsic part of effective support of dyslexic students has to be the building of confidence. As noted by Gilroy and Miles (1986), Hampshire (1990) and Edwards (1994), dyslexic students have a history of difficulty which frequently results in a loss of confidence in themselves and sometimes their ability to learn. One of the essential roles of the support tutor is to build that confidence by enabling students to find their own particular way of learning.

It becomes increasingly evident in this work that it is impossible, and indeed undesirable, to be prescriptive about methods, since the nature of dyslexic difficulties is so diverse that teaching needs to be equally diverse in its methods in order to serve the needs of learners. With this in mind, tutors are recruited more for their flexibility, creativity and sensitivity to adult dyslexic learners than for their adherence to particular methods, which might indicate an undesirable rigidity.

As a postscript to the overview of methodology used in the college, two tutors have, in a limited way, begun to pilot the Davis (1994) method of orientation counselling. At the time of writing, this method is entirely new to this country, although well established in California. All students taking part are volunteers and it is a method only started in June 1996 but early results are very exciting. The students who have started this programme are very enthusiastic about it and are amazed at their learning speed and success. Davis' (1994) explanation for dyslexia is:

> At dyslexia's root is a natural ability, a talent which allows the individual to disrupt sensory perceptions and replace them with conceptualizations. Dylexia is not a complexity. It is a compound of simple factors which can be dealt with step-by-step. (Davis 1994)

His methods involve a technique to establish accurate sensory perceptions and a series of steps to undo the inaccurate perceptions and solutions of the past, leading to a mastery of the basics of the symbols of language and mathematics.

Other methods of support

But what of students' day-to-day college experience? It would be naive to suggest that it is anything but tough for dyslexic students to survive and succeed in a further education college. Gilroy and Miles (1983) recognized this some years ago when working with dyslexic students in this environment. At East Berkshire College there are initiatives towards addressing these issues. A Dyslexia Support Group which meets on a weekly basis has had a promising start and will be introduced at the second of the three sites of the college in the next academic year. The support group provides a forum for discussion of topics that the students want to explore, and a means of mutual support to minimize possible feelings of isolation in a college environment which is not ideally equipped to accommodate dyslexic students' needs.

One-to-one support sessions are not the only method used in the college. In-class support is sometimes more appropriate or is used as an additional means of supporting students.

Note-taking in class presents a difficulty for most dyslexic students. If the student has severe writing problems but can cope with other aspects of the course, learning support provides a note-taker for some or all of the student's sessions. Students with less severe writing difficulties can borrow a dictaphone for the academic year. In addition, spellcheckers can also be loaned on request.

Examinations and tests are a problem area for most dyslexic students. Many of the dyslexia staff at East Berkshire College are trained to do assessments (for public examinations these are endorsed by an educational psychologist). Examination arrangements are made for dyslexic students on the basis of what they require and the nature of their difficulties. These arrangements range from allowing students extra time to providing the services of an amanuensis (reader and scribe). Although it is possible to lobby examination boards to endeavour to create a fairer system for dyslexic students, the college has little control over the arrangements for external examinations. However, it is possible to design internal tests, assignments and methods of assessment which do not present dyslexic learners with an impossible barrier to achieving accreditation (Klein 1995). This is an equal opportunities issue which few colleges will have addressed and East Berkshire College is no exception.

The support process

Following the initial interview with students requiring support, details of the support offered and any important information regarding students is sent to the course tutor. Liaison between support tutor and subject lecturers, although desirable, is rarely achievable in any great measure. This is more a reflection of further education at this time than of a lack of will on either side.

Twice a year, supported students have a chance to give their opinions of the help they have received and to make suggestions for possible improvements. In addition to this, a system of observation and feedback is currently being devised for support tutors in order to constantly improve the quality of the support being given.

Future developments

There are a number of ways in which East Berkshire College's support for dyslexic students could be further improved. One of these is the need to improve staff awareness of dyslexia and of dyslexic learners' needs. It is a challenging, if not daunting, task in the light of all the other pressing needs for staff development in an ever-changing educational environment and with an ever-decreasing staff development budget. However, this is a key factor in the learning experience of dyslexic students and is urgently needed if this and other colleges are to provide total access to the curriculum.

The nature of the flexibility of the further education curriculum on offer can militate against being able to provide adequate support to dyslexic students. If students are studying at a distance or are only attending college for one day a week, all of which is spent in the classroom or workshop, there is no time for support - a problem yet to be resolved.

It is fitting that this chapter should end with a short 'pen sketch' of one of East Berkshire's dyslexic students. Susan's is only one of the many positive comments support students make. She has experienced support with her learning for the first time this year. Last year, at another college, she described herself as 'just scraping through'. There was no support on offer. This year, with regular specialist support in language and in numeracy, she gained a credit on her ITEC Sports Injury Therapy Course and is intending to study A level human biology next year. She says she would not have considered this step had she not had the support this year. She has now gained the confidence to continue and is optimistic about her future career.

CHAPTER 12

Staff development in further education

CYNTHIA KLEIN

Introduction

> We need a match between how people learn, their learning goals and the learning environment. (Professor John Tomlinson, Chair of FEFC Specialist Committee on Students with Learning Difficulties and Disabilities)

> People who look like having trouble with simple, ordinary things may be very skilled at other complex things. (Tom West, author, and himself dyslexic)

> What's hard is dealing with other people because they don't understand it [dyslexia]. (Dyslexic student at a Futher Education college)

What do these three quotes have in common? There are probably many answers and there are no prizes, but my vote goes to Tomlinson: 'Teacher expectations and attitudes are as influential as technical equipment and individual ability'. In other words, when it comes to the success or failure of dyslexic students, it is the staff who count.

Further education: ugly stepsister or princess?

Generally speaking, further education remains the most undervalued and under-recognized sector in British education. However, it has a particularly interesting and important role in the education system as the home of the 'fresh start' for adult returners, for those who failed academically at school and for those with practical or vocational leanings which did not have a full outlet at school. Staff are therefore dealing with a wider range of students and courses than in any other sector of post-16 education, and also with a greater variety of learning styles and needs and levels of literacy and learning skills. This range includes a considerable number of dyslexic students whose dyslexia was not identified at school and who were instead seen as lazy, careless or not very bright.

The Further Education Funding Council (FEFC), through the Tomlinson Committee's three-year enquiry into provision for students with learning difficulties and disabilities, acknowledged this range and the need to extend it. The Committee's report is centred on the concept of 'inclusive learning', the notion that whatever a society decides to offer its citizens in the way of learning must be available to all its citizens. This involves a shift in emphasis *away from students with special problems* and *towards the learning environment and the importance of matching this to the student* rather than expecting students to fit in with what is available - and this is for all students, not just those with learning difficulties and disabilities.

The Committee also recognized the implications of this change through one of their most urgent recommendations: a major, national staff development programme supported by earmarked funding.

Here is the 'Cinderella' sector taking the lead in a major shift in thinking - about disability, teaching and learning. But what exactly does this shift mean in practical terms for the issue of staff development?

Staff development: for whom?

'It's not my job.'

This is a common cry. But exactly whose responsibility *is* it to support dyslexic students? If dyslexia is seen as a difference in learning style, with specific difficulties in accessing and retaining verbal and written information and producing written work, then it is clear that curriculum requirements, materials, course delivery and assessment will all have an impact on the dyslexic learner, either as a hindrance or a help.

A learning support tutor complained not long ago that the whole of his weekly support session with one student was spent deciphering and organizing the notes dictated by one of his lecturers. Others tell how their students are unable to make sense of three-page typewritten assignments or lengthy instructions. Even more worry about dyslexic students who are not identified until their second or third term because subject tutors do not know how to recognize dyslexia so leave students to flounder or fail.

In a model of inclusive learning which focuses on the ability of the learning environment to meet the needs of all the students, promoting student achievement is everybody's job.

'I have too many more important things to do.'

Lecturers are besieged by many and conflicting demands as qualifications and accreditation specifications change and monitoring requirements increase. However, it is too easy to ignore the important for the sake of the urgent. Student drop-out and underachievement are major concerns for colleges; addressing the learning needs of dyslexic students means addressing *learning,* and addressing learning means more success for *all* students, not just the dyslexic ones. If the work of teachers is not about learning and teaching, what is it about? Many would say that assessment has dominated the curriculum and learning has been lost as a focus. The Tomlinson Report has re-established that focus for the future; this is as important for teachers and managers as for students. The new inspection framework also puts more emphasis on the quality of learning in the classroom and the extent to which teaching meets the learning requirements of all students.

The role of managers, and their perceptions of staff development, are central. Managers need to see and value - by committing time and resources - the link between staff development and curriculum development, between time given to staff for reflecting and developing more effective teaching strategies and the improved retention and success of all students, and consequently the improved confidence and commitment of staff. Acquisition of new skills, knowledge and understanding gives staff energy and confidence; this is communicated to students who then learn more effectively and become more confident and interested as learners. It is a sort of 'parallel processing'; teachers' own confidence and interest in learning are mirrored by those who learn from them.

'*I don't have time to do all this extra work for one student.*'

Underlying this comment is a hidden myth, that of the 'typical learner'. This is a dodgy notion, certainly not backed up by the frequently commented on, persistent 'long tail of underachievement' among learners in British education. Precisely because dyslexic students are *not* 'typical learners' and do not learn the way others do, they challenge our assumptions about learning and force us to address the role of learning styles in achieving learning success. Strategies that help dyslexic learners can therefore often help other learners, particularly those who do not respond well to traditional methods.

Time spent developing and introducing a more effective and accessible course delivery and embedding strategies to improve learning is easily recouped by not having to spend so much time covering the same ground over and over again, as well as by improved participation and success from previous low achievers. Investing in the present to reap rewards in the future is about time as much as money.

'*She shouldn't be on this course if she can't do the work.*'

On the face of it, this seems fairly obviously true; unfortunately, it doesn't hold for two reasons. The written language skills of dyslexic people can be improved considerably with appropriate support; however, in most cases these will never be commensurate with their other abilities. Indeed, this is one of the classic indications of dyslexia: a discrepancy between verbal and/or performance skills and written language skills. Dyslexic students frequently get frustrated and demoralized by being told to improve their 'basic skills' before being allowed on a course in their chosen vocational or academic area. As many will never reach the required literacy level, they are condemned to underachievement; whereas with knowledgeable support and special examination provision, they may do well, some achieving success at a high level in a field where they have talent. A student who continues to have difficulties recognizing simple words, such as *the*, and who cannot copy accurately off the board may be quick at reading three-dimensional plans and grasping principles of engineering.

It is also important to note that the dyslexic learning style is such that students develop literacy and learning skills most effectively when these are context-bound, especially in a personally meaningful context. This affects ability as well as motivation. Recent research with highly successful dyslexic adults in a range of fields has shown that they are able to read in their own subject at a much higher level than when reading texts of a general nature (Fink 1995).

When asking who staff development should be for, we need to remind ourselves of everyone who contributes to students' placement, success and progression. Staff development for managers is vital; there are still some who do not really 'believe' in dyslexia (do they 'believe' in deafness?) and many others who do not realize the full implications of dyslexia for assessment and learning. Such managers are unlikely to ensure adequate resources for dyslexic students or to use staff and additional learning support hours in the most effective ways.

Lack of knowledge by those involved in initial advice, assessment and placement at the pre-entry and entry phase can lead to failure, drop-out or wasted time and resources. Students themselves do not always know enough about the courses on offer or their own learning needs to select the best course, type of accreditation or progression route. A recent example concerns two dyslexic students doing media studies. They were wrongly placed in that they were having difficulties with certain aspects of the course and neither was on the course he really wanted to do anyway. One had wanted to do performing arts but was afraid he wouldn't be able to remember lines; the other had wanted to study music but thought he wouldn't be allowed because he couldn't read music. Both wasted a year which could have been avoided by appropriate advice, discussion and planning.

Careers advisers are equally in need of staff development if they are to explore with students the most appropriate courses, qualifications and career routes in order to maximize rather than limit the realization of potential. Dyslexic young women who did poorly academically have been led to take up office skills or business studies, which rely on skills where dyslexic people are particularly weak, by unaware or thoughtless careers advisers who failed to seek out their aptitudes. Less crudely but with just as devastating consequences, other dyslexic individuals have been discouraged from pursuing their chosen careers because of their poor literacy skills or not helped to access the support to which they are entitled.

Without trying to be exhaustive, other staff such as librarians and technicians can, with genuine understanding, also help ease dyslexic students' struggles to achieve success.

Additional learning support: remediation or progression?

Additional learning support funding offers an opportunity for the provision of the specialist individual support vital in enabling dyslexic students to achieve success; but for this to be effective, staff giving support need a thorough understanding of dyslexia and dyslexic learners in order to help them develop their strengths and use these to compensate for weaknesses.

We now know something of the processing problems of dyslexic people; that these are neurological and developmental. What can be developed neurologically at six with regard to, say, discriminating or segmenting sounds, cannot be developed at 16 or 60. Attempts to 'remediate' thus often flounder with adults and young people who describe school remedial classes as a repeated experience of failure. '*I was a hard-core member of the remedial class*', said one. The learning support teacher who tries to teach phonics and rules or uses worksheets, wordlists, exercises and such will usually find students become bored, frustrated and often stop attending. But more importantly, nothing will be done to develop a sense of *mastery*, which dyslexic students get from finding their *own* strategies for remembering and from discovering that they have strengths as well as weaknesses. With such an approach, shy students with little confidence in themselves as learners have blossomed into class leaders and have even been found teaching others their memory strategies! Also, perhaps more importantly, their written work has improved noticeably. A class lecturer recently called the change in one student's work 'a miracle', a comment echoed by many, even if not quite in such extreme terms.

Consequently, the kind of training specialist tutors receive is crucial to student success and motivation. Such training needs to be about teaching adult dyslexic learners; child-based courses are not appropriate, nor is basic adult literacy training, which even now does not readily acknowledge that language processing difficulties are a major reason for failure to acquire literacy skills and rarely has even the smallest component on dyslexia.

Since the aim of additional learning support is to enable students to achieve their primary learning goal; it needs to be thought of and planned – not on the basis of what students haven't learned in the past, be it rules of spelling or grammar or how to decode when reading, but on the basis of what students need to enable them to achieve success on their course. Tutor training must therefore include diagnostic methods for determining students' strengths as well as weaknesses and teaching strategies which use the diagnostic assessment to form and implement an individual learning plan clearly linked to students' coursework and assessment requirements. The thinking, planning and strategies taught must always be aimed at progression and developing learner autonomy, not about remediation.

What staff need to know: assumptions and answers

> He claims he's dyslexic but he's really just not very bright.
>
> She's not dyslexic; she can read.
>
> Just give him a spellchecker.
>
> It's just a middle class excuse.

Identification and referral

'*There's lots with worse problems than him.*' It is the *nature* of the difficulties which need to be identified and the extent to which these affect achievement of individual potential. A seemingly minor problem may prevent students from realizing their goals and undermine their confidence. Staff need to be able to recognize indications of dyslexia and refer students early for an appropriate asessment as the identification and understanding of their difficulties is crucial to dyslexic students' success in learning and in raising self-esteem, which affects learning. This is particularly important as so many dyslexic students in further education were never diagnosed at school. One former student went home, took out a recipe book and baked a cake when she found out she was dyslexic; the diagnosis alone, with the explanation that'. . . *it had nothing to do with me being stupid*' gave her the confidence to have a go with the recipe book. Another former student was able to do an Access to Law course instead of being shunted into a Basic Skills class because her difficulties were identified as dyslexia through a diagnostic assessment; she now has her law degree.

Understanding dyslexia

'*Now you see it, now you don't*'. The nature of dyslexia is itself an obstacle for staff and needs illuminating. Misunderstandings abound, making students even more confused about their learning. Staff may think dyslexia is only a problem with reading and spelling and be sceptical when students mis-copy, muddle instructions, turn up late and get lost. They may be unsympathetic when a student seems to be able to read the required texts, understands the ideas, contributes to discussion and then turns in an unreadable assignment with the same word spelled three different ways (all of them wrong) on one page and muddled sentences which make no sense.

Implications for teaching and learning, course curriculum and delivery, assessment, achievement and progression: all and everything

A learning environment to match the learning styles and goals of all students clearly has ramifications for all aspects of the curriculum. Some of these include only simple changes, such as writing legibly on the board and when marking work; others challenge us to more thought about the way we communicate to students both course content and, even more, our expectations. Dyslexic learners do not automatically acquire the conventions of written language; therefore they need everything to be made explicit within its appropriate context. They also require us to be aware of how we set up learning activities and to think about how we measure and validate achievement and enable progression. Students with motivation and support will often surprise us by succeeding against all our expectations. We need to keep the path open for them by making the learning environment as dyslexia-friendly as we can and by destroying the barriers of our negative expectations.

Dyslexic students also need help from staff at each stage in finding their way through the system, what support they are entitled to and how to get it.

There are three hurdles to be overcome in trying to implement a staff development strategy: getting people interested, getting them to listen and getting them to take action.

Experience and belief: changing minds

There are still considerable numbers of teachers and lecturers who do not believe dyslexia exists or who are unwilling to acknowledge that any of their students might be dyslexic, preferring to blame lack of progress on laziness, poor teaching at school, lack of intelligence or even parental pressure.

There is a Nasruddin story where he borrows a neighbour's cooking pot and returns it with a second smaller one. To the neighbour's surprise he explains that the cooking pot 'had a baby'. When he next borrows the neighbour's cooking pot, he fails to return it. When the neighbour asks him about it, Nasruddin explains that 'the cooking pot has died'. To the neighbour's exclamation that cooking pots can't die, Nasruddin comments that the neighbour was prepared to believe that one could have a baby, so why couldn't it die? This story has many layers of interpretations but one possible one is that we are willing to suspend disbelief when we perceive it to be in our interests. It is in teachers' interests to 'believe' in dyslexia when they see learning support working and students' performance, confidence and exam results improve.

Experience is the most effective way to counter unfounded beliefs; as teachers we all know that our students often need to experience something for themselves in order to learn. One of the most profound 'conversions' I've witnessed was a 'disbelieving' tutor who was given an essay by one of his students which described dyslexia, its emotional and social effects, his early experiences at school, and gave an analysis of what was wrong with remedial teaching; all beautifully expressed but with numerous examples of peculiar spellings and unexpected grammatical and punctuation errors. The tutor was so moved that he became the student's most committed advocate.

Capturing the golden fleece

Preconceptions of why students fail to learn generally underlie refusals to recognize dyslexia. We all feel threatened by ideas - and even evidence - that challenge our frameworks of belief. If the new idea demands too much readjustment, or forces us to admit we have been wrong, we can become extremely defensive and hostile. In the story of Psyche and Eros, one of Psyche's tasks was to collect some golden fleece. She was advised by the reeds not to try to collect the fleece from the fierce golden rams in the heat of the midday sun but to wait until the cool of evening and gather the fleece from the branches where it had caught when the rams passed by earlier. Good advice for avoiding confrontation and waiting for a time when people are 'cool' and relaxed before trying to collect the gold of their attention.

I first started doing dyslexia support at a college many years ago when there was much less recognition of it. I did all my staff development informally, by hanging out in the staff room and chatting to lecturers about individual students, making small suggestions or pointing out something they might not have noticed, or an interesting article or bit of research, or offering to talk to their class about getting help with spelling. I found I began to get staff coming up to me and asking me about dyslexia because they thought they or their children might be dyslexic or because they had noticed an improvement in a student's work and were curious as to how this had been brought about.

My other most successful tactic was to use my diagnostic reports on students. A copy of the report would, with the student's permission, be given to the tutor and I would then offer to talk to the tutor about the report and recommendations; this gave me the chance to explain a little about what dyslexia was, how it affected the student and why what I'd recommended should help. Often this was enough to get tutors interested, especially if they then talked to the student about it, at which point I would suggest they might like to find out more about it.

When offering formal staff development sessions, it helps to remember that we are all interested in ourselves; sessions on learning styles and the brain always go down well. Simulations of difficulties dyslexic people experience often make the most impact, as do students themselves when describing their difficulties or the complicated strategies they have to resort to for what seem to be simple tasks. Time helping students understand and articulate their difficulties to their tutors is time well spent by dyslexia support staff. It is often one small experience or connection which makes sudden sense to a tutor that starts a major change in thinking.

Carrots, sticks and levers

Getting people to take action may need more than carrots, even if honey covered. Fortunately, the Tomlinson Report recommendations backed by the inspection system offer useful levers for affecting both practice and policy. The Disability Discrimination Act of 1995 also provides levers, requiring colleges to publish disability statements which include information on policy, admission arrangements, access, specialist equipment and support services. A current bill will increase colleges' responsibilities to disabled students.

One of the problems in getting colleges – and schools and universities – to put dyslexia on the agenda has been its history of exclusion. Disability groups have not traditionally seen it as a 'real' disability and special needs teachers had little or no training about it. Even last year, two academics argued in a quality newspaper that 'dyslexic' children were taking scarce resources away from those with 'real' disabilities. Dyslexia, or specific learning difficulties, has often been subsumed under 'literacy problems', although training in the teaching of reading did not even mention it as it was seen to be a 'special needs' issue, if indeed it was seen as an issue at all. It is only by its inclusion in recent policy that ignoring it or not acknowledging it as a genuine disability has ceased to be an option. The eligibility of dyslexic students for additional funding has had and continues to have an impressive impact. A colleague at a London college told me the other day in an amazed voice how there was now a special room for dyslexia support on each site of the college and they had a budget for resources and equipment, as well as hours to provide the specialist tuition needed, all of which had been previously denied as too costly, or indeed 'impossible'.

The Tomlinson Report helped to shift the ground on disability, a shift which will continue to affect education for many years to come; the changes in thinking that it requires affect us all, staff and students alike. It is a genuine opportunity for dyslexic students to contribute to constructive changes in the learning environment, in teaching and learning in and out of the classroom. We need to encourage the dropping of worn-out stances and create opportunities for their voices to be heard. To quote Professor Tomlinson again, it is 'a mistake to think you can change education by changing qualifications'. To create real change, we have to 'energize from within'. Good staff development is an essential source for that energy.

Strategic approaches to staff development for dyslexia support staff

When planning an approach to staff development, it is useful to consider the appropriateness of different strategies; these depend on who the target groups are, the level of current awareness, management support and the timing in relation to college planning. There are three general approaches, each with advantages and disadvantages.

Follow the student

- Use student processes through the system, such as the diagnostic report, individual learning plan, request for special examination provision, as a basis for discussion, and explanations about why the student has difficulties with certain aspects of the course.
- Include students in discussions or encourage them to talk to their tutor, explain their problems and what would help them.
- Follow up discussions with ideas or offers to help, suggesting tutors might be interested in finding out more about dyslexia.

Advantages

Students can be a very powerful tool for making significant changes in perception and attitude, and also help in the creation of allies.

Disadvantages

It is a slow process, only addressing small numbers of staff.

Colonization ('drip, drip, drip' or 'a finger in every pie')

- Use allies, both staff and students, to put the issue of dyslexia into everything and 'ride the coat-tails' of all curriculum and policy discussions, documents, plans, strategies, events (e.g. diagnostic assessment, drop-out and retention, funding, disability, learning and teaching, key skills, inspections).
- Offer to give input or help at every opportunity.
- Circulate information, articles and anecdotes, keying in to individual staff members' interests and concerns.

Advantages

This approach avoids confrontation and gradually wears away opposition as well as increasing allies throughout the college.

Disadvantages

It relies on persistence and lots of energy, so it can be discouraging without good support from allies, and it is not very systematic.

Strategic campaign ('flooding')

- Use a team of allies to launch a concerted and staged 'attack' on targeted groups throughout the college through making sure dyslexia is officially on the agenda of management, governors, the college development plan, self-assessment reports and quality and disability statements.
- Write reports and make formal recommendations and presentations to senior management meetings, governors' meetings and the academic board.
- Write a college dyslexia support development plan, analysing current provision and drawing up a model and strategy for a quality provision.
- Contribute to equal opportunities, inclusive learning and key skills policies - also student and staff handbooks, news bulletins and staff development days.
- Bring in outside 'experts', set up student support groups, initiate projects or action research and link up with community organizations.
- Encourage students to articulate what they need and why, to talk to staff and to participate in staff development sessions.

Advantages

A well thought out and executed campaign targets all levels of staff in a systematic and overt way, making dyslexia a legitimate area of concern.

Disadvantages

Such a campaign can be confrontational and may offend some people so it needs care and a 'team' of allies, including managers - and it may be better at getting action but not as effective in changing attitudes.

A dyslexia staff development action plan

It is useful to draw up an action plan, especially when a task seems overwhelming, unclear or riddled with obstacles. The following is a suggested model of such a plan:

- What is my overall strategy?
- Who are my target groups? Which are key? Which stage are they at (e.g. 'interested but not really listening' or 'sympathetic but do not see it as a priority')?
- What opportunities do I have and in what context? (e.g. curriculum or policy issues or initiatives, meetings, particular events, staff development plans or days).
- Who are my allies and how can I use them?
- Staging: What are my objectives and over what periods of time (by what dates)?
- What are my favoured tactics?
- How shall I measure my achievement (what are my 'performance indicators')?

Resources

The best resources are dyslexic students (and staff), what they say, demonstrations of their difficulties and abilities, and examples of their writing. First-person accounts, videos of dyslexic people and television programmes are all helpful.

Research is useful in counteracting false beliefs, especially research on the brain and learning styles. As ignorance is the result of limited information, knowledge is a great asset: find out as much as you can about dyslexia so you can make information available as well as be seen to be knowledgeable and confident.

Characteristics of dyslexia, implications for teaching and learning, and suggestions for supporting adults can be found in Morgan and Klein (2000) and in Krupska and Klein (1995). The latter also has resource sheets for staff development and a section on useful resources.

CHAPTER 13

A learning styles and memory strategies questionnaire for the identification of SpLD in higher and further education

DOROTA ZDZIENSKI

Introduction

Colleges of further and higher education in England and and Wales are currently required to make provision for the identification of students with specific learning difficulties (SpLD). There has been a growing demand in such colleges for a quick and effective way of identifying students with SpLD so that appropriate support can be put in place sufficiently early to be of use to the students concerned.

In most universities a full assessment by an educational psychologist is required in order for students to be granted any concessions or support (Singleton 1999a). Dyslexic students whose problems have been well documented throughout their school years can refer themselves appropriately on entry and ensure that they receive the support to which they are entitled. However, not all dyslexic students are being successfully identified and supported prior to entry to higher and further education. Practitioners in this field are aware that quite often it has been only with the failure of the end-of-year written examinations, or the handing in of the long dissertation in the second or third year, that dyslexia comes to be considered as the likely cause of their problems.

In higher education institutions any general screening procedures used to identify students with any kind of study skills limitations or difficulties tend to be operated primarily for the benefit of the first-year intake and are fairly broadly based tests targeted at the English as a second or other language population, who are then offered extra English support. Within that context, tutors may identify the essay answer of a dyslexic student because of the typical errors of spelling reversals and misplaced words or syllables as described on a dyslexia checklist.

In further education, study support tutors frequently administer their own literacy-based assessments and then make recommendations resulting in a programme of individual or group support. However, the focus in these assessment procedures may well be of a more general nature in order to identify learning difficulties. Since the provision of study support (for which funding is available) is the main objective, the assessment is likely to result in an adequate arrangement.

Students may have a number of special learning needs, and dyslexia may be one of several, which may include lack of familiarity with the English language, lack of appropriate study skills or inadequate training in certain basic skills. A questionnaire has been constructed as part of a large-scale study to identify any, or a combination of the above, difficulties in learning and offer recommendations to students, in addition to giving some practical tips on study skills.

The rationale for the large-scale study involved a response to the reported drop-out rate at Kingston University of between 10% and 17%, largely among the first-year intake, and to the assumption that it would be helpful to ascertain from that group how many students were dyslexic, how many had a general English language difficulty and how many lacked certain basic skills in literacy, numeracy and study.

This chapter summarizes an investigation into the effectiveness of a procedure for screening for identification of this range of difficulties, including SpLD, at 16+. The procedure involving a questionnaire is entitled *QuickScan* (Zdzienski 1997).

Research background

When considering carrying out any screening procedures with large numbers of students one of the greatest obstacles proved to be the effect on staff time of marking all the scripts. There are several dyslexia checklists and lists of symptoms available with reference to SpLD/dyslexia, but some of these could be deemed too general to be systematically implemented at this level. However, the widely known British Dyslexia Association *Adult Checklist* (Chasty 1987), which is recommended by the Adult Dyslexia Organisation was selected for use in an adapted form suitable for issue to large numbers of students. For its intended audience, the adaptation was intended to offer the checklist a more appropriate and accessible format, namely that of a questionnaire about individual learning styles and study skills.

The research of Vinegrad (1994) supports the reliability of the *Adult Checklist* as a means of identifying dyslexia among adults. Indeed, from personal observation of over 60 students who had had independent dyslexia assessments within a university population, rarely was there any significant mis-match between the results of the *Adult Checklist* and the consequent confirmation of dyslexia by the educational psychologist (Zdzienski 1998, p. 165). In some cases students selected perhaps fewer of the positive indicators, but still enough to alert the tutor's attention to the existence of memory, sequencing and directional difficulties.

QuickScan

This new questionnaire, *QuickScan* (Zdzienski 1997) places dyslexia within the context of a wider learning continuum. It includes questions relating to many of the commonly accepted and researched positive indicators of dyslexia interspersed with a range of other questions which relate to students' perceptions of their strengths and weaknesses in relation to study. In this way it is hoped that *QuickScan* will provide all students with a tool for examining themselves as learners, getting some practical and immediate feedback and, more importantly, receiving some indication as to whether they may be dyslexic. In such cases they would be recommended to make an appointment with the study support tutor.

In Vinegrad's (1994) research, an additional finding was the 'extreme hesitation' of dyslexic individuals when responding to the *Adult Checklist* compared with others who tended to tick the relevant boxes in a 'rapid fashion'. The difficulties that these particular individuals experienced in having to make quick decisions was regarded as being a 'powerful indicator of dyslexia'.

Although *QuickScan* contains over 100 questions, compared with 20 in the *Adult Checklist*, it takes non-dyslexic students between eight and 15 minutes to complete it. Depending on individual reading and decision-making speeds, it is likely to take dyslexic students longer.

On the basis of experimental results during development it has been interesting to note that for dyslexic students the length of time taken to complete *QuickScan* does not increase in linear proportion to the greater number of questions. Although there are five times more questions than on the *Adult Checklist*, it does not take dyslexic students five times as long to complete. So far as has been observed, dyslexic students complete *QuickScan* in about 20 minutes.

As *QuickScan* is now available on computer it will be possible to check the total length of time students take to respond to all the questions as well as the number of times they amend their answers. This will yield some further data concerning one of the important issues in both the diagnosis and support of dyslexic students, namely their speed and efficiency of processing written information compared with non-dyslexic students.

In addition, the advantages of *QuickScan* include the fact that it is self-administered, automatically analysed and can provide immediate feedback to each student in the form of a printed report.

Description of *QuickScan*

QuickScan is Part One of a two-part computer-based assessment program, named *StudyScan Suite* (Zdzienski 1997) which can be purchased by institutions of higher and further education.

QuickScan, the 15-minute questionnaire, is devised for use on a computer network. It is a tool for adults who want to explore the way they learn in terms of their individual learning preferences and study habits. The results of the completed questionnaire are computer analysed to produce useful personalized study guidelines on screen or in printed form. The resulting profiles indicate whether students need study skills support and/or whether a full dyslexia assessment is appropriate. The computer program includes the facility to outline the services and contacts available in the institution where the student is registered.

QuickScan is not a test but a self-reporting questionnaire. It has been constructed in the format of a 'Yes–No' item model with more than 100 items. The only departure from a 'Yes–No' response is the inclusion of eight 'Left or Right' responses where students are asked to indicate their preferred hand or eye for a given function (e.g. '*Do you write with your left or right hand?*').

Clearly, the main disadvantage with this model is the necessity to simplify both questionnaires' responses. However, it is emphasized that for questions where respondents might validly chose either answer, they should opt for the one which is generally the truer response. The questions have been worded carefully; for example, they are expressed in the following terms: '*Do you tend to . . .?*' or '*Do you generally find that . . .?*'

The on-screen computer instructions ask students to respond with the first answer that comes to mind and to work their way quickly through the program as questions are presented. A bar graph indicates the percentage of items completed. The formulation of questions has been refined after a first pilot and ambiguities minimized.

Students can select the font size they see (10-, 12- or 14-point) and background colour of the screen (white, yellow or blue) and can change them if desired during the questionnaire.

There are 110 questions in total, which are presented in a randomized sequence in any sitting. This has been done to minimize the possibility of students remembering previous sittings and thus to provide the most spontaneous response possible.

Sample of ten questions selected from different sections of *QuickScan*

This random selection of 10 questions illustrates responses given by students (Table 13.1). Responses coded D are the answers given by one of the dyslexic students and those marked X are from a non-dyslexic student.

The information gathered from the student responses is categorized and cross-referenced as they complete the questionnaire. The program produces the results based on the proportion of positive indicators, including difficulty with, for example, memory, sequencing, laterality, self-image as a learner, reading, study, etc. The emerging profile shows students' preferred sensory channels for learning, namely, predominantly visual, auditory or kinaesthetic or any combination of these.

A consistency scale is being refined which will show the extent to which students respond in the same way to a question when it has appeared a second time using different wording, for example, '*Do you consider that for general purposes your reading is fast enough?*' and '*Would you describe yourself as a fluent reader?*

Consistency of response is a particularly relevant factor in establishing individuals' preferred learning styles. Practical suggestions for study are based on the emerging patterns of results from the questionnaire.

Table 13.1. Selected questions

Question	Answer code			
Do you consider that for general purposes your reading is fast enough?	Yes	X	No	D
Do you tend to hum, or to talk to yourself?	Yes	X	No	D
Is English your first language?	Yes	X	No	D
Can reading actually cause you to get headaches?	Yes	D	No	X
When you can't remember a particular spelling do you try to picture the word in your mind's eye?	Yes	D	No	X
Do you tend to mix up numbers, e.g. 281 for 218?	Yes	D	No	X
Have you on occasions been described by others as a talented person?	Yes	D	No	X
When you look back over your handwritten notes do you tend to find them difficult to read?	Yes	D	No	X
Do you write with your left or right hand?	Left		Right	X D
Are you quite quick and efficient at copying information down by hand from a board or screen?	Yes	X	No	D

Learning styles

Of the total of 110 questions in *QuickScan* nearly 30% relate to investigating students' preferred learning styles. Questions are based on the observable behavioural characteristics which have been researched as indicators of students' dominant sensory systems (Barbe et al. 1979). These are categorized into the three modality strengths: visual, auditory and kinaesthetic. In the process of practical group experimentation it was found that many students have a mixed learning preference rather than a single one. The *QuickScan* output has been refined to accommodate single, double or even triple modality. This facet of modality was examined in the Hornsby Neuro-Linguistic Programming course (De Luynes and Zdzienski 1992).

It is quite surprising to find that students are frequently unaware of their stronger sensory channel(s) for learning and they sometimes follow less personally appropriate ways of learning. It can be a liberating and positively helpful experience for them to discover the best way of approaching any aspect of learning from the perspective of their strengths. From experience of supporting dyslexic students in higher education, it was frequently found that particular students were unaware of their strengths. One student, not realizing that he was a particularly good visual learner had, for example, been continuously underachieving because he kept trying to use verbal methods for learning and was getting frustrated at the difficulties he was experiencing. Once he discovered that visual learning in fact involved a different approach, he was able to carry out tasks with greater ease and confidence, and to apply the concepts of visualization and imagery to a range of study situations. For further examples taken from case studies of teaching to modality strengths and developing memory strategies, readers are referred to Zdzienski (1994, pp. 45–66).

For the purposes of illustration, the dyslexic student to whom we can refer as 'Student D' who completed *QuickScan* as seen in Table 13.1 was found to be a predominantly visual learner, and the study suggestions shown in Table 13.2 were provided for him by the computer program printout.

In addition, Student D's responses gave a clear indication of SpLD and, therefore, the information shown in Table 13.3 was also presented to him.

Student D did, in fact, make an appointment for a full assessment with an educational psychologist and was found to be dyslexic, with above average ability (*Wechsler Adult Intelligence Scale*), but with particular weaknesses in auditory working memory and coding processes. Additionally, the full assessment process revealed that his reading comprehension skills (*Scholastic Abilities Test for Adults*) were above average when tested under untimed conditions, but when timed, his results fell into the below average category. His spelling was low average, and his handwriting was described as 'slow and inefficient' with a 6% spelling error rate in written composition. Speed of processing was generally below average.

Table 13.2. Study suggestions for a predominantly visual learner

Visual key words:
see, watch, imagine, picture, visualize, draw, look, display, clear sight

A visual learning preference means you learn best by seeing for yourself and watching others demonstrating a particular skill. You need to look at materials which you are studying and to be able to see the connections between different aspects of the subject.

Planning, colour-coding and categorizing information in a visual way is very effective. Highlighting important areas of text, creating flow-charts, diagrams and, in particular, mind-maps would be a good way of storing materials, planning essays and revising for tests. People who are very visual learners can often study for long periods with a high level of concentration and intensity.

Reading can be a very enjoyable experience and can be interspersed by moments of vivid imagination on behalf of the reader.

Learning, therefore, can be very effective when set within the context of a particular scene, and visual reminders can act as a good memory trigger.

Awkward spellings are most accessible by sight, and difficult words, specific terms and definitions, or various formulae can be remembered by visualizing them.

Revision of such information is most memorable when produced on small cards which can be looked at frequently and regularly throughout the days before an examination.

If you are very visual then you can, and might at times, prefer to think in pictures and images rather than words.

Problem-solving, memorizing and coping with stressful situations can sometimes be more easily achieved using mental imagery.

Thorough planning, and a meticulous and professional (neat) level of presentation are strengths.

Concentrated study is best carried out where there is a minimum of distracting movements and disorder.

Table 13.3. Recommendations made to Student D

Recommendations		NO	YES
1. To have a consultation with the Learning SupportTutor			X
2. To make an appointment and do a full assessment			X
3. To enrol on a study skills course			X
For a consultation please contact:	....		
location	....		
tel. no. etc.	....		
For a full assessment please contact:	....		
Additional information: e.g. English Language Centre is at:	....		
For study skills support please contact:	....		

The bottom section of this form is automatically completed by the institution's program from data entered during the installation process.

- Reading at 95 words per minute (wpm) compared with an adult average of 250 wpm.
- Writing at 19 wpm compared with an adult average of 20–30 wpm.

Laterality functions were as follows:

- Handedness: Right
- Eyedness: Right

showing a right-sided lateral organization for eye and hand function/co-ordination. Left/right awareness was rather confused.

Two recommendations were made with regard to written examinations. The first for additional time to complete each paper (at the rate of an additional 15 minutes per hour) and the second for allowances to be made for weaknesses in spelling and handwriting presentation.

A summary of Student D's responses to *QuickScan* are presented in Table 13.4. These show a reasonable match with the findings of the independent assessment report.

An exploratory pilot study

Before carrying out a pilot study of *QuickScan* using computers, a series of mini-studies was carried out with groups of students in a sixth form college and in higher education, and several adults were referred through the Adult Dyslexia Organisation and the Hornsby Dyslexia Centre.

Table 13.4. Summary of student D's responses to *QuickScan*

Learning profile scale (indicating increasing difficulties from mild to severe)	Mild – Positive – Severe
Positive indicators of general learning difficulties	------------------------------
Positive indicators of SpLD (dyslexia)	---
Memory-related difficulties	--
Sequencing problems	--
Visual problems which affect reading	----------------
General reading difficulties	---
Problems with writing	---

Further indicators:	NO	YES
Problems with spelling		---------
Mixed laterality functions	---------	
Left/right confusion		---------
Difficulties with maths		---------
Creativity		---------

A group of 30 students made up the first pilot group. The students were split into three groups: dyslexic, non-dyslexic and English as a second language (ESL), with ten subjects in each group. The variables from this dataset were split into two types: continuous (scores) and categorical (i.e. yes/no, left/right).

Statistical testing

For each continuous variable, tests were carried out to explore the range of results between the three groups and to establish whether the differences between the means were statistically significant. There were eight such variables in the first draft version of *QuickScan*:

- Kinaesthetic (total/12).
- Auditory (total/12).
- Visual (total/12).
- Self-image as a learner (total/10).
- Sequencing problems (total/10).
- Memory-related difficulties (total/17).
- Adult dyslexia checklist (total/14).
- *QuickScan* dyslexia checklist (total/30).

Results

A summary of statistics for the variables for 30 subjects is presented in Table 13.5.

Analysis of variance

Analysis of variance (ANOVA) was carried out on all three groups for each given variance. Since there was sufficient statistical evidence to suggest that the mean scores were different on all of the categories listed above, pairwise comparisons were also carried out for each pair of the variables and *p*-values obtained.

In order to see if there was any relationship between the variables in the dataset, correlation coefficients (*r*) were obtained. These are presented below (Table 13.6). Where any significant association between two variables exist (a correlation coefficient > 0.7) these are briefly discussed.

In the case of self-image as a learner, the Adult dyslexia checklist and the *QuickScan* checklist, there was a significant difference between dyslexic and non-dyslexic students, and between dyslexic and ESL students. However, mean scores between the non-dyslexic and ESL student groups were similar. The relevant confidence intervals for these five subcategories are presented in Table 13.7

Table 13.5. Summary of statistics for the variables for 30 subjects

	Dyslexic	Non-dyslexic	ESL
1. Kinaesthetic			
Mean	7.7	6.5	7.7
Median	7.5	7.0	7.0
Standard Deviation	1.7	2.5	1.4
Range	5–11	2–10	6–10
2. Auditory			
Mean	6.7	7.7	7.3
Median	6.5	8.0	7.0
Standard Deviation	1.7	2.3	2.4
Range	4–11	4–11	5–12
3. Visual			
Mean	7.6	7.1	8.7
Median	8.0	7.5	9.0
Standard Deviation	2.1	2.0	1.9
Range	3–10	5–10	6–12
4. Self-image as a learner			
Mean	5.7	3.3	4.3
Median	6.0	3.0	4.5
Standard Deviation	1.3	1.6	1.2
Range	4–7	1–6	2–6
5. Sequencing problems			
Mean	8.2	1.2	2.5
Median	8.0	1.0	3.0
Standard Deviation	0.9	0.9	1.1
Range	7–10	0–3	0–4
6. Memory-related difficulties			
Mean	12.8	1.9	3.8
Median	13.5	2.0	4.0
Standard Deviation	2.8	1.0	1.3
Range	9–16	0–4	2–6
7. Adult Dyslexia Checklist			
Mean	11.2	1.3	2.8
Median	11.0	0	2.5
Standard Deviation	0.8	2.1	1.3
Range	10–12	0–6	1–5
8. *QuickScan* Dyslexia checklist			
Mean	23.7	3.9	7.2
Median	24.0	3.0	7.5
Standard Deviation	1.4	2.8	2.4
Range	21–15	0–8	4–10

Variables 1, 2 and 3, which relate to learning styles and sensory channels, indicate that there is no evidence of any difference between each sensory preference for the three groups. Variables 4 to 8 all indicate significant evidence of a difference between the mean scores for the three groups.

Table 13.6.

Correlation coefficients for the variables for dyslexic subjects

	1.Kin	2.Aud	3.Vis	4.S-I	5.Seq	6.Mem	7.Adul	8.Quic
1. Kin	1							
2. Aud	-0.2260	1						
3. Vis	0.78336	0.05685	1					
4. S-I	0.44392	-0.0926	0.59522	1				
5. Seq	0.32661	-0.5254	0.33951	0.23504	1			
6. Mem	0.68979	-0.6006	0.35204	0.60941	0.27827	1		
7. Adul	0.62863	-0.4466	0.19094	0.37913	0.39854	0.78004	1	
8. Quic	0.64872	-0.2254	0.67517	0.88455	0.22168	0.74380	0.45690	1

Correlation coefficients for the variables for non-dyslexic subjects

	1.Kin	2.Aud	3.Vis	4.S-I	5.Seq	6.Mem	7.Adul	8.Quic
1. Kin	1							
2. Aud	0.41400	1						
3. Vis	0.71927	0.45623	1					
4. S-I	0.46607	0.41701	0.74823	1				
5. Seq	0.61653	0.40602	0.41753	0.54678	1			
6. Mem	0.46016	0.52824	0.57307	0.77156	0.51067	1		
7. Adul	0.46455	0.62564	0.66025	0.51789	0.48117	0.70401	1	
8. Quic	0.71205	0.66757	0.69587	0.57974	0.73073	0.66348	0.87483	1

Correlation coefficients for the variables for ESL subjects

	1.Kin	2.Aud	3.Vis	4.S-I	5.Seq	6.Mem	7.Adul	8.Quic
1. Kin	1							
2. Aud	-0.0033	1						
3. Vis	0.48704	0.3121	1					
4. S-I	-0.0067	-11778	-0.3987	1				
5. Seq	-0.3264	10218	-0.3963	0.04435	1			
6. Mem	-0.5713	0.34339	0.10405	0.18924	0.07813	1		
7. Adul	-0.2737	0.70109	0.14741	0.26202	1	0.48717	1	
8. Quic	0.28702	0.36911	0.37932	0.09796	0.08763	-0.0934	0.51767	1

Table 13.7. Confidence Intervals

	Parameter	From	To	Mean difference	95% confidence interval
1	Self-image as a learner (total/10)	Dyslexic	Non Dys	= 2.4	-1.5, 6.3
		Dyslexic	ESL	= 1.4	-2.3, 3.2
2	Sequencing problems (total/10)	Dyslexic	Non Dys	= 6.0	5.5, 8.5
		Non Dys	ESL	= -1.3	-3.1, 0.5
		Dyslexic	ESL	= 5.7	3.9, 7.5
3	Memory-related difficulties (total/17)	Dyslexic	Non Dys	= 10.9	3.3, 18.5
		Non Dys	ESL	= -1.9	-4.3, 0.5
		Dyslexic	ESL	= 9.0	0.7, 17.3
4	Adult Dyslexia Checklist (total/14)	Dyslexic	Non Dys	= 9.9	5.5, 14.4
		Dyslexic	ESL	= 8.4	6.3, 10.5
5	*QuickScan* Dyslexia Checklist (total/30)	Dyslexic	Non Dys	= 19.8	10.9, 28.7
		Dyslexic	ESL	= 16.5	9.9, 23.1

In the case of sequencing problems and memory-related difficulties a significant difference was found between all three student groups, indicating that in these two important areas related to learning, dyslexic students can be identified as a clearly separate and distinct group. These results reveal other associations which may merit further investigation are as follows:

- Dyslexic students: self-image as a learner and the *QuickScan* checklist (r = 0.8850); memory and the *QuickScan* checklist (r = 0.7440); memory and the Adult checklist (r = 0.7800).
- Non-dyslexic students: self-image as a learner and memory (r = 0.7700); Adult checklist and *QuickScan* checklist (r = 0.8748).

Discussion

It is emphasized that the results reported above are produced from a small student group and that further piloting is under way, this time using the *QuickScan* questionnaire on screen with a group of 60 students currently in higher education, of whom 30 are dyslexic. This work is being carried out with the co-operation of the Psychology Department of Ulster University and the School of Education and Student Support Services of Leicester University. The estimated reliability of *QuickScan* in its first administration via the computer screen has been measured to be 0.9. The comparison of means of the two groups (30 dyslexic and 30 non-dyslexic students) by use of a one-way analysis of variance (ANOVA) clearly confirms that the questionnaire data is capable of discriminating between the dyslexic and non-dyslexic group (Zdzienski, in press and in Zdzienski 1998, pp. 377–378).

Laterality

Difference between mixed laterality, right- or left-sidedness and left/right confusion for the three student groups has been noted but not yet statistically tested. It was considered advisable to include a larger group for the study of these variables. However, the original study results are confirmed by a similar trend in the Leicester University study group comprising 19 dyslexic students and 16 non-dyslexic students from which the following figures emerge (Table 13.8).

Table 13.8. Laterality (%)

	Right side dominant	Left side dominant	Ambivalent/ mixed laterality	Left/right confusion
Dyslexic students	26	16	58	37
Non-dyslexic students	57	18	25	18

Further analysis needs to be carried out on larger groups to confirm or amend these findings. Many tutors and other professionals working with dyslexic students for a number of years confirm it is their experience that more dyslexic students appear to have ambivalence of laterality functions when compared with their non-dyslexic peers.

Currently, because of a lack of research evidence, many educational psychologists no longer consider it relevant to even report on the students' laterality in their dyslexia assessment reports. In fact, this topic features under the subheading 'What are *not* signs of dyslexia?' (Turner 1997) and the McCarthy scales (McCarthy 1972) are referred to, at which time it was found that 40% of the general population was 'cross-lateral', thereby seemingly negating its relevance, as either a predictor or a significant symptom of dyslexia. The issue of laterality is thus dismissed by Turner (1997) as a feature 'likely to proceed from a different origin from dyslexia'.

In the light of the early findings of this study, it may be considered difficult to dismiss the possible relevance of laterality to dyslexia. It will be possible (through the *QuickScan* computer program) to gather more data on this controversy-riven topic.

Familial factors

QuickScan asks students to indicate whether there is any incidence of dyslexia in their family, and this is taken as a strong indicator of dyslexia for students who are experiencing difficulties.

It is generally accepted that a positive family incidence is the first major risk factor, as 80% of cases can be identified in this way (Vogler et al. 1985). It is interesting to note, therefore, that in the results of the study (including Leicester and Ulster students) 80% of the dyslexic students answered positively, compared with only 5% of the non-dyslexic students. From the non-dyslexic group a few students emerged who participated in the tests because they had difficulties but had not been assessed before, and they indeed may be dyslexic students who have compensated to a greater or lesser extent. The figure therefore could be closer to 1%.

Spelling difficulties

One of the most persistent difficulties dyslexic people encounter is in spelling (McLoughlin et al. 1994). It is interesting to note that 95% of the dyslexic study group reported continuing problems in this area compared with 20% in the non-dyslexic study group.

Learning styles

Interestingly, there appears to be no difference between the three groups in the mean assessments for kinaesthetic, auditory or visual sensory channels, although the more recent results from the Leicester student group shows 10% greater preference for a kinaesthetic mode of learning among dyslexic students. However, there is clearly a benefit in raising students' awareness of their preferred sensory channel in learning for the purposes of more effective study and improved scholastic performance.

Sequencing and memory

In this study, significant differences between the groups' means are noted in the sequencing, memory and dyslexia categories. The most relevant distinction between dyslexic students and their non-dyslexic peers in higher and further education may well be in those areas that are most affected by any deficiency in sequencing and memory skills.

Conclusions

The main implications for teaching are for training in sequencing and memory skills to play a key role in study skills support for dyslexic students. There is strong case study evidence from the results of the HEFCE project carried out at Kingston University (1992–1994) to support the value of training and development programmes in sequencing and memory skills for dyslexic students at 18+ (Zdzienski 1998, pp. 72–137 and pp. 341–347).

In summary, current evidence supports the view that the administration of *QuickScan* as a first filter for large numbers of students can lead to appropriate further action as determined by the students in consultation with their study support tutors and that the *StudyScan* suite may prove to be an effective and accessible resource.

Acknowledgements

With thanks to Morag Hunter-Carsch for her encouragement and interest in this study in her role as PhD supervisor, and to Ranjit Lall (University of Sheffield) for her advice and consultation regarding the statistical analysis carried out. Further thanks to the organizations and staff involved in the piloting and to the individual students for their time and interest in this project.

CHAPTER 14

An approach to specialist learning support in higher education

MARGARET HERRINGTON

Introduction

The primary purpose of this chapter is to record an approach to providing specialist support to dyslexic learners, which has been developed and refined during my work with higher education students at the universities of Leicester and Nottingham in the 1990s. Here I shall explain the practices and processes involved and reveal some of the theoretical underpinnings in an area of professional practice, which is undertheorized. References to individual students will be anonymous.

The main rationale for attempting a descriptive analysis of my own approach stems from a concern about the continuing dominance in higher education of a deficit paradigm for dyslexia, based both on a medical model of disability and on some rather simplistic ideas about literacy 'skills' and their relationship with academic ability. Despite two excellent conferences organized by the University of Plymouth at Dartington Hall in 1994 and 1996 which explored a broader view, many practitioners and policy-makers still appear to view dyslexia as a set of 'problems' stemming from a neurological impairment. However, though dyslexic students experience a number of specific learning difficulties (SpLD) which appear to have a physiological basis, and which may even feel 'physical' (Poussu-Olli 2001), it is unlikely that these difficulties represent the complete cognitive profile of dyslexia (West 1991; Hetherington 1996; Steffert 1996). It is also the case that much of the suffering endured by dyslexic adults stems from how such difficulties are, or have been, viewed by others. The 'disability' has, in effect, largely been constructed socially (Barnes and Mercer 1996), influenced by the nature of the literacy and learning practices and contexts in which dyslexic learners are assessed, and by the dominant cultural norms about literacy and intelligence. This chapter describes an approach to learning support which actively addresses contextual factors and explores processing 'differences' rather than viewing dyslexia solely as a cluster of in-person processing weaknesses.

A second reason is that there are still very few written analyses of what actually happens within dyslexia support provision in British universities, despite the growth in this type of work in recent years (Singleton 1999a). Some pioneering accounts are available, which reveal both the general approach taken (Michelson 1995; Gilroy and Miles 1996; Preston and Gorbold 1996) and specific aspects of practice (Morgan 1995). There are also accounts from dyslexic students about the nature of their difficulties in higher education and the kind of responses they have found valuable (Hinton 1993; Somerfield 1993; Moss and Cairns 1995; Morgan 1995; Pollak 1996; Riddick et al. 1997). Powerful insights into effective approaches have been provided by Clarke (1994), Cottrell (1996), Stacey (1996, 1997), Stephens (1996), Thomas (1996) and by Goodwin (1996a,b). From these it has been possible to identify the range and type of services provided within learning support contexts; and also the recurring elements of good practice which acknowledge the interface between individual learners and their personal and learning contexts:

- The fundamental importance of individuals gaining the confidence to describe and explore their own thinking and learning styles and processes, both for practical reasons and in the pursuit of fundamental notions of identity.
- The significance of developing meta-cognition and meta-linguistic awareness; and ways of making the literacy and learning tasks in higher education explicit and manageable within the time limits allowed.
- Support with the emotional effect on learners deriving from both past experience and from the continuing ignorance about dyslexia among educators in higher education.

Despite these commonalities there appear to be discernible differences in emphasis. Some staff focus on enabling students to 'fit in' as best they can within existing higher education conventions. Others are either more prepared to think critically about the implications of what may be a fundamentally different cognitive style or they recognize from a 'radical literacy' perspective (Barton 1994), the kind of challenge which dyslexia presents to traditional ideas about literacy practices and their assumed relationships with intellectual competence.

The approach described here can be located on the more 'challenging' wing of current practice. It incorporates much of what has been found to be effective elsewhere but tries to move forward in two respects: first, it involves a clarification of the kind of 'wide angle' and 'zoom' lenses tutors need if they are to avoid a deficit-laden, technicist approach. Second, it includes a fuller description than usual of the nature of the interaction between tutor and student. This demonstrates that by bringing a 'criticality' into the learning support sessions, the results for students and tutors may be revelatory and empowering. Though essentially it is one exemplar of practice, it carries clear practical implications for specialist tutor training.

The role of the learning support tutor in higher education

The dyslexia support described here occurs within a generic learning support unit context rather than a special dyslexia or disability unit. Learning support in higher education is still an under-investigated professional activity (Rivis and Herrington 1994) and there have been few serious attempts to expose the theoretical underpinnings of current practice in higher education (Wolfendale and Corbett 1996). For some staff, learning support is seen simply as the response of the organization to those who are struggling with some aspect of their studies within a particular higher education institution. For them, the learner has the problem and the institution will help where it can, through separate learning support facilities and through the pastoral functions of staff. For other staff, learning support is an intrinsic part of teaching and if teaching/assessment methods do not anticipate the diversity of learning styles and stances and are therefore not supportive of learning then any changes may need to start with those methods rather than with individual students. This view is essentially an 'inclusive' learning development approach (see Chapters 17 and 18 in this volume).

In each higher education institution these different views co-exist and the role of learning support personnel will therefore depend very much on the teaching/assessment culture and methodologies of the institution, on the way in which 'support' is viewed by the institution and on the philosophy and organization of the support service itself and its personnel.

Though there are considerable variations in these respects within the university sector (and not just between traditional and non-traditional universities), it would appear that in quite different contexts many learning support tutors working with dyslexic learners are at least engaged in helping students directly and in explaining the higher education contexts to the student. They help with advice about learning ,writing, time management, IT, examination arrangements, Disabled Students' Allowances etc. (Singleton 1999b). They may also 'represent' students to the institution, explaining to staff what dyslexia is like in general as well as clarifying the implications of individual clusters of dyslexic characteristics.

I shall focus on the kind of service which actively engages dyslexic learners in dialogue about their styles of thinking, learning and writing. The role of the tutor in such a setting involves a mix of teaching, counselling, advocacy, organization and staff development tasks. It is thus a demanding and unfolding hybrid professional role. It requires enthusiasm for learning from dyslexic students themselves, assumption of some responsibility for using the knowledge gained and willingness to clarify for the institution how its practices may be 'excluding'. Tutors thus have a function at some level as 'change agent'. This goes beyond notions of 'skilled helper' or 'reflective practitioner' or even 'reflective teacher' and acknowledges explicitly the dynamic interactive relationship of the professional with the institutional contexts.

An holistic/analytical/dynamic approach

This approach draws directly on two traditions within adult literacy practice: 'student-centredness'; and a recognition of the significance of the social construction of literacy and illiteracy (see Chapter 8 in this volume). These focus, respectively, on enhancing the power of learners in terms of curriculum content and process and on challenging the power of those within the social, educational and political contexts who defined literacy 'standards' to suit their own preferences and abilities, without any reference to the excluding nature of some literacy practices.

Although the higher education context is often characterized by a teacher-led curriculum in the main, many academics create considerable opportunities in their teaching and assessment practices for student determination; and there are more variations and flexibility within higher education with regard to literacies than many imagine. Yet when students come to a learning support unit, loss of personal power in relation to learning and academic literacy has often been experienced and a student-centred support curriculum is vital. This does not mean just asking students what they want and responding with standard study skills methods. It does imply starting with thc issue which the student wants to address and jointly analysing how the student is thinking and learning, and together devising effective ways forward. Tutors must focus on the explanation of, and 'conscientization' in relation to, the context (Freire 1972). They must work to re-connect learners with their own resourcefulness and to develop their own 'voices'.

Two distinct but related elements of 'voice' are important here. The first concerns an appreciation of the intrinsic significance of individual perspectives and motivations for effective learning, and the articulation of these in the learner's voice being seen both as a means to, and an outcome of, effective learning. The second refers to the issue of whose voices are heard. In higher education it is important to acknowledge the issue of unheard groups in order to give people sufficient power to challenge literacy practices if and where necessary. In her study of students' writing in higher education, Ivanic (1998) has usefully distinguished between the autobiographical, discoursal and authorial selves to reveal the kind of journey which writers may have to make as they gain an integrated voice for their academic work. I focus in learning support work explicitly on building the kind of learner self-confidence necessary for such a development to occur.

A successful way of releasing and developing the voices of dyslexic learners is to establish exploratory partnerships between students and learning support tutors in which presenting issues are analysed in depth, in some cases over considerable periods of time; the nature of dyslexia is explored and the past and present are 'reframed'. Implications for the future are worked through. Power issues within the institutional/cultural context are deconstructed, options are shaped, decisions about curriculum and process are made by the student and actions are pursued and reviewed.

This will sound familiar enough to most experienced practitioners, but there are few accounts of actually how this can be done. For a newcomer to the field, the task can be daunting and so I shall now identify three key elements in my own practice. These deal in turn with: developing the support tutor's 'gaze'; the tutor's 'professional hinterland' and the nature of the student/tutor interaction.

Developing the support tutor's 'gaze'

For me it is essential that if tutors are to assist dyslexic students in deconstructing the impact of confining values and practices they must have an understanding of how these constrain or encourage learners and shape their experience of dyslexia. Thus, the tutor's 'gaze' requires a conceptual framework in which individuals and their personal contexts are seen within broader contexts (institutional, social, political, economic etc.). Consider Figure 14.1.

At a glance, this simple figure shows the students and tutors operating with their individual, personal constellations of characteristics and contexts but also within larger institutional and social contexts. It also shows several co-existing dimensions of time to suggest both the changing nature of these contexts in time and the complexity of learning support situations when ideas about time appear irreconcilable.

Using this diagram, it is possible for tutors to 'hold together' the exploration of specific individual characteristics and circumstances (personalities, feelings, goals, cognitive styles, clusters of SpLD), the effects of the personal

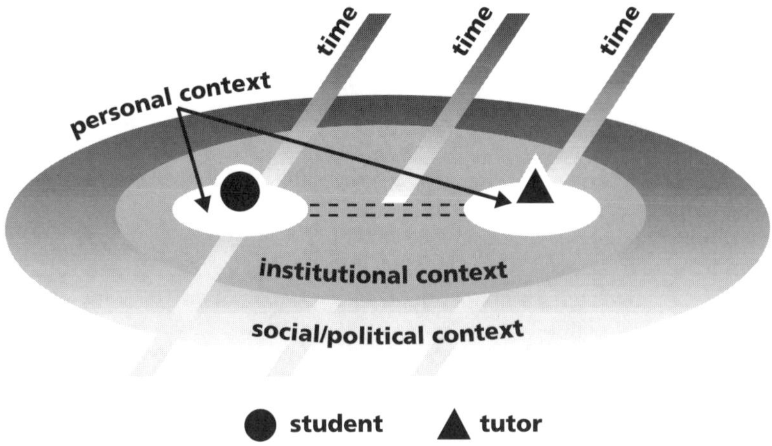

Figure 14.1. Students and tutors in contexts and time dimensions.

and educational backgrounds, the impact of the higher education setting and the cultural and politico-economic values about literacy.

This larger framework enables tutors to understand the very different student stances they will encounter. Individual students arrive not only with their immediate and particular requests (Table 14.1) but with a different vertical slice through these layers; not just different dyslexic clusters but a different experience of these shaping contexts. If students have a very positive personality, a strong belief in their own value as a person and have had an early 'diagnosis' and background support from family and friends then their position in terms of self-knowledge about dyslexia can be enhanced and their ability to cope with new demands in new situations is often increased. Dyslexia for such students is often not experienced as the crushing, disabling burden so frequently described, even when the degree of dyslexia is relatively severe.

Similarly, if the impact of the values and workings of educational institutional contexts is also understood then assessment can take account of quite different experiences in this respect. The learning stance of a dyslexic student who has had a major struggle against negative stereotyping by teachers can differ dramatically from that of someone who has had consistent support, even though the nature and degree of the dyslexia may be similar. The insidious effects of earlier misunderstanding and dismissals by schoolteachers can still affect the learning confidence of some of the most resourceful and determined dyslexic learners in higher education. The effects of positive earlier support are less frequently recorded, but can be equally long-lasting and powerful.

Table 14.1. Issues brought to a tutor in a learning support unit in a UK university on one day in November 1998

Handling dyslexia and depression
Seeking ways of finding dissertation topics which would use dyslexic strengths/ developing self-advocacy
Problem with finding ways of moving between the different kinds of 'story telling' in academic writing
Unravelling unfamiliar literacy formats
Handling anger and frustration at word-finding delays
Endeavouring to understand the culture of higher education in the UK: expectations and practices
Dyslexia and multilingualism, distinguishing between mother tongue interference and dyslexic characteristics
Applying for a Disabled Students' Allowance
Handling a department position which appears 'anti-dyslexic'

The presenting issues brought by students to learning support settings are always underpinned by the contextual interplays and sometimes overtly so.

Given the challenge dyslexic students face in the new complex environments (see Chapter 18 in this volume) they commonly seek, from all higher education staff, the acknowledgement that they are able people who have a right to be at university despite certain literacy, memory and/or motor weaknesses. They seek some recognition of just how hard they have to work to handle the information-processing demands (accusations of 'carelessness' with literacy are experienced as very hurtful). They also seek some flexibilities and responsiveness to their styles of learning and writing. And they require explicit information whenever possible in accessible form about what will be required of them and about how all aspects of the system work.

Tutors are in the frame, too, with another personal life history, a position of authority within systems which may not be supportive for dyslexic learners and without a great deal of power to change them. Dyslexic students do not always know what to expect from learning support tutors. Though some of the most vulnerable seek tutors' help, they are also afraid of 'being judged again' by a figure in authority or they may expect immediate answers to all their difficulties. This needs to be worked through. Whatever is done, tutors should not act as if this is a non-issue. At the very least they should explain to students the basic philosophy and practice of learning support, both at the individual level and as it concerns changing the disabling contexts in higher education.

Developing the 'professional hinterland' of attitudes and knowledge

In responding to the individual and institutional demands which emerge in learning support settings, tutors need some understanding about their own stance and some key areas of knowledge and skill. Specialist training requires far more than specialist knowledge about SpLD. I have found the following three pointers to be particularly useful in this work.

Tutors' views and expectations about the qualities, skills and roles of individual dyslexic learners are key

These can be far too general and even stereotypical if the learning support tutor's training and experience has been narrow. I cannot be the only tutor in higher education who shudders inwardly at discourse which includes sweeping generalizations, such as '*The dyslexic learner is like this*', and recent research on heterogeneity within dyslexia would support such a challenge (Ellis et al. 1996). Alternatively, tutors can be completely 'blind' to dyslexia if they have not had the opportunity to learn about what dyslexia can encompass. Identification can be missed.

In my case, I start with a general understanding of the power of teacher expectations in relation to successful student learning and always have strong expectations that students will achieve more control. I have a positive framework of expectations about all adult learners as well as some specific ideas about dyslexic learners. I view dyslexic learners in higher education as generally able, not by virtue of their dyslexia (which is independent of general intellectual ability) but because they have cleared the entry hurdles. I tend to look for a 'creative' approach to issues and problem-solving and anticipate a strong 'logical' sense. I have often experienced dyslexic learners in higher education as resourceful, determined and needing a sense of 'control'. I also anticipate different mixes of dyslexic characteristics and know that the classical dyslexic profile is not the only SpLD to be encountered. I expect individuals to change over the time I work with them.

I also expect that if they experience auditory memory difficulties they will be more appreciative of clear and succinct communication, and that if they prefer to think in visual terms then they will want teaching approaches which respond to this. I recognize that they may need to learn about learning support because many have not encountered this type of student/tutor relationship before. The idea of fellow learners sharing power in particular areas with their tutor will be new.

I expect that learners will be my teachers both about themselves and their dyslexia and about the syndrome of dyslexia in general. The fact that I make this explicit at some point means that the learner gains power in the relationship. I actively provide examples of what other dyslexic students have taught me.

I also have a lifelong learning framework in mind and so am always ready to encourage learners to see the longer view of their continuing development beyond the university. For example, a dyslexic literature student in her third year discussed the stresses of her workloads. In discussing possible self-balancing activities, the question of what she loved most emerged. She had always loved sculpture but had been discouraged from thinking of this as a career. Our discussion focused on locating this particular passion and strength within her future working life.

Students sense the tutor's personal values, beliefs and motivation as they relate to the professional role

Students have frequently commented, '*You treat me as an equal*' and have indicated that they value this highly. It seems to go beyond the appreciation that 'someone in your position takes me seriously' and so I have started to try to unravel this for myself. It appears to challenge professional boundaries and barriers because in terms of positions of authority within the institution we are not equal. Yet, quite apart from my political commitment to equality of opportunity and a radical 'literacies' perspective, there there are at least two other factors which may contribute to this. First, I have a background in adult basic education in which I was alongside and learning from those who had been written off by mainstream school educators. There was always the sense that the learners were teaching us, drawing from our existing skill and insight but always showing us the important steps forward. This recognition of the learners' gift to the development of my professional knowledge shaped this 'equality'.

Second, my encounter with Martin Buber's description of the *Ich und Du* [I and Thou] relationship (Buber 1958 and in English 1937) has helped me to articulate a fundamental feature of my way of working. Buber was seeking to understand the kind of relationship he had with his deity and drew a distinction between relationships in which both participants are viewed as subjects (I and Thou) and those in which one objectifies others, I and He/she/it. Buber discussed the relevance of the distinction to many different kinds of relationships, including those of teachers and pupils:

> In order to help the realisation of the best potentialities in the pupil's life, the teacher . . . must not know him as a mere sum of qualities, strivings and inhibitions, he must be aware of him as a whole being and affirm him in his wholeness. (p. 132)

However, Buber indicated in his postscript that he did not believe that the conditions for a full mutuality of an I and Thou relationship could exist between student and tutor and thus considered that such a relationship was impossible. Nevertheless, I found the basic distinction illuminating from a tutor's viewpoint, and suspect that this is what some students have particularly valued when they have previously been objectified in a negative way by a series of significant and powerful others. A kind of 'mutuality' is possible, involving not equal power in all respects but an openness to sharing, and a mutual generation of, particular kinds of power.

The tutor requires a deep understanding about how learning occurs both in general and, in the case of SpLD, within the higher education framework; and a range of key professional and academic skills

An appropriate body of knowledge would include:

- The philosophy and practice of adult/lifelong learning.
- Thinking, teaching and learning models, approaches and styles.
- Literacies, academic literacies and numeracies.
- Participative research and practice methodology.
- Models of counselling.
- Parameters, concepts, research, assessment and teaching methods regarding SpLD and dylexia – first-hand accounts by dyslexic adults.
- Social and medical models of disability.
- The higher education curriculum process, practices, cultures and underlying rationales.
- Epistemological issues and the dominant paradigms within disciplines.
- Disability and employment issues.

Without these key bodies of knowledge the tutor's gaze is too limited and limiting for the dyslexic learner. For example, without an awareness of a range of teaching models at one's disposal, a tutor may not be able to respond fully to a learner's preferred stance. If a student has a strong preference for analogy and metaphor as a means of making meaning ('*I think all the time in metaphors*' Nottingham student 1999) a tutor needs to know that a 'synectic' method may be most productive (Joyce et al. 1997). Similarly, without an understanding about the nature of knowledge and its generation in different cultures it is difficult to explain the underlying ideas about 'argument' as it is used in British higher education (Costello and Mitchell 1995). If tutors do not understand the literacy and power issues at the heart of higher education practice, it is difficult to assist students to reframe their experience of feedback from some tutors (Houghton 1996).

Such knowledge is also important when engaging staff in discussions about dyslexia and its implications for their own assessment and teaching practices. Academic staff frequently ask challenging questions and are not fobbed off with facile explanations (see Chapter 18 in this volume).

The key skills required include interpersonal, analytical, facilitating/ teaching, clear verbal, visual and written communication, negotiating, advocacy and research. Academic confidence is also essential if the institution is not to regard this work as remedial for a minority of students with 'problems'.

Developing the dynamic of the interaction

Tutors must be able to bring the knowledge, skill and expectations described above into a dynamic interaction with students. I will now attempt to characterize this informal process under four headings:

- Structured and structuring 'conversations'.
- The 'spirit of enquiry'.
- Specific processes.
- 'Moments of development'.

Structured and structuring 'conversations'

I choose the term 'conversation' because it best describes the relaxed and exploratory process which enables students to feel relief from tension, to be comfortable and free to be themselves in open communication. It allows both tutors and students to learn and teach.

For me a conversation implies a 'coming together to talk and listen'. Theories of conversation identify minimally defining communication characteristics but I am more impressed by possibilities and unpredictability in conversation. Harste (1994) suggests how some of these actually emerge:

> Conversations have both connections and edges. The presence of connections means that the thinking of others lives on in your text. The presence of edges means that something new has been added. It is in fact the edges which keep the conversation going.

A recent example illustrates this point. A student and tutor were discussing the subtext of a range of essays set for a vocational course, namely that of 'professsional stance'. All the essays were essentially concerned with encouraging the learner to begin to construct a view of professionalism for herself. The student felt that she could write about this from her heart but that she was being required to switch to writing about this from her head and was not entirely comfortable with this. The tutor began to ask questions about what the distinction meant to the student. The student said:

S *As you are speaking, I am getting a picture in my head.*
T What of?
S *I am putting my head inside a professional hat and am looking round inside the hat at the different elements. I can turn my head around inside the hat.*

T Do you mean like this? [tutor draws a sketch]
S *No, like this.* [student draws her view of it]
S *Yes, and I can see the different bits of the role as pictures.*
T Can you bring your heart into it anywhere?

This kind of conversation (Figure 14.2) enabled the student to make sense of her particular concern at the time. It gave her a quality of space for thinking and visualizing. It lived in the tutor's text as part of a store of visual imaging which could be suggested to other students and alerted her to the student's preferences for three-dimensional visual metaphors.

Within student/tutor 'conversations' it is possible to structure time, 'affect' and analytical content as part of the dynamic. Although tutors may start the structuring process by, for example, reassuring students that emotional release is a legitimate part of a learning support session and indicating options as the session continues, students, with experience, take this over, indicating their priorities, making judgements about these as they go and monitoring progress.

There is a time constraint on any session but the particular significance of time for dyslexic students (Herrington 1997) means that tutors must be aware of the stance they are taking themselves. Are they simply reinforcing the institutional and cultural values in relation to time or will they alert students to the cultural nature of the constructs and how they affect a dyslexic person in particular? In my case I actively suspend institutional time within the session and tune into students' sense of time. Although the issue under analysis may be how to fit written assessment into given time, students do not have further tutor time pressures imposed upon them during the session itself. In fact, over a number of sessions, students develop a sense of the time they have within a session and will declare priorities at the start. I do

Figure 14.2. HE student's visual image emerging during 'conversation'.

alert them if they appear to have moved so far from their issue of concern but this is not really to do with time. It is part of the summarizing, shaping and signalling mentioned below. Towards the end I will say that we have nearly run out of time so that the essential decisions are made and recorded before the student leaves. The overall 'relaxation' of institutional time allows the conversation to move in and out of work on the task in hand to maintain comfort and stimulus.

There are also issues to do with place. It is possible to 'structure' the experience of space for learning by:

- Analysing and discussing preferred learning environments.
- Organizing learning support space in such a way as to maximize students' sense of 'power', e.g. open access areas in which they can make coffee and use computers.
- Acknowledging that individual sessions in a learning support unit do not 'contain' the learning support processes. The nature of the input does have to be sufficiently empowering for students to be able to work with it outside the session.

The structuring of 'affect' starts at the beginning. The first issue is always that of the emotional stance of the learner. Students are usually looking for a 'place' to experience release from some level of anxiety (not necessarily severe). They will intuit whether or not tutors can assist this process and usually will not return if they cannot. What appears to help this process is an ability to recognize the level of feeling and to enable them to wind down a little. This can be achieved with close listening as students pour out accumulated anxieties, in a peaceful and sometimes humorous atmosphere. For some students it is humour which lightens everything.

However, this is not just an emotional atmosphere and tuning-in issue. Stress and dyslexia is a well-documented area (Miles and Varma 1995) and questions about the relationship between cognition and affect in dyslexic students are an ongoing feature. Some may well be intrinsic and others are closely connected to the reactions of others. There are different kinds of interplay, for example, seeking supportive emotional responses from others as a literal prerequisite for communicating verbally ('*He's not interested, I am not talking to him.*', when the tutor may simply have been too busy at that moment to listen). There is logic to this. Students are trying to maximize the probability of success in communication and know that they may need some 'give' from the listener. If that can be identified first, the communication will be more effective. However, it can (ironically) be self-limiting in terms of developing communication skills and also underestimate the amount of supportive listening available. Tutors thus need to know about these relationships.

The 'spirit of enquiry'

These conversations are clearly investigative, the questions of *How?*, *Why?* and *What do you mean?* (Gee 1988) are repeatedly posed in relation to students' concerns, whether they be personal, practical, academic or epistemological. Several writers have discussed this fundamental enquiry principle (Mace 1992) and Harste's 'spirit of enquiry' seems particularly useful for the higher education setting.

In proposing this, Harste (1994) was arguing for a different curriculum paradigm in general for higher education. Though he acknowledged the contributions made by 'disciplines', Harste (1994) argued for more emphasis on fundamental questions which cut across disciplines. The three questions relevant to this discussion were about the nature of knowledge; the role which language and other sign systems play in knowing; and about learning and the more inclusive nature of enquiry (everyone can ask questions). As noted above, these can form the meat of discussions with dyslexic students who, for example, may be questioning the present valuation of sign systems:

> The other sign systems are not held in as high esteem as forms of literacy even though they do help us to conceive, express, communicate and interpret, dream, record and create our world as we think it is and we think it might be. (p. 1226)

This idea that knowledge can be expressed using different sign systems, seeing something as something else, is particularly relevant in dyslexia support. Such examples can fire imagination and insight.

Harste's three propellors for enquiry are:

- Openness: learners being free to pursue their own questions.
- Personalized construction of meaning: no one can make anyone learn. It relies on 'finding patterns that connect' (Bateson 1972, in Harste 1994).
- Collaboration: involves using ourselves and others to outgrow ourselves.

Harste's (1994) theory of learning shows the significance of difference, 'connections, conversations, tensions, anomalies, in short anything that supports difference, becomes the propellors of enquiry' (p. 1224).

These ideas are particularly helpful for generating the appropriate support with and for dyslexic students. They help to set a scene in which there is an open invitation to question and analyse.

Specific processes

We can usefully identify the following processes within the conversations.

Welcoming/relaxing/enjoying

The welcome is important. This must give students a feeling that they are going to be heard. The opening welcome and question can be, '*Hello Jo, come on in, have a seat . . . [informal chat] . . . what can I do for you?*' This is open ended and allows students to talk freely and move towards a definition of their concerns.

Listening and unravelling

For myself, I purposely avoid the terms 'diagnosis' and 'assessment' in this context because it is a joint investigation and the former terminology implies something done by the professional to the student. 'Close listening' and 'unravelling' are more appropriate terms and processes. Questions can find the end of the ball of wool and start the unwinding process, but it must unravel according to how it has been wound. There is no way of knowing this beforehand and it has to be discovered by learner and tutor. Checking for classic indicators of dyslexia is not difficult, but understanding the interplay between them and the integration of these with the whole person in all contexts is an unfolding 'story' which can take time to unravel. No educator should feel apologetic about this because it is this complex mix which will determine effectiveness in learning.

One specific example of this process is when a student declares himself to be a slow reader. The unravelling will involve a search for his particular approach/response to text; and his experience of reading (past and present). This process can reveal many factors which may be slowing the student down: visual disturbance on the page, decoding and phonemic segmentation issues; tracking difficulty; and text factors such as font type and size and right justification. However, the student is usually using linguistic and semantic cueing to comprehend the text and to have the process made explicit, '*You are actually using your intelligence and your existing knowledge of language and of your subject, to get round these delaying factors*', can be extremely helpful. Further, to discuss the processes of 'active reading' and also the various ways in which information is presented in our culture (it suits some to present information in this way) enables the student to move from an 'over-technicist' approach.

The unravelling can also produce from the students important and illuminating descriptions of parts or of the whole process:

- Reading as two distinct processes: '*It's as if there is a delay between processing the print and the meaning.*'
- On the need for a particular visual layout of text in order to read comfortably: '*I need corners to find a place on the sides. I need all the corners to find out whereabouts it is*' (Nottingham student 1997/8).

- On the delays when having to switch between words and pictures: '*I have to look at each word to make it connect to the next one . . . I draw pictures in my mind of what people are saying in order to understand it. I have to go slowly and have to re-read to fill in . . . I create a visual image and then go back to the words to fill in*' (Nottingham student 1996/7).

The term 'unravelling' is useful because it signals the complexities in any individual's dyslexia cluster. This kind of data goes beyond scores for processing weaknesses, is revelatory for the student and leads directly to strategies for particular purposes.

Analysing

An example of this was provided by a student who experienced a kind of reading 'shutdown' after a particularly heavy period of work. This had never happened before and he was afraid. He was an articulate and successful person and did not consider himself to be dyslexic. However, the unravelling had revealed that during his schooldays he had been regarded by his family as being a bit 'dreamy' and it was clearly possible that he had used these periods for self-balancing. The dyslexia had only really emerged explicitly when he was faced with an intensive timetable which did not allow any 'dreaming' time. An overload hypothesis was one possibility. Another was that the student had an organic disease. It was clear from the ensuing discussion that the student wanted to work with the overload hypothesis first. He was recommended to go home for the three-week vacation and do absolutely nothing in relation to reading and writing and to do something which would use his most comfortable kinaesthetic modalities. He proposed to mend cars for the period. When he returned he found that his reading ability had reappeared. We then arranged for a formal dyslexia assessment, which indicated that he was indeed dyslexic, and arranged support which involved taking pressure off written work by using a note-taker and encouraged him to do self-balancing activity each day. The student graduated successfully and with the kind of self-knowledge which would prevent him experiencing a 'shutdown' again.

Conversations can also be useful for analysing a situation in which a student reveals little evidence of conceptualization on paper and may be judged by academic staff as not capable of this. Conversing about a whole range of matters can reveal that in fact the student does conceptualize and this can be used as mechanism for making explicit the concepts we use in everyday life and for drawing the links between the two.

Learning, teaching and exploring

Some practitioners find it difficult to see how teaching can be incorporated in such informal facilitative processes and yet there is a teaching element in every session. Recent examples have included punctuation and handwriting. The teaching always stems from questions raised by learners and will include, for example, sharing historical information about the development of punctuation marks and/or research findings such as those by Ivanic (1996) in relation to punctuation. This contextualization of the issue prevents wasting of time on inappropriate instructional teaching and encourages exploration of why the notion of full stops or commas is difficult to master in one's own writing. This can show, for example, how 'streams of consciousness' are the meaning units for some people and that sentences may be experienced as alien structures. Simply showing basic sentence structures does not always provide a sufficient bridge across the void.

Similarly with handwriting, appropriate responses can be essentially practical in that use of technology is explored and/or the teaching can usefully involve the introduction of letter formations and writing styles which will use the writer's most comfortable movements. However, sharing insights about perceptions of handwriting can release a broader perspective within which students can make more sense of their own difficulty. For some students the comment by a dyslexic artist has been enlightening and has served to remove some of the negative connotations attached to their handwriting:

> If only someone had told me that writing was a form of drawing! (Adron, Arts Dyslexia Trust Newsletter 1997)

And, of course, there are references to different learning modalities and multisensory methods. A final-year student who was struggling to memorize pages of equations eventually succeeded because we analysed carefully how her memory worked best. The breaking down into meaningful and manageable (small) chunks the sequential cycle of: seeing/speaking out loud/writing/repeating; use of optimum energy bursts and regular reviewing were used. However, these were not presented as a set of techniques but as a 'meta-cognitive' way of solving a problem, that is, '*Your present approach is this but it is not working for you. Think about the other ways in which you can take in information.*'

Counselling

Current recommendations about dyslexia support in higher education (Singleton 1999a) identify specialist counselling as an essential part of any institution's package of support. It is far from clear what this would involve and who should do it in higher education settings. Meanwhile, counselling skills and an eclectic use of certain approaches can be very valuable in learning support (Goodwin 1996a, b).

Shaping options and decision-making

A key activity is reducing a mass of possibilities to a few options and facilitating a decision. The practice of 'spraying out' possible methods for students to choose between is usually ineffective. Instead, an hypothesis-testing approach with students in control of monitoring the process of discovery is most useful. The tutor's task is to synthesize options and give students confidence to make the decision and follow up with review. All decisions and processes are reviewed. If a decision has not proved effective for the learner, the fundamental confusion is re-analysed.

'Moments of development'

Finally, these are moments in any session or learning support path in which there is an option either to settle for a limited explanation or response or to select one which is 'empowering' in the sense of alerting students to the broader context. Three examples of the latter are described below.

Time and dyslexia

Recurring claims are made about the issues surrounding time and dyslexia. Diagnosis involves tests in relation to time and dyslexia appears to involve certain sorts of processing delays. Dyslexic people are sometimes thought to have an uncertain sense of time passing and to find time management difficult. Dyslexic learners find organization difficult and time is one more thing to organize. Time may be another void for which an accessible structure is not easily available.

I usually explore these issues before helping students to consider new ways of scheduling time, *'How is time a problem?' 'In what circumstances?' 'Is there anything you do manage well in relation to time?' 'How is time actually experienced?'* For example, Student C described himself as someone who could lose time:

> I can arrange to see someone at 5.30 about a flat . . . and I do need the flat . . . but something else will have attracted my attention and I have no sense of time passing. When I come to I am way into the evening.

We had to discuss the nature of this 'blank' in order to ascertain if anything could be devised to help. We devised some possible strategies to do with vigilance and signalling to self about key events but I was not convinced that these would work because I was not sure that either of us had the necessary insights/vocabulary to describe what was happening. The student went off to think more about the precise circumstances in which this tended to happen.

I mention this provisional decision to indicate that sometimes the explorations do not lead to immediate solutions and that only the ongoing investigations by tutors will reveal ways ahead. I am therefore grateful to Susan Parkinson of the Arts Dyslexia Trust for permission to use her comment (personal communication 1999) that, for her, time appears two-dimensional. Moving from her usual three-dimensional activity feels as if one is having to literally (almost physically) move into another dimension to come back into time. Time for her is not therefore a blank; rather a different place which cannot be inhabited at the same time as certain other activities. Retrospectively, I saw that this could have generated another set of hypotheses with the student concerned.

Structuring essays

A second example of it being necessary to bring broader/deeper factors to bear in the face of a presenting problem is provided below. Many dyslexic students experience difficulties with 'structuring' essays. These can be experienced in a number of ways and at a number of levels. Tutor responses vary from the relatively superficial to those based on deeper analysis and exploration.

An example of the latter involved a student who always arrived with masses of notes and seemed completely disorganized. He was completely confused by the quantities of material and the literacy requirements he could not seem to meet. The proposed structure of his essays was always an assembly of points in no particular order. Discussion about the set topics and his thinking about them always produced an outline but the student could rarely write to that. After several failed attempts on my part to make any headway, I said, '***Put all this stuff on one side and tell me what you think about when you first see an essay question.***'

> Lots of things. The main question is in the middle and I can see it link to other questions and further links.

He started to draw an example of where an imaginary question about the sun would have led him (Figure 14.3).

This indicated that the student did create structures in thinking but that they were essentially dynamic three-/multidimensional networks which were almost impossible to turn into a two-dimensional linear form. It is not just a matter of numbering each place to give an order because everything was so dynamically connected and it was difficult to write as if they were disconnected. Direction did not really signify; you could start anywhere on the matrix. I reflected this back to him but also encouraged him to value his initial fast creative response which might involve connections that others

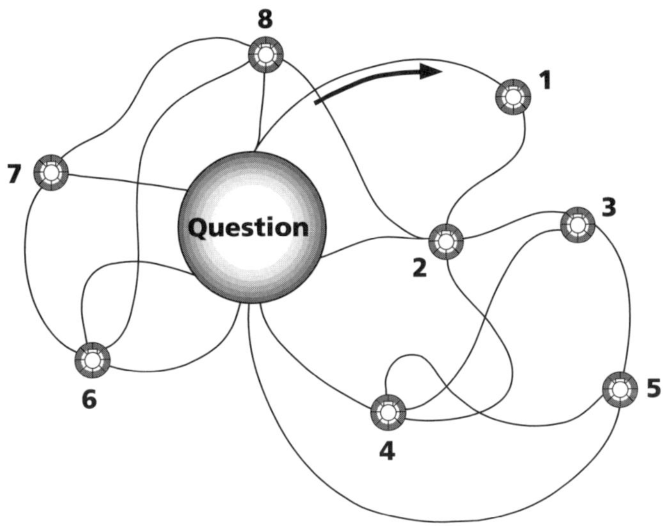

Figure 14.3. Rapid, dynamic, multidimensional thinking.

may not make. I then clarified the question that this structure was actually answering, '*Tell me everything you are thinking about this question*' and offered other questions and subquestions which could lead to a linear 'story':

- '*What is the essay question getting at?*' '*What is the issue?*'
- '*Why is it an interesting issue for this course?*' (put the student in the place of the question setter).
- '*Who thinks what and why?*'
- '*Whose ideas challenge these positions?*' (the unfolding story).
- '*What do you think is the answer . . . why do you think so?*'

I also offered different diagrams and used gesture to show the development of an answer.

This approach provides a scaffold across what can be experienced as a void or blank. Students can literally have no idea at all where to start and this is often interpreted as an inability to think when it is an absence of a route map in unfamiliar territory.

In addition to providing this kind of scaffolding, the task always involves a discussion about literacy practices in higher education; not only making them explicit and clarifying the rationale for them but also locating them within traditions and cultures. Students may always have difficulty with some forms of literacy but they are freed from a failure paradigm if they can see exactly how and why their style conflicts with what has been required by those who operate in a different way.

Challenging student positions

Finally, development for both student and tutor can emerge from challenge within conversations. For example, students invariably compare themselves unfavourably with the most accomplished and fastest readers and writers among their peers. This is used to compound feelings of failure (Rack 1997), to confirm a sense of 'unfairness' and can lead to the feeling that if only they could be like that then they would be top of the group. No one ever seems to compare themselves with anyone who appears average to them. When I have asked why, several reasons have emerged:

> I am attracted by the beauty of this person's writing. It is so good. I want to be able to write like that.

This echoes remarks made by others about seeking 'beauty' or eschewing ugliness in relation to words and text. Students have also identified the most able in the group as being their equals:

> I am as clever as they are but they get the marks.

They then think that literacy-based assessments prevent them from taking their rightful intellectual place in the group.

Both of these are worthy of further exploration but the issue can become problematic if students deduce that the process of composition for everyone else is relatively easy. It may be just as difficult but for quite different reasons. It appears to me that there is a general tendency among dyslexic students to assume that literacy is far easier for students who are not dyslexic than is in fact the case. Hence I challenge such general assumptions by referring to the writing experiences of other students and their challenges with academic literacy practices.

I have also begun to think that the best speakers and writers may also be noticed because they require less effort from the dyslexic students who are already in a multi-tasking situation and who may have less spare processing capacity and more need of clarity and succinctness.

This process of using 'moments' in an informal way allows the interweaving of a critical awareness of context within the learning support curriculum. It frees the student and adds to the professional development of the tutor (Figure 14.4).

Outcomes and conclusion

This approach is essentially exploratory, investigative and power-sharing. There is much more for us to find out about learning 'differences' and there is

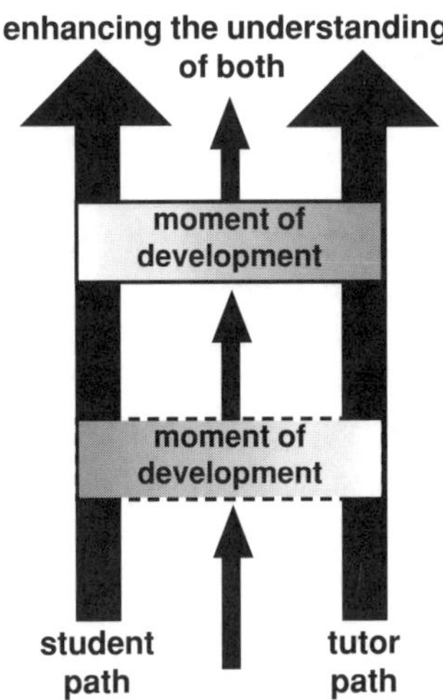

Figure 14.4. Moments of development within student/tutor interactions.

a great deal of work to be done on changing practices and contexts to ensure that *differences* are not perceived as *deficits*.

Students find the approach described here interesting and they regularly mention outcome in terms of enhanced literacy and learning and increases in marks, and a growth in general confidence and self-advocacy skills. They value the opportunity to have discussions about meta-cognition and meta-affectivity. They mention an increased awareness about their own dyslexia and, for some, a restoration of 'self'.

Two questions emerge from this: first, is this approach merely desirable or is it actually necessary for dyslexic learners? I would argue that it depends on the outcome sought by a student and tutor. If someone does not have too much difficulty with essay writing then a technicist approach from the tutor can succeed in helping the student to produce the essay for a deadline. However, if there is a more deep-seated difficulty and/or if a long-term gain in 'power' is sought in relation to learning then this joint investigative approach is sometimes the only effective option.

The second question concerns whether or not this is essentially different to what is necessary for non-dyslexic students coming to learning support sessions. I reviewed my caseload for one term in 1996 to seek an answer to this. Many of the issues raised by dyslexic and non-dyslexic students were identical. They formed a core curriculum for which the broad contextual analysis described here is particularly suited: academic practices (literacies, teaching methods, conventions of curriculum organization etc.) and personal transitions. However, dyslexic students more frequently raised particular vulnerabilities with regard to affect/cognitive relationships and with particular aspects of literacy and speech. They also described short term processing blanks, voids and absences more frequently and much work had to be done simply to manage short 'delays' without panic. Increasingly, they produced powerful descriptions of very different types of processing experience. A deeper knowledge of how both the difficulties and differences were being experienced, and an investigative stance in relation to them, were required. I concluded that the basic method was desirable for both groups but that it had been essential for students bringing the deeper dyslexic stories. Only joint investigations of this nature could expose the issues and devise the most productive responses.

CHAPTER 15

Conversations about spelling in higher education

MARGARET HERRINGTON

Introduction

The purpose of this chapter is to describe a particular approach to the teaching of spelling in higher education. The approach was developed with students in adult basic education in the 1980s–1990s and has since proved relevant and effective with dyslexic students in higher education. It is informed by fundamental notions about literacy and power, both in the community at large and within the higher education context, and has at its core the investigative partnership of student and tutor and the central analytical and decision-making role of adult learners. The approach described here has proved useful for any adult learning to spell but in particular for dyslexic learners. Dyslexic students at two British universities have helped to refine it.

Background

The issue of the levels of spelling accuracy expected from students in British higher education remains for the large part unresolved. Attitudes of British academic staff to spelling accuracy among undergraduate and graduate students vary within and between departments and disciplines (Moss and Cairns 1995). Some who regard the first degree as reflecting particular 'standards' of both basic and academic literacy, regularly express concern at what they perceive to be falling standards in this respect; others, more concerned with subject knowledge and intellectual skills, do not view errors in students' spelling as anything too important, especially if the nature and quantity of the errors are not too unusual. Hence, some go as far as to include spelling within the designated marking criteria for coursework, others mark down for spelling but do not reveal this to the students, and others still, simply ignore spelling errors altogether for marking purposes.

To some extent this reflects attitudes to spelling in the community at large: on the one hand, those who insist that 'standards' (by which they mean adherence to standardized spellings) should be maintained and that those who deviate should in some sense be 'called to order'; and on the other, those who think that standardized spellings are a 'convenience' but that regular deviations from them are 'normal' and usually not too serious, provided that most readers would find them comprehensible. Even a passing glance at literacy in the community shows that variations in some contexts are the norm and rarely have any significant impact on the comprehensibility of the message. However, what is interesting about the diversity among higher education tutors is that this is the very place where one would expect the commitment to 'standardized forms' to be at its highest and most uniform.

Needless to say, this situation can be confusing for students. They can have no effective way of knowing how spelling is viewed unless they ask the staff who mark their work. It is particularly difficult for students who have never been told about their weak spelling at school and thus have no idea that a tutor could be penalizing them once they are in higher education.

However, it is not just confusing. Many of the comments now made on essays and reports about spelling, by those who are extremely concerned about falling standards, are imbued with a set of negative associations, viz., carelessness and sloppiness. Assumptions are sometimes made about the intellectual abilities of those who experience spelling difficulties in general and about the precision, care and effort of the individual concerned. For individual learners who are very able and who devote great efforts to producing accurate spelling, this can be extremely demoralizing:

> . . . spelling was and still is a millstone for me. Even in my third year I have been held up for it. I have a lot of trouble and feel that if it was better, with some tutors I might have gained more marks in essays. (Benson et al. 1991, p. 3)

The view that it could be useful to teach spelling strategies rather than making comments such as '*Take more care with your spelling*' or '*Use your dictionary*' is not widely held in higher education. To some extent this stems from uncertainties about the role of higher education teachers in relation to literacy teaching: most would not regard the teaching of what they would deem to be basic literacy as part of their remit. In addition, a lack of teacher training for higher education staff (though this is now developing rapidly across the sector) may have meant that even if they did believe that they should not ignore such literacy errors, they would not have necessarily felt equipped for the task of teaching students how to address them.

In the face of uncertainties, negative labelling and an absence of teaching, many students resort to spellchecking devices. These have clear limitations but they are often 'good enough' for most coursework assignments or dissertations. Students also report a double benefit of actually learning to spell by frequent use of a spellchecker. The use of a PC keyboard and screen has also been reported as a helpful aid to visual memory. So, the interesting questions for tutors are: is there any case at all for devoting time to the teaching of spelling in higher education; is there a case for teaching dyslexic students to spell when they are often struggling to fit their work into narrow time constraints, and when specific arrangements can be made to disregard spelling errors in examinations.

Reasons for teaching spelling in higher education

There appear to be at least four reasons for doing so:

- The value of understanding the notion of spelling as part of an 'ideological' rather than an 'autonomous' model of literacy (see Chapter 8 in this volume). Dyslexic students can gain from learning about the way the language and literacy conventions have developed. Without a sense of how, why and in whose interests these conventions are maintained, it is difficult for them to reshape and reframe their perceptions of their spelling difficulty; away from an undue emphasis on personal failing and towards a broader understanding of the educational and the socio-political contexts in which forms of literacy are generated and contested. Such knowledge can also help students to enhance their self-advocacy skills and to challenge some of the cultural values which attach to perfect spelling.
- The practical reality that examinations in higher education are still largely done by hand rather than on PCs. If spelling is a struggle, and especially in timed conditions, then the student is at a disadvantage. Tutors who have been used to spellchecked coursework may be taken aback by the extent of poor spelling in an exam and the student will often not know how this is being taken into account in any marking. This can be further complicated in the case of some dyslexic students who may take substantially longer to write than others and may thus experience associated physical strain. It can be helpful for such students to have more spellings automatically at their disposal.
- There are also many circumstances in adult life when dyslexic graduates may need to commit key words to memory. Past experience of poor teaching of spelling should not be allowed to hold back adult learners and the opportunity to analyse their own learning and memory strategies. To enhance their own 'toolkit' in relation to spelling is important and this is particularly true if there has been no prior opportunity for them to do so.

- In higher education 'key skills programmes' relating to graduate employment and employability include reference to communication skills and literacy in general (Murphy et al. 1997). There are also a number of vocational settings in which spelling conventions are deemed to be particularly important (e.g. medicine) and dyslexic higher education students aiming for those vocations will find it useful to have both technological aids and some strategies for acquiring essential spelling vocabulary.

Ultimately, the students themselves have to be convinced that these are good reasons for allocating time to spelling. If they are, then it is essential to address the questions of:

- What are the appropriate methods and why?
- Who should be responsible for teaching spelling?

An effective approach

There are many approaches to the teaching of spelling available to us (see Chapter 5 in this volume) and, in relation to dyslexic students, the structured multisensory approach is usually advocated by dyslexia specialists. Within adult basic education, tutors did not traditionally start with such a prescription; their task was to explore methods of remembering spellings with their students. They would be able to offer a range of methods using different combinations of senses and also be able to contextualize the spelling conventions in general. However, the learners would essentially teach the tutor about what would be effective.

Based on such work, this chapter proposes first an integrated 'analytical-logical-sensory' approach which works explicitly with knowledge of the context noted above. It involves students in a co-exploration in which their perceptions of words in general can be discussed. Difficulties with particular words, selected by them, are analysed and 'logical' solutions found. Hypotheses are generated about the memory for a particular word at the start but then, over time, general hypotheses can be developed about how students will remember spellings.

The approach works by using 'an exploratory conversation' framework. Tutor and student engage in an informal, relaxed conversation in which both teach and learn. Many descriptions of approaches to spelling do not attempt to describe the real-life interactions in which tutors and students work together to find actual ways forward. In this case there is an attempt below to give some idea of how this can work. First, some of the essential elements which must be included in the conversation are identified, and then snippets of stylized conversations, based on real conversations between the author and higher education students, are shown. The limitations of the snapshots are obvious: not all methods nor stages of the process can be illustrated but a taste of the exploratory partnership can be obtained.

The exploratory conversation

Key elements:

- The student's personal history of spelling. Not just a list/passage of what they can or cannot spell but what has gone on before in terms of experience with spelling, of prior teaching, of personal effort expended etc.
- The nature of the process of spelling for students. What happens when they try to retrieve a word . . . and in which contexts? Always difficult? Sometimes easier? How is the process described?
- The words which are already automatic for them, about which they never falter, and memories of how they may have learned these.
- Words which resist learning and an analysis of why.
- Identifying what students now want to know and why.
- Ways of tackling the new material.
- Ways of memorizing and reproducing words on demand.
- Reviewing memory and progress over long periods.

The following guide and dialogue illustrate some of the stages in the approach as it unfolds. It is difficult to reflect the pace and rhythm of these interactions in such abbreviated snatches of conversation. Suffice it to say that the conversational framework allows humour, and informal digressions, to allow for 'mental rests'. It is also difficult to illustrate the extent of the visual presentation of words in colour and on coloured paper and yet a discussion about colour, perception and memory is almost always included in spelling conversations at some point.

Tutor and student interaction

Encourage the student to clarify and prioritize his objectives and to explore feelings about spelling, previous teaching and the fear of tedium. Place the student at the centre of decision-making about content and process.

T You have said that you want to try and have a go at some spellings. Is there anything in particular that you would like to start with?

S *Well, it might be good to get a few of these words I'm really supposed to know for my course.*

T Is there any **one** word you'd like to tackle first? It really is important not to overload when you are starting to work out how your memory works . . .

S [Student laughs] *One word!*

T [Tutor laughs] I'm serious! One word is all I ask!

S *Mmm – well there are a lot of medical terms, but I would really like to be able to spell a fairly common word . . . it is the word 'available'. I never get this right.*

T How have you tried to learn it before?

S *I cannot really remember . . . but I do have some awful memories of doing tedious exercises . . . with vowels in pairs . . . a waste of time really . . .*

T Well, I can promise you that this will not be tedious. [Laugh] You are finding out how your memory works and this will put you in a better position when you want to learn something. You decide what you want to learn. No one will set you any exercises. What I will help with is the analysis of why a word is difficult for you to remember . . . but you will have to decide how it will be learned. You will have got some strategies already anyway.

S *I suppose I must have for the words I can spell.*

T Yes, these will probably come out more clearly as you go along. What you are looking for are new ways of tackling those words which will not stick in your memory using your existing strategies . . . whatever we come up with, only you can say if it works.

Place spelling in its appropriate perspective: historical; linguistic; and cultural.

S *I do find it a bit of a nuisance to be pulled up for spellings because I suppose I do not think it is so important. The content of what you say is what matters . . . surely . . . as long as they can tell what you mean . . . isn't that enough?*

T Well . . . I suppose for some people the sight of inaccurate spellings takes their mind off your meaning temporarily . . . and breaks their concentration . . . but this probably all goes back to ideas about literacy 'standards' and the place of standardized spelling within those.

S *What do you mean? What's standardized spelling?*

T The convention . . . the 'agreement' . . . that there will one correct spelling for any particular word. Sometimes it is important to bear in mind that we haven't always had this convention.

S *Oh?*

T Well, Shakespeare managed to spell the same words in different ways even on the same page! Standardization came in with Johnson . . . a few hundred years ago [provide more examples about the history of particular words if appropriate . . . very interesting for some students]. Because it is always evolving . . . all people cannot maintain the same spellings all the time – there are occasional outcries about standards slipping.

S *So are you saying you don't really think we need to agree how a word will be spelt?*

T Well . . . I think such agreements are valuable but I now think that some degree of deviation should be seen as a normal part of the way literacy develops.

> People who generate such differences should not be seen as transgressing some standards which are cast in stone. Otherwise, the ability to spell can be used as by those who can easily stick to the conventions . . . to make quite inappropriate judgements about those who cannot. But I accept that at any one time there will be some contexts in which it is vital that agreement be reached and maintained. [Discuss examples, perhaps the names of drugs if working in medical settings, discussion about literacy on the wards and how it works . . . who has to write what and who checks.] I am not convinced though that spelling has to be perfect on all occasions and I certainly do not think that spelling capability reflects intellectual ability.

Analyse the chosen word for the bits known by the student. Start by presenting the correct spelling.

T I'll write it out first
a v a i l a b l e.
Are there any bits of the word you would have known?

S *Not a clue – well – maybe the first letter* [pause] *or the first two* [pause] *and the last.*

T [Ticking the bits known as the student identifies them.] So you knew this . . . and this, even though at the start you were not sure you knew anything . . . this tells you that if you will be patient and wait for the bits to come in . . . you can manage the delay instead of panicking.
The bits you don't know are here and here [pointing]. Have you any idea why?
av ail able

S *I usually get the letters but in the wrong order – I half know that there is an* 'I' *in there somewhere. I can get* 'ai' *the wrong way.*

Analyse what needs to be done to make it memorable. The tutor makes suggestion: split the word into more manageable chunks and in a way which attaches the uncertain bits to the known bits. The tutor reassures that there is no right way of splitting the word; the task is to find a way which works.

Try a first hypothesis: split the confusing 'ai' combination . . . explain why this is necessary . . . the sound of a long 'a' in this word cannot predict the 'ai' combination . . . it is too imprecise. Try a new way of breaking up the word. The tutor writes in large clear letters, in colour and/or on coloured paper. Sometimes boxes are placed around the chunks to separate them carefully.

T ava / il / able
[tutor checks]: Does this make sense?

S *Yes . . . it is different somehow.*

T Well, you're OK on the end bit so the task is to ensure that these two first bits are got hold of . . .
Will you remember it if you say **av a** [a blend of the sounds of 'a' and 'v' and then the letter name 'a' on the end]
or is it easier to say **a.v.a** [individual letter names]?

S *a.v.a I think* [writing it out and saying it] – yes, a.v.a.

T What about the **il**? Do you want to say it as it sounds or by names of letters as well?

S *I think* *i.l.* [letter names] *because I know how to spell* ***ill*** *and I might put a double 'll' in.*

T OK so it is a.v.a.i.l. able [write it out and say it]. Have a go and see how it feels to you.

S *a.v.a.i.l. able* [speeding up at second and third time].

T Can you see why there is a good chance that you might remember this? It is because you are giving yourself a precise sound clue . . . you are telling yourself the name of the letter you need. The general long 'a' sound is not precise enough for you to retrieve an 'a' and an 'i' together.
The task now is to see if it sticks. A way of doing this which works for lots of students . . . you can start with this if it makes sense to you . . . is to do what you have just done for six days – just once a day for six days. You do not have to get out your papers or folders. You just need to say it and write it out once a day . . . the back of an envelope will do. No exercises – no big deal – one word! Then stop for a few days completely and try it again and see what you remember. You'll find out whether it really was the best way of chunking the word and the best way of remembering it.
When we next meet let me know what you've found out.

S *OK, I'll give it a go!*

Review the process together:

T Did it work? Can you remember how to spell it now?

S *Yes it did!*

T Did you do exactly as we agreed or did you do other things to help you to remember?

S *I did post it up in my room with it broken up in this way – so I could see it whenever I arrived back.*

T So you were giving yourself a frequent visual reminder . . . Would it have worked without this do you think?

S *I don't really know – it just seemed to help.*

T Do you think you needed the six days or would a few days have worked?

S *No – I think I definitely needed the six . . . I'll think about that more next time.*

T Did you really stop altogether after the six days?

S *Yes . . . and took the cards down . . .*

T And it was there easily when you tried to retrieve it four days later?

S *Yes it was [grin].*

Building the next step: prepare for ongoing learning and review:

T You seem to have learned quite a bit already about how you need a precise sound clue for the chunks you are trying to remember . . . and you are beginning to find out more about how much reinforcement is necessary . . . What is next?

S *I have a number of words here that I really should learn for work.*

T Which do you want to try first? Which is most urgent or which would be most useful?

Repeat the process, remaining open to new ways of remembering. Do not expect a student to learn about his own learning immediately:

T Do you want to try two words today? I wouldn't recommend any more until you are far more certain that you will retain what you've started to learn.

This approach goes beyond the offering of a range of methods for remembering words but helps students to focus on the residual problem within the word and to ask precisely why it cannot be remembered. The following conversation with a different student illustrates a further stage of review when the student is looking back on a number of words he has learned and the approaches he has used for each:

T Looking back over the work you have done so far . . . you have already given me some idea of what spelling can be like for you . . . you feel reasonably confident if the sounds are clear to you because even if you do not spell the word correctly, you will be able to find enough letters for the reader to know what you mean . . . if you experience blanks and then letters 'float in', but not in order, you can sometimes work with your memory of the shape of the word to find out what is wrong.

S *Yes, I can often tell from the shape that something is wrong but that does not help me put it right necessarily.*

T No but it is useful to have that awareness of shape . . . not everyone does.

S *I can sometimes get an idea of whether the word is long enough . . . whether I have the right number of letters in it from the shape.*

T Yes it is a useful backstop for some words, especially those with distinctive or unusual shapes . . . [pause]. It might be worth checking over the methods you have now used to get things right . . . what was the first word you did?

S *It was the spelling for my middle name* ***John****. I have always been a bit embarrassed that I could not spell it.*

T Oh yes, I remember. You knew the first letter 'J', but were not sure about the order of the others. We discussed it and you decided that it would have to be split into two **Jo hn**.

S *Yes I got* ***Jo*** *easily . . . the sound is clear to me . . . but the only way I could get the order of the other two in the end was because I knew that 'h' on the end made the wrong picture.*

T You couldn't get it from saying the names of the last two letters . . . **h.n.** which had worked with other words?

S *No . . . and the shape was something I already had an idea about.* [Chat about other words with distinctive or non-distinctive shapes for the student.]

T What about some of the others . . . the next one was **pound** wasn't it?

S *That was easy once the split was between* ***po*** [with a long 'o'] / **und** *I could say it like that and get the spelling right.*

T So you could get **und** from your pronunciation?

S *Yes.*

T You split the word **chemistry** as well . . . You started with **cheistery** and the split which worked was **chem / is / try** [tutor reading out and writing at the same time].

S *Yes, I could say* ***ch*** [like the sound at the start of **chicken**] *with* ***em*** *and then I know the words,* ***is*** *and* ***try****. I needed only one check on that one. It was so clear.*

T One of the interesting things was when you tried to learn two words together . . . the topic for your project . . . **bacillus subtilis** [chat about the project and how it has gone].

S *My first go was to break it into* ***ba cill us sub til is***.

T It did not work did it?

S *No, I would get* ***basillis subtillis***.

T The chunking did not lead you to the correct spelling and your sense of shape could not really help. You were not getting a precise enough sound/symbol cue from the soft 'c' sound, in the first word . . . and in the word **subtilis** there was no clue from the sound that there was only one 'l'.

S *Another thing that happened was that when I started to write* ***bacillus*** *I would want to put in a 't' sound from the next word and put* ***bactillus****. It was as if my mind was going ahead to the next word.*

T So, what worked in the end?

S *I learned the words separately, starting with* ***bacillus***. I broke the word into **bac** [hard 'c' sound] ***ill us***. *Once I got the* ***bac****, it was fine because I could spell the words,* ***ill*** *and* ***us****. I did the usual five days of practising once a day . . .*

T And now you get it right?

S *Yes, it makes sense now.*

Implications of the process

The conversations involve an unfolding, unpressured exploration of feelings, motivation, cognition and effective learning by student and tutor but with a focus on the student as decision-maker and evaluator and with some precise analysis of what could be going wrong. Though these conversations are distillations of one-to-one conversations, the same approach can be used in small groups. In my experience, the group setting can show learners how other students choose quite different ways of chunking words. This reinforces the view that there is no single correct method of remembering for all.

Ideally, any tutor working in this way should have:

- Knowledge about the history and nature of spelling; the range of methods available.
- Knowledge about the nature of spelling difficulties experienced by learners with SpLD.

- Values which include power-sharing with regard to the content and process of the curriculum.
- Commitment to 'a spirit of enquiry' and exploration in each case (we have much more to find out about memory in general; only an ongoing exploration will uncover individual students' ways of remembering).
- Views about the process - informal, humorous and respectful of learners as co-explorers.
- Personal qualities and skills, e.g. listening, analytical, investigative.
- Recognition of individuals' constellation of strengths and weaknesses - not attempting to impose a standard method. Sharing with students the knowledge and recognition of the variation between all of us in the way we perceive and recall visual symbols.

It is reasonable to expect such expertise in 'off-course' learning support settings in higher education. The issue of what can be expected from academic tutors who are marking piles of scripts is more problematic. However, these conversations reveal some key messages which could easily be taken on board by non-specialists. It would not be difficult for a tutor to underline the error within the word and to write out the correct spelling. Nor would it prove too onerous to point out that there are a number of ways of remembering the parts which are proving difficult. Any learning support unit should be able to provide the appropriate back-up with this.

Recurring features

Conversations with dyslexic students over many years about spelling have revealed a number of recurring issues. First, their sense of panic at what can be experienced as a 'blank' in retrieval. There can literally be the feeling of nothing there. Yet these blanks are often not as complete as they seem. Methods which allow for the 'half-known' to emerge and for the management of delayed recall are very effective. Encouragement not to panic and to make space or find forms of words which will give them some time to draw out what they do know is essential. The notion that letters and words may emerge or pop in over a few minutes is often in itself revelatory to students.

Second, it is important to note that some methods of breaking up words often make no 'sense' at all: syllabification can be a complete mystery. The task is to find a way of chunking which does make some kind of sense to the student. However, it is not just a matter of 'not making sense' for some students, particular ways of breaking up words can be very 'uncomfortable' and 'unpleasant' for them to look at. Sometimes letters can be added so that the word becomes more 'pleasant' (e.g. adding 'e'). This kind of response can sometimes be helpful for understanding why some students with SpLD simply do not want to write some letter combinations (a recent student did not like to look at double 's') or why, for example, a student places 'e's on the end of lots of words. Without a discussion which covers these, learners could experience considerable frustration.

Third, many students have said that though they have a spelling difficulty in general, and often do not know what their mistakes are, they can spell some words if that is the only task in hand. Invariably, they are having to think about content when writing and the attention to surface features cannot be maintained at the same time (the automaticity/multi-tasking problem). Then if they can bring themselves to read what they have written (and it is quite common for dyslexic students not to read what they have written unless they have to), they will be focusing on meaning and may not notice even the spelling errors they could correct. Hence, though single-word analysis is key in the above approach it is always crucial for the tutor to be aware of the complex multi-tasking involved in writing. Checking whether or not the words can be retrieved during writing is important.

Finally, and most important, the conversations have also revealed that other students help dyslexic students with study in general and with proof-reading, grammar and spelling in particular. This confirms previous findings about the support provided for each other, in general, by students in higher education (Rivis and Herrington 1994). It also suggests parallels with the literacy 'brokers' identified by Barton and Padmore (1991) in their community literacies research. This showed the extent to which adults helped each other within families and social networks; not all completed their literacy tasks alone. In higher education, too, where writing is assessed, there are students who are prepared to assist others with their literacy tasks and not just the official group writing tasks.

Conclusion

It seems clear that the teaching of spelling in higher education may be both necessary and desirable in some circumstances. In general, students will use spellcheckers whenever possible but for some students in some contexts, these will not be adequate. It is also clear that there are effective methods which employ the analytical powers of students and tutors working together and which contextualize spelling within a broad literacies framework. Although these should be known and understood by specialist tutors, it is also possible for spelling awareness to be introduced within general higher education teacher training as part of 'academic language and literacies' awareness. Such work will have an important place as the higher education sector continues to widen participation.

Acknowledgements

With thanks to Morag Hunter-Carsch for her suggestion to record, transcribe and analyse the exploratory conversation; for her method of analysis of the dialogue and discussion of early drafts of this chapter.

CHAPTER 16

Students' views of learning support

JAMES PALFREMAN-KAY

Introduction

I am dyslexic and I received learning support as a final year undergraduate and postgraduate student at Leicester University between 1993 and 1995. This support helped me to develop the necessary academic skills and self-esteem for success in higher education. In this chapter I shall draw on my experience of learning support in secondary, further and higher education, together with that of other dyslexic students, to identify key elements of effective learning support. I shall argue that despite some disadvantages, personal accounts provide valuable information for policy-makers about the nature and value of existing provision.

Objective, rationale and method

Objective

My overall objective for this chapter was to contribute to the debate about effective learning support for dyslexic students by identifying some outstanding questions and by seeking answers from available personal accounts by dyslexic learners. The questions which seemed important included:

- Have dyslexic students in higher education received prior learning support?
- Do all dyslexic students require learning support in higher education?
- What do dyslexic students receive in this respect?
- What do students think about learning support tutors/sessions?
- Has learning support helped dyslexic students to be successful in higher education?

Rationale

I decided to focus primarily on the assistance provided by learning support tutors, whilst recognizing the significance of support provided by academic tutors. Academic tutors often give guidance on the subjects being studied, on some aspects of academic literacy and often on pastoral issues. This is in contrast to learning support tutors, who provide 'one-to-one guidance on ways of studying' (Gilroy and Miles 1996) with explicit reference to the impact of dyslexia and the development of cognitive and self-advocacy skills. I hesitate to make such a generalization about learning support practice given the fact that not all universities have learning support personnel/units and there is still limited evidence about the actual nature of such practice in higher education in the UK. However, I think it is a useful distinction to make for this chapter.

In focusing on personal accounts of learning support I recognized both their value and their limitations. In education, the former has long been recognized (Graham 1991). Such accounts provide a:

> . . . complete life history [which] attempts to cover the entire sweep of the subject's life experience. It is inevitably long, many sided and complex. The multiple biographies approach, by abstracting dominant themes, makes it possible to generalise to one type by showing that certain biographies have, for all the idiosyncrasy, some common elements. (p. 45)

and so, for this chapter, I anticipated that they could be used to 'help understand what was significant' (Lummis 1987) to the dyslexic student. They would allow dyslexic students 'to describe, evoke and generally recreate the development of the author's experience' (Abbs 1974) of learning support through a process of self-reflection. As student views are 'distinctive, [they] add their voices to those of other 'outsiders' whose viewpoints' (Walmsley 1995) will assist in the future direction of this support provision. Personal accounts seem to have the potential both for empowering students and for providing recommendations for developing more effective forms of learning support.

There are also several disadvantages in the use of autobiographical material. Butt and Raymond (1989) show this when they state that autobiography reveals 'personal bias and selective recall'. Furthermore, it involves 'stories according to dispositions'. Depending on the dyslexic students' experience of learning support it can possibly result in a distorted picture being portrayed. Further, they can prove to be a very weak tool for answering general questions about a large sample. The approach clearly requires caution but I anticipated that such personal accounts as were available would provide useful preliminary information from the student perspective.

Method

My approach involved three stages of information-gathering.

Revisiting my own experience as a dyslexic student

This involved two steps:

- Constructing a written account of my educational experience in which I described and analysed experience across the sectors.
- Arranging to be interviewed about the experience so that the talking could release more memory.

A literature review

A library search revealed seven autobiographical accounts by dyslexic adults in the literature, three of which concerned experience of higher education (Gilroy and Miles 1996; *Dyslexia Contact Journal* (BDA) and the *Journal of Learning Disabilities*, USA). Most of these, however, tended to focus on experience in primary and secondary education and so I extended my search to the internet.

Seeking other personal accounts through world wide web mailbases

The search of the world wide web mailbases involved sending out a general e-mail message over a two month period in 1997 to members of 'Dyslexia mailbase', 'Dis-Forum' and 'Disability-research'. The question I asked via e-mail was: 'I am presently writing a chapter in a book entitled *Dyslexia and Effective Learning*. My chapter is on Dyslexia and Learning Support. I was wondering if you could help me by possibly giving me an account of your dyslexia and what help, i.e. learning support, you received while you were at school, college and university.'

The 'Dyslexia mailbase' was the most useful as it allowed me to contact directly dyslexic students who were currently receiving learning support. I also searched the archive facility of this mailbase to see if I could collect other personal accounts from dyslexic students.

I obtained a total of 34 personal accounts from dyslexic students world-wide. Twenty of these accounts showed experience of higher education; nine were from dyslexic students within the UK and 11 from outside. Eighteen accounts focused mainly on general experience of higher education and highlighted the differences in secondary and tertiary systems. Only two accounts provided an experience of learning support within the UK higher educational system. Both these accounts also revealed experience of receiving learning support during secondary education. Another account from the UK revealed one respondent receiving learning support while in secondary education. Outside the UK there were two personal accounts which provided an experience of learning support in American and Canadian universities.

Findings I: key observations from my own experience

Experience in the school context

My own account revealed a range of experiences, some of which were echoed elsewhere. In brief they included:

- An ongoing path of self-discovery about the nature of my dyslexia and its implications for study.
- An absence of specialist support until the later stages of secondary school.
- A lack of academic support from most teachers who seemed to have neither knowledge nor curiosity about these learning difficulties.
- A handful of exceptional teachers, and in one school a majority of the staff, who were curious and helpful.
- My own responsiveness and progress as a learner whenever I detected genuine interest and patience, and my complete humiliation at the hands of one or two others.
- My own determination not to let dyslexia restrict me from achieving the success I wanted.
- The value towards the end of my secondary education of having both supportive academic staff and a learning support tutor.

In brief, the following observations are particularly important.

Staff were too ready to link difficulties to literacy problems alone

My difficulties were in learning from my teachers' styles of teaching. The impression given was that if you could not learn from their specific form of teaching, it was you, the pupil, that had the problem. This, of course, created difficulty because the teachers thought you were either lazy or simply experiencing some form of literacy problem.

Teaching styles were too prescriptive

On the whole, the teaching styles I experienced during my secondary education were very prescriptive. My experience of this was felt particularly when I attended my first secondary school. An example of this was when teachers expected me to fit into their ideas of learning and in particular when they wanted me to learn long lists of information, visually. I had difficulty with this method of learning because I could not learn large amounts of information in such a manner. This created conflict and when experiencing such problems, it was difficult to discuss alternative methods of learning. The effect of this was to dent my self-esteem.

Some teachers were not prepared to help

Some teachers during my secondary education were unwilling to help me with my dyslexia. I particularly experienced this when I entered secondary education. It must be noted that the lack of support was before anyone knew that I was dyslexic. I would attribute the lack of support to the fact that I did not conform to their prescribed patterns of learning.

Lack of recognition of dyslexia among teaching staff

For the majority of my secondary education I felt there was little awareness of dyslexia. At school many teachers viewed me as someone who tried hard, but would not get too far. Even when it was confirmed that I was dyslexic I felt the level of awareness only slightly increased, because I had to go to the majority of my teachers to inform them about dyslexia.

It was noticeable that when I returned to certain secondary schools there was an increased awareness of dyslexia. This was illustrated with support tutors being brought in to support dyslexic students. On discovering support was in place after I left, I had mixed feelings, as I would have benefited from such support but I was pleased it would benefit other dyslexic students.

Interest in you as a person was key

During my secondary education I was aware of teachers who took interest in me as a person. On reflection this was because I displayed an interest in their respective subject(s). As a result, the teachers were prepared to give you additional time to discuss particular subjects or to allow you to discuss any difficulties you might be experiencing. I found such support helpful, as it encouraged me to work harder.

Encouragement to find your own way of learning was vital

Another positive experience in my secondary education was that I was encouraged to find my own way of learning. The encouragement only really came from the tutors who I felt took interest in me as a person. Examples of this would involve teachers allowing me to discuss with them different ways of learning their particular subject; they would also provide guidance and specific methods of learning. The end result would be for me to develop a learning style which brought me success.

Small class sizes were helpful

I found the small size of classes helpful throughout my secondary education.

Their value was that they gave me the self-esteem to answer and ask questions and they allowed me to receive additional help with areas of difficulty. With class sizes being small they allowed me to establish a working relationship between myself and the teacher. I did this by approaching the teacher to seek either further clarity or help with subject topics.

Staff communication with parents was important

Staff communication played an important role during this period of my education, as it resulted in the discovery of my dyslexia. I made the first step towards discovering I was dyslexic as a result of my personal tutor being aware of spelling difficulties through my English language tutor. This led him to suggest to my parents that I might be dyslexic, and that it would be worthwhile confirming this either way through an assessment.

The value of the learning support tutor was very clear

The value of the tutor was that she helped me to develop the necessary skills which allowed me to make the transfer to higher education. This involved help in developing an effective essay writing technique which allowed me to achieve success with my GCSEs and A levels. The support the tutor provided was taking me through the various stages in putting together an academic essay at these particular stages of my secondary education. This was help with planning, structuring and proofreading an essay. Other areas of support included providing advice on different methods of learning; through discussing such methods I adopted a new learning style which was suitable for the subjects I was studying.

The 'emotional' environment the tutor created was important, as it was a relaxed and friendly atmosphere. Possibly I was comfortable in such an environment because the tutor treated me as an equal person. Because the tutor created the impression that she was generally supportive, it helped in the development of my self-esteem. The support made me even more motivated towards success, because I did not want to let down someone who had displayed confidence and faith in my abilities.

Experience within higher education

The overall issue to emerge from my reflections about higher education was that I had had to focus on reducing the gamble involved in submitting academic work.

The support I received from some academic tutors was important in this respect. The support initially varied between tutors and this can be attributed to the differing levels of awareness about dyslexia. However, by the end of my higher education experience at Leicester University, the staff with whom I had had contact were positive and were prepared to help in any way possible. Examples of help included providing additional help with essay writing such as help with the planning and structuring as well as recommending important references. There was a minority of tutors, who took longer to develop a dialogue with me about my dyslexia. The delay seemed to stem from their preconceived ideas of dyslexia, for example, the notion that it was a psychological problem.

Learning support tutor

It was during my final year as an undergraduate and as a postgraduate that I received learning support. My experience of this was that the tutor was unravelling the difficulties with my academic work. For our first meeting, I remember asking the learning support tutor what it would take to achieve a good degree. Initial thoughts were that I would have to develop a more analytical essay writing style to achieve success. On the whole, this is the area with which I received most help, and I was also given guidance on essay planning, organizing and proofreading. By the tutor taking me through the various stages of organizing the 'argument', I felt I was reducing the chance of submitting a poor essay.

The growth in my confidence was shown in the learning support sessions. Initially, the tutor would 'control' the structure of the sessions, but as I grew in confidence I took control. The support provided was essential because the tutor helped me to develop confidence in my essay writing style. A sign of my growing confidence was that after a while I only submitted my essays to be proofread by the tutor. I viewed this as a safety net before I submitted them to my academic tutors.

Learning support environment

The 'personal environment' created by the learning support tutor contributed to my success within higher education. Four key features stand out:

- **I was always treated as an equal person**. The impression given by the tutor within and outside the learning support sessions was that she viewed me as a person of equal value. By being given this impression, it gave me the self-esteem to talk to the tutor about the various ways to answer essay questions. The learning support sessions were informal and relaxed and they gave me the confidence to discuss with the tutor different methods of learning and to learn from my mistakes.
- **The tutor was wanting me to do well**. I was constantly being encouraged by the tutor which helped to develop my self-esteem. The faith being displayed by the tutor motivated me to do well, as I did not want to disappoint an individual who had displayed so much faith in me.

- **The tutor and I would discuss matters apart from academic work**. By discussing non-academic matters I realized the tutor was interested in me as a person. These discussions helped to create a relaxed atmosphere which helped me to work.
- **I did not feel I was receiving counselling**. Although I was receiving learning support I did not feel that I was receiving counselling. This is because I was receiving help in developing an effective essay writing technique which would bring me success in higher education, instead of receiving help for a psychiatric problem.

Support from other students

Other students played a supportive role in my experience of higher education. Support would be provided by friends reading through essays and making helpful suggestions about how to improve essays further. I found this useful as it would show a different perspective on work which I had not previously considered. On the down side, some students resented the additional support that I received; this was based on the assumption that the additional support that I was receiving was providing me with an advantage.

Findings II: personal accounts from the internet

The personal accounts which I collected, confirmed and added to the above observations. I will highlight the additional key issues which emerged.

Support in secondary education

The majority of those who went into higher education had already received support in their primary and secondary schooling. The experiences recorded about secondary education confirmed those which had emerged from my own personal account. However, unexpectedly, four accounts gave a less than glowing account about the quality of their learning support. Two examples illustrate the point:

> At school I had always been an awful speller and had even been in a learning support system for 4 years, they just tried – unsuccessfully to teach me to spell.

> I was immediately put into these remedial English lessons,and this is really where I learned to read, although it wasn't an awful lot of help apart from learning to read.

Hence, there appeared to be some variation in the experience of learning support among dyslexic students during their secondary education. The problem with negative experiences is not only that students fail to progress but also that they may not seek help at a later date as a result.

Only one respondent referred to support in further education but this did confirm my own experience of such support:

> When I started my second year of A levels, I went to . . . [a learning support tutor] . . . who was in Northwich and who is a specialist dyslexia teacher. She helped me very greatly indeed.

When the dialogue was extended to higher education, the experience of others matched my own. Some additional issues did emerge and these are described below.

Not all dyslexic students require learning support

Five accounts identified learning support from a learning support tutor in higher education and, in general, they were appreciative:

> The Learning Support Office was really good to me. . . . They also arranged a special needs tutor to help me with my work.

> The essays proved the most difficult tasks and I often turned to the Dyslexia Unit for help.

> The Disability Office . . . supports a dyslexia discussion group for students within the university, through this group we get help with spelling, presentations etc. . . .

However, a small minority of respondents felt that they they did not require specialist learning support while at university. One account noted:

> There is learning support at university, as yet I have not called upon it. But I am thinking of looking into it this year. My marks so far have been excellent, but it has probably taken me a lot longer to produce the work.

Another account suggests the respondent did not require learning support because he felt his dyslexia did not affect his reading and writing:

> The problem I face is that people automatically assume dyslexia means you have trouble reading and/or writing, but I am a voracious reader of all types of literature, especially science fiction.

However, the majority considered it important to have learning support available for dyslexic students, as at some point of their higher educational experience they may require it:

> . . . our systems of education are not individualized but are standardized on the learning patterns of the 'average person'. Our individual differences are not always going to fit with that standardized approach given our various backgrounds and neurological differences.

Accessing learning support

The personal accounts showed two main ways in which dyslexic students had obtained help.

Referral by a supportive lecturer or tutor

This occurred when students who were largely unaware of their dyslexia were spotted by tutor or when the student had presented particular types of problem to the tutor. One respondent recorded:

> It was only when I met a professor in university who was dyslexic and started working for him that I thought I might be dyslexic. He recommended for me to get tested.

Another account showed referral in response to problems:

> Just before my first set of exams I went to see my personal tutor and told him that I was worried because in exams my writing, spelling and reading got much worse. I was worried that the markers wouldn't be able to read my work and I would be marked down for it. He then referred me to the university learning support unit office who did a short assessment and from the results of that sent me off to a educational psychologist to be formally assessed and it came back - after my exams - that I was dyslexic.

> A sympathetic tutor referred me to the Dyslexia Unit, where a formal assessment was arranged for me, and I was given information and help.

Each of these rested on prior awareness among academic staff about dyslexia and about the available learning support facilities. The problem with this process of referral is that it is not sufficiently reliable if academic staff are unaware of available support.

Self-referral

This method of accessing learning support depends on students awareness of the support services which a university is able to offer and their perceptions of what such a service may be like. One respondent tried to access support but left it very late in his course:

> The Disabled Student Services didn't want to help me because it was my last semester. The best they could do is if I stayed another two years they could start helping me if I paid for a lot of tests to be done on me.

Self-referral also seems to depend on prior knowledge about the learning support among students and also on their own confidence and self-esteem.

Clearly, some students could fall through the net and a more systematic approach may be necessary.

The issue to emerge from these accounts is that dyslexic students need to be aware of the provision of learning support when they enter higher education. The accounts identify the need to develop effective referral procedures and to move away from either an informal referral or relying on students to be automatically aware of such support.

Role of the support tutor

Two of the personal accounts made reference to the nature of the support tutor's role. The students' perception of the role of the tutor was to assist them specifically with their academic work:

> I can also remember meeting a learning support tutor, who for the first time offered me help with my essay writing technique.

> We started with the Instrumental Enrichment (IE) program . . . which is a program designed to teach thinking skills. This was a 60 minutes session and then a 30 minute session on spelling and writing. We also had outside work on spelling and writing on which we were tested in the next class.

However, the accounts show tutors also adopting a generally supportive role:

> I was able to start work with this tutor because she made me feel comfortable. I felt this because . . . I was not viewed as someone stupid, but as a person who was intelligent and capable enough to obtain a good university degree.

First impressions were important in this respect. The responses show respondents coming away from the first session feeling very positive because they were given the impression by the tutor that they were:

> [At] . . . least as good as other students and with a little help . . . might do even better.

This general stance helped students to develop their self-esteem and have the confidence to seek success at university.

It could be argued from this that learning support tutors were, in fact, combining academic guidance with a counselling and practical advisory role. Students discuss '. . . living arrangements, . . . flat-mates not understanding , . . . problems with money' with their tutors (Gilroy and Miles 1996). Hales (1994) argues that 'We cannot – must not – separate an individual's dyslexia from other aspects of existence . . . and should be, a part of our service to the individual dyslexic person' (p. 73). Gilroy and Miles (1996) suggest that the approach of a tutor should be ' . . . to support the student as a person: this means encouraging her motivation by developing . . . self-confidence and feelings of self-worth, while at the same time supporting . . . ongoing academic work - coursework, dissertations, and essay writing.'

Variations in learning support by subject

The respondents show the level of learning support provided varied with the subject studied; dyslexic students following arts courses were more likely to obtain comprehensive learning support than those following science courses. Students enrolled on arts or social science courses reported:

> The support given was in improving my essay writing technique; this would be help in planning, structuring and proofreading essays.

whereas science students noted:

> She was a very good special needs teacher but the maths certificate she had only covered my work to a certain level and after a while she wasn't that useful and unfortunately there are very few special needs teachers of physics so next year I will probably be without one.

There is a need to provide an equal learning support service to dyslexic students enrolled on either arts and science courses. Clearly, it will be difficult to achieve this as there is a limited number of support tutors with a science specialism. To an extent this issue is being addressed through learning support units using either academics or postgraduate students to provide help. However, such individuals would not be able to offer the specialist help of a support tutor.

Frequency of learning support sessions

The accounts referred to some variations in the frequency of learning support sessions:

> When I returned for my final year I had three one hour lessons (one to one).

> . . . about the tutor, well I would see her an hour every week. She was a special needs tutor with a certificate in maths.

> I would see the tutor for one hour either every week or every two weeks.

This variation seemed to depend on the degree of dyslexic difficulty, the timing and circumstances of its discovery, and the point in the course at which students accessed learning support. A pattern of support which involved intensive weekly sessions at the outset and then fortnightly/three-weekly meetings as confidence developed was reported favourably. In general, decisions about the frequency of learning support sessions were made flexibly and in consultation with students.

Type of help with academic study

The respondents revealed the specific areas in which they received help. Not all required help in all areas.

Essay writing

The majority of the accounts show that learning support tutors provided specific help with structure and proofreading for essay writing, within a general framework of helping students to identify their learning strengths as well as weaknesses:

> She gave me pointers on essay writing, i.e. writing plans, paragraph headings and sentence construction.

> I would normally give an outline of the topic I was being asked to write about, and from discussing it we would set about developing an essay plan and structure.

Tutors helped students to create:

> . . . structure . . . and firmly abandon ideas that are irrelevant to the questions. I have often come up with a novel approach to an answer.

One account suggested the importance of tutors explaining the nature of the dyslexia:

> These sessions were important, as the tutor helped me to understand my dyslexia. I identified my dyslexia affecting me in the structuring and organizing of my essays.

Help with proofreading was also noted:

> Proofreading . . . was helpful as it would allow me to work on other areas of my essay writing technique which would not be shown at the first stage.

and it was important to timetable this properly:

> After a couple of days I would discuss the essay with the tutor which was helpful, as I could look at the essay in a more objective manner.

The respondents also identified help with note-taking techniques and with organization of notes:

> I was given help with various things but mainly sorting out my notes and writing letters to the biochemistry department . . .

This support helped to develop organizational skills.

Time management

The role of a tutor, as shown by the accounts, was also to provide advice on time management to dyslexic students:

> She went through all the work she could with me, she gave me advice on how to handle time management in coursework and exams - such things like never put things off start them straight away so you don't panic and hand in naff work. This enables you to work at your own pace and have plenty of time to ask for help or correct any mistakes.

It clearly takes dyslexic students longer to produce academic work and so the development of time management skills is vital.

Value of information technology

Six respondents noted the value of using computers in organizing, structuring and presenting their work in a readable format:

> Another thing I did which helped improve the readability of my work was to use word processors to write up projects and coursework.

> A talking word processor does help here, it's like a proofreader, if you can hear the mistakes.

> My comprehension of the written word is slow, if I can read out loud or the computer reads it to me, it makes a hell of a difference. My grammar is useless, but is getting better, I put this down to computers.

Information technology is able to play a role in providing effective learning support as it can help dyslexic students to organize, structure and present their work in a readable format. There is a need to provide support to dyslexic students to develop their IT skills, as such technology can play a supplementary role to the support provided by the learning support tutor.

An emergent framework

By drawing together the issues emerging from this evidence, I was able to draw up a framework which grouped together expectations, attitudes, values, skills and processes which are relevant for effective learning support (Table 16.1).

Table 16.1. Emergent key elements in effective learning support

Students' expectations of self	Environmental factors	Students' expectations of tutor
Strong motivation to learn and do well	A place to feel welcome	Genuine interest in the student as a person
Willing to form a good relationship with tutor	Friendly relaxed atmosphere	Being a hearing, listening and responsive individual
To be prepared to learn from your mistakes	An atmosphere to work in if needed	Not talking down
To feel confident in your own ability	To be comfortable enough to improve your learning	To be treated as a normal and equal person
To determine not to disappoint yourself and your tutor	The opportunity to drop in for a chat with the tutor and to focus on work	-
To be a self-advocate	-	Be encouraging of the student
To be confident enough to explore new methods of learning	-	Deep understanding about the nature of dyslexia
Need to be clear about what you want to achieve	-	To give the student clear advice on: (1) Planning essays; (2) Structuring essays; (3) Note-taking; (4) Time management skills and (5) Advice on different methods of learning
To establish a dialogue with academic tutors	-	To convey to the student that the support is not counselling, but academic guidance
-	-	To give the student a sense of confidence
-	-	For the tutor to liaise with academic tutors

Conclusion

With regard to my initial questions this evidence has provided a useful starting point. It underlines the importance of learning support within secondary schools for students who go into higher education, its value in further and higher education, and the range of key factors which are essential in the provision of effective learning support in any sector. This evidence also reinforces the point that dyslexic students are helped by certain attitudes and skills among all staff in schools and colleges and that learning support is not restricted to learning support staff alone. It therefore provides valuable feedback for schoolteachers and for higher education service providers.

The personal accounts have shown that each dyslexic has an individual experience of learning, and that if learning support is required, it should be focused on responding to individual needs. It is appropriate to have general factors in place, such as an informal and relaxed atmosphere when providing support, but it is important to remember that learning support has to be provided on a focused, individual basis. The proposed framework shows the mix of student, tutor and environmental factors which facilitate this.

These accounts have also proved valuable because they provide students with an opportunity to assess their own progress while in education and to clarify their thoughts on how learning support has helped them, through a process of self-reflection. This assists with ongoing development as learners.

Finally, the value of communicating through information technology has emerged clearly. In this case it allowed me to reach a wide range of dyslexic students, who have had different experiences of education. By comparing the accounts from a diverse sample, it provided an opportunity to give a broader picture of the key issues involved in providing learning support.

Acknowledgements

With thanks to Margaret Herrington and Morag Hunter-Carsch for discussion of an early draft of this chapter

Chapter 17

Developing positive learning environments for dyslexic students in higher education

Stella Ni Ghallchoir Cottrell

Introduction

Although there has been a rise in awareness about dyslexia in higher education, and many more British universities offer a dyslexia service of some kind, the quality of such support varies widely across the sector. Most dyslexia units or services are relatively new phenomena and are subject to great financial restraints. Staffing levels are usually much lower than required, and expertise is hard to find. Even where mainstream teaching staff are concerned and willing to support dyslexic students, the issues raised are but a small part of a very wide range of new responsibilities which staff are expected to comprehend and absorb into every aspect of their work, but without additional time or ongoing training. Among their other responsibilities may be an ever-growing number of students with study, language and life difficulties. Dyslexia is only one subcategory of such need.

Thus, an emphasis on continuity in support for all students can be a useful strategy for developing curriculum accessibility for dyslexic students. A positive environment for dyslexic students may depend critically on the distribution of this support across a wide range of university personnel, departments and processes. In particular, processes related to transition, admissions and preparation for higher education may be key. In this sense, a positive experience of higher education is influenced by what happens long before arrival at university.

Pre-entry guidance and transition

The first step towards creating positive experiences for students is to ensure that applicants have an understanding of how universities are currently constituted, of the changes or adaptations which may be necessary in the current context, and of the kind of baseline preparation necessary for success.

Students arriving from school (or from further education) are typically used to small classes, where the tutors and other students on the course know each other's names. Students may be used to working together with staff and a group of students for the whole course, sometimes for years. In such conditions, the tutor can opt for progressive marking strategies, selecting, for example, some areas of grammar or sentence construction to comment upon in a current piece of work, and building upon key elements over many subsequent assignments.

Further education staff tend to meet in course team meetings, discussing students' progress and the factors which may be affecting students outside college. Nurturing environments may develop. Students sometimes mention that they received help from tutors at college with writing letters to their council, help with completing UCAS forms, even with gas bill disputes; they may be used to discussing their personal problems with the course tutor. Both further education and schools employ trained teachers who, it is hoped, have some understanding about the philosophy of teaching and learning, and about the needs of learners, whether dyslexic or not.

The transition to higher education is a shock to many students and for these reasons:

- For the first time they may be in a group of 200 or more students on a course, with perhaps two tutors responsible for that course. Universities are about 'mass' education rather than classroom teaching. The lecture hall may seem vast; it may be daunting even to walk to the front where they can hear better or set up a tape-recorder, strategies typically recommended to dyslexic students. There may be nobody who remembers them by name for several weeks; the lecturers may never recognize them by both name and face. On modular courses, there may be new lecturers every 10 or 18 weeks, depending whether courses last a term or semester; and not only the lecturer changes, but so does the group with whom the student worked, and to whom they may have talked about their dyslexia.
- With the demands made on teaching staff, the time available for a personal tutor to spend with each of the students allocated, may be very restricted. Rivis (1994) noted that the personal tutor system was under considerable stress. Some departments have dispensed with personal tutors altogether.
- Each study module is a world unto itself. Each may be distinct in terms of its teaching methods, assessment strategy, specialist vocabulary and language style. The total number of assignments required for any module may be low - often only two or three pieces of submitted work. This

means there is very little time or opportunity for students to develop the 'habits' required for each module; and the opportunity for tutors to monitor progress can be very restricted.

- The tutors may be lecturers in a very formal sense – 'delivering information' from notes or from their heads, rather than having been trained in the art of teaching.
- Lecturers are traditionally researchers rather than teachers; their interests may lie with their research in a way that is unusual in further education or school. Moreover, in higher education, funding is linked to research so that the pressure to produce research publications can be overwhelming.

The traditional expectation in universities is that students arrive ready to work in the way that universities teach. This is usually lecture- and seminar-based for most courses, and almost always requires academic writing, even if the course could be regarded as creative or practical. Although there has been a lively movement within higher education to change the emphasis to learner-based approaches and trained teachers are becoming more common, a number of contradictory processes have militated against substantial change. These include institutional inertia but, perhaps more often, the consequences of the rise in numbers, the cut in budgets, the decline in staff, the pressure for research and publications, and the greater needs and special requirements of much higher numbers of students, without commensurate increases in financial support to meet such needs. Even the willing and helpful staff members can find themselves unable to help.

Developing more realistic expectations

In order to address this contrast with previous experience, teaching staff or psychologists advising students on higher education entry or undertaking needs evaluations should ensure that students understand the difference between school (or college) and university. They need to be explicit about the kind of support that is realistic for individual students' patterns of strength and difficulty, for the course they are selecting and for their level of IT competence. This may involve greater liaison between further and higher education sectors, and between higher education and the professionals undertaking dyslexia assessments for those aiming at higher education entry.

Three examples illustrate the kinds of issues that can arise in such liaison work. First, at a transition workshop, a further education-based dyslexia support tutor mentioned that one of her students, 'John', currently received four hours of language support a week for grammar, vocabulary, spelling and sentence construction and insisted that this would be essential when he transferred to university. Second, a dyslexic applicant, Amanda, brought the educational psychologist's report to her initial interview at the university. This stated that 'Amanda's tutors need to go through her notes with her, and check that she has understood the point of the lectures and seminars and what she has read'. The report does not indicate, for Amanda's benefit, that she could expect her notes to cover 20–30 hours of lectures and reading per week. Third, a higher education lecturer contacted the dyslexia unit to ask what could be done about a student, Matthew, who was struggling with the course and likely to fail all units. The tutors found it hard to give any marks at all for his work. They were worried because the student's arrival was preceded by a letter to the department, from his former college of further education, stating that although he had failed his BTEC course, he had the ability to do very well at university and recommending that he be offered a place.

In these, and in many other cases, students were led to believe they could succeed at university at their current level of performance, often because a cognitive profile suggested they had the 'ability' or 'intelligence'. They may well have had the 'intelligence' indicated. However, in all three cases, although a range of support was provided for the students, the students were not sufficiently prepared to make adequate use of what was available. None had developed IT skills prior to university entry. They could all have developed their study and language skills further. They had not developed the appropriate study habits and organizational skills to be able to survive at university. They had poor general knowledge, had read (by ear or eye) very little over their lifetimes, had little sense of language structures, and though their oral skills were good, they were not strong enough for oral assessment purposes. They each had been led to expect that they could rely on using a level of support which was untenable in the present higher education context.

In John's case, it would not have been impossible to arrange for four hours of language support if he had really wished to continue with it. However, this would have depended upon factors such as the student's eligibility for the Disabled Student's Allowance and the support of the local Education Authority for his claim (which the university cannot guarantee in advance of admission). However, the demands of a higher education course are such that students are extremely unlikely to be able to maintain an additional half-day's study in language support as well as coping with the usual demands of their course. This is especially the case for dyslexic students who already are likely to spend much longer than other students on their course studies, before other support work begins. It is all more the more important that severely dyslexic students have experimented with different types of support before they begin university as it is difficult to do this in combination with a university course.

Similarly for Amanda; her note-making skills were weak and listening comprehension poor. Her written notes contained many gaps or were illegible and hard even for her to understand. She was distressed to find that the ratio of staff to students, coupled with the incidence of many students having a wide range of needs on that course, precluded the possibility of tutors going over lecture notes with her for more than a few hours per semester. As she regarded the psychologist's recommendation as indicating a special entitlement to her lecturers' time, she lost study time and a great deal of lecturers' goodwill in arguing for 'rights' which could not be met.

Matthew was also disadvantaged by his false expectations. His identity became wrapped up with success on his course. Because people wanted to reverse his pattern of failure, many hours of additional support were arranged for him over the first year. However, he was unable to find the time or organizational resources to attend those sessions. He believed his tutors were 'picking on him' when they offered detailed feedback on how to improve his work. It was manifest from his scripts, from his behaviour and from speaking to him, that he was not ready to grasp at even an elementary level what was required of him.

For these students, university was a negative experience from the start because they had been given false expectations of what university is like. This is not to argue that universities could not make changes, or be more supportive. However, it might be more helpful to offer accurate information about what is expected of university students, as well as on-campus visits, tasters of university life, and discussions about the implications of working in such different environments.

There is a need for longer access courses and for bridging courses for dyslexic students entering higher education. This is especially true of mature students who often have only a brief, nine-month access course to make up for years of lost schooling and the loss of study habits during their absence from school, as well as studying the equivalent of A level for university entrance. In addition, such students may be told for the first time that they are dyslexic; yet their further education colleges may lack the money for a full assessment and specialist tuition and counselling may not be available. The student has to cope with the additional emotional demands of coming to terms with the revelation of their dyslexia. One student at the University of East London has, after two years at university, decided to return to the first year on a different course; she feels that she is now at the stage she should have been at when she first applied. Although she passed the first two years, this was with low passes, extraordinarily high levels of support, and enormous personal costs in terms of time, stress, interests, health, parenting and relationships.

Evaluating needs for higher education

Once students enter university, it is important that they are offered an evaluation of their needs for the particular higher education context. The coping strategies developed for managing the school or further education context may collapse in the new setting of higher education. This is not just because the support structure is different, but because the levels of reading and writing, and above all the demands for personal organization, are much greater.

Course considerations

What students need or require in higher education will differ very much according to the particularities of that context. If a student's spelling and grammar are weak but the ideas flow well and the writing can be understood, all that the student may need is for teaching staff to agree to mark work for content and to ignore mechanical writing errors. If the teaching staff argue that this is not possible for their subject area, the student will need a more extensive support package. This may involve word-processing facilities with spellchecker, possibly voiced software so that errors can be heard, and personal support on developing writing skills or learning to use the ICT.

On a course such as architecture or fine art where the ratio of dyslexic students may be very high, the most effective support may be a reconsideration of the demands of the course. It is not reasonable to expect art courses, for example, to request 30% or more of their students to have additional ICT and study support, paid through the Disabled Student's Allowance, when the needs manifested are to be expected for a large proportion of that intake. In such instances, a departmental or institutional approach to dyslexia is required!

Individual preferences

Individual preferences must nevertheless be established if an appropriate support package is to be devised. There is a tendency to consider that all dyslexic students will take to ICT, that all need to work at home, and that all will need a tape-recorder in lectures. However, the flashing computer screen can exacerbate difficulties for some students; others do not take to the keyboard. Some find that working with tape-recorders is too difficult, as they cannot find their place on tape very easily, or that they develop time-consuming habits such as trying to transcribe lectures onto paper or to listen to all lectures again at home.

For some students, especially those living in shared accommodation, the allure of owning their own computer fades when they find that it is difficult to escape distraction from their peers. Universities need to provide good ICT facilities in a quiet space on campus. This would include dyslexia-useful ICT, such as screen reading facilities, computers with talking spellcheckers, optical scanners, printers, headphones, and computers where workspace colours can be altered. Equally important is easy access to support and training from staff who understand their needs.

Other variables

When considering the support that students need, other factors need to be taken into account: eligibility for the Disabled Student's Allowance, staff:student ratios on their course, the number of students with a 'special need' of one kind or another on that course, and the preferability of individual, small-group or whole-group solutions. It also needs to be considered how much time students have to develop new skills and also the stage of the course they are at when they present for support. Third-year students may need to be offered proofreading facilities because they have insufficient time to learn ICT and keyboard skills. A more long-term approach can be taken with first-year students.

The evaluation also has to walk the difficult tightrope between recommending what is actually available, what may be feasible, and what individual students need in ideal circumstances. As ideal circumstances are unlikely to pertain, it is important that whoever makes such an evaluation is familiar with higher education, with the particular university the student will attend, and with the demands of the course the student will be following.

Changing university environments

Although many universities have developed support services, students and support services lament the slow progress of awareness and supportive attitudes across institutions at large. Some lecturers take a 'sink or swim!' attitude towards all students or argue that 'some people are just not very bright'. Although this may be true of some students, it is all too easy to make such judgements on the basis of weak technical writing skills or errors in oral work. With invisible disabilities such as myalgic encephalitis (ME), repetitive strain injury (RSI) or dyslexia, some staff feel that they are entitled to pronounce about the very existence of the condition or difficulties. It is clearly important that students' needs are not left to the mercy of such individual whims.

Policy and appeals procedures

University policies on equal opportunities, disability and dyslexia are essential. The disability statement can give added weight to these. Guidelines on what should be included within such policies are outlined in the report of the HEFCE National Working Party on Dyslexia (Singleton 1999b). As has been widely discovered in the implementation of equal opportunities statements in employment, policy is ineffective unless accompanied by a series of other measures which give it teeth, such as a grievance or appeals procedures with clear lines of referral and named personnel.

Staff awareness and training

Many staff may appear to be unhelpful because they are not aware of what dyslexia is. Dyslexia is a very complex syndrome. Many people assume that dyslexia means either that a person cannot write, or cannot read, or sees all letters, if not the whole world, 'in reverse'. When a student has well-compensated written skills, it can appear particularly baffling that they ask for support or consideration for dyslexia. However, it is clear to those working or living on a day-by-day basis with dyslexia, that the ongoing effects of dyslexia on organizational difficulties, new learning, study, stress, tiredness, social skills, self-esteem, and on many facets of everyday life can be very great. Unless all staff are aware of the wider effects of dyslexia, of why it is thought to occur and of why there is such debate in the area, then misconceptions will continue to plague dyslexic students.

A number of key points can be stressed in relating staff development to the creation of positive environments. Participant feedback on many staff awareness sessions in over a dozen universities and further education colleges consistently mentioned both dyslexia simulations and case study work as the most helpful part of the training. Involving course staff in the process of identification, referral and evaluation of needs is also important. Teaching staff can contribute valuable information about the skills or equipment essential to a student on their courses (such as statistical packages which a student would need if working at home). Similarly, they can identify why certain types of support may not be feasible at present within their department and whether this arises from staffing, financial constraints, or attitude.

Course staff may use the knowledge of dyslexic students in their own area to identify patterns of difficulty which known dyslexic students encounter on their own courses. They can then use these patterns to identify other potentially dyslexic students for referral. In this respect, staff need guidance in how to broach the subject of dyslexia with students and some awarenesss that students may not be ready to 'hear' that they are dyslexic or may not want to take up on an assessment or support. It is important that staff respect the students' position, support them in the ways they can, and do not feel angry or rejected if students do not welcome intervention.

Staff awareness also needs to include reassurance that dyslexic students have a combination of strengths as well as difficulties. A lecturer recently asked, in all innocence, whether it was not true that dyslexic students were weak across the board. Information should be disseminated about successful dyslexic adults, and where applicable, retention rates and grades of successful students.

Integrating dyslexia support into institutional support for all students

Local provision of support and learning development

'Local provision' means bringing the support as near to the students' everyday place of study as possible. However good a central support service might be, students are likely to spend a very small proportion of their time in direct contact with that service. The typical student experience of such a unit is that there are perhaps 200–300 students in contact with one or two specialist dyslexia staff. Most student contact with the institution will be in their department, lecture halls, laboratories and libraries. Whether their experience of higher education is considered positive or not will depend greatly on overall university structures and attitudes. The evaluation of needs for individual students, and a good staff awareness programme, should include recommendations and suggestions on how all staff could support dyslexic students. Dyslexia-aware teaching and library staff can help identify where their course or teaching environment creates barriers to learning or fair assessment for dyslexic students.

A shared responsibility

There can be a tendency on the part of lecturers or other university staff to consider that students with dyslexia are somehow the 'responsibility' of the dyslexia support units. For example, dyslexic students may find it difficult to learn ICT skills alongside other students. They may not be able to decipher on-screen directions; they may need help in identifying ways of presenting data on screen in a way that minimizes the effects of the dyslexia; they may need more visually based materials to work from; and they may find they need a break when others are ready to learn the next vital step. The additional help they require may be perceived as the responsibility of the dyslexia unit, rather than of the ICT unit's responsibility to respond to a diversity of student learning needs and styles.

Increasingly, it is becoming clear that specialist dyslexia staff can be most usefully engaged in training a range of staff to recognize the implications of having dyslexic students within their 'client group'. Table 17.1 offers an indication of ways in which responsibility for support can be disseminated across university services.

Table 17.1. Disseminated responsibility for dyslexia support

Who	Indicative tasks
Former education establishment	Identifying dyslexic students
	Liaison with higher education about progression
	Inform students about higher education
	Develop IT, keyboard and organizational skills
	Offer longer access course/bridging courses
	Careers education/course choice guidance
Publicity/outreach	Accurate information about support in Prospectus
	Handbook/leaflets to distribute at schools fairs
	Open days/organize visits and tasters
Outside experts	Is money available to pay others, e.g. hardship funds for dyslexia assessment/tuition?
Admissions	Liaision between department, specialist staff, former institution and applicant
	Information on support available
	Specialist advice to applicants and staff
	Appropriate admissions procedures
Course/subject area	Initial screening, help, referral
	Teaching methods/lecture handouts/overheads/ glossaries
	Clear marking schemes and assessment criteria
	Constructive feedback for work
	Advice on selecting essential texts
	Variety of assessment modes
Student services	Advertise service/induction events
	Dyslexia-aware counselling
	Send out pre-admissions letters to those indicating dyslexia on UCAS form
Successful students	Staff development
	Feedback to courses
	Meet new students
Student Union	Organize events
	Support a dyslexic student society
	Disseminate information
	Volunteers and 'buddying'
	Finance certain equipment
	Raise issues within the university
	Ensure information is available in dyslexia-friendly modes
Library/Learning Resource Centre	Arrange longer loans
	Allow loans of additional books on short loan to try out on scanner
	Subject specialists advise on texts
	Help find texts
	Set up photocopying cards/invoices for Disabled Students' Allowances

(contd)

Table 17.1. (contd)

Who	Indicative tasks
ICT	Supportive ICT inductions Dyslexia-aware support and training Distribute open learning worksheets designed for dyslexic students Maintain software on network, e.g. Texthelp Maintain equipment such as scanners Advise on new software/hardware
Local education authorities (LEAs)	Visit universities Clarify position on what they will award Liaise with other LEAs to provide consistent approach
Charities, etc.	Support projects Support individual students Support purchase of equipment National Listening Library for taped books
Dyslexic student society	Mutual support Newsletter Share strategies and tips Organize speakers and events Lobbying role in the institution Contribute to staff development

Support by lecturing staff

One example of this is provided by the Fashion and Marketing Department at the University of East London. Staff in this department have a commitment to improving learning and teaching for all students. Lecturers noticed that that almost all of the dyslexic students had difficulties with pattern cutting. They discussed this with the students and the learning development unit, to identify where the difficulties lay. For some, the difficulties arose in remembering the instructions, and the sequence of operations that was required. Staff responded by clarifying instructions, offering written instructions in formats which suited students' needs, and offering additional help and moral support. Fashion lecturers now use pattern-cutting difficulties as an indicator of students who may have an unidentified dyslexia and whose studies may be at risk in other ways. Staff offer help in the early stages of writing assignments, to ensure students have understood the task requirements. In order not to pathologize dyslexic students, this facility is also available to students who are not dyslexic.

There are a number of ways which departmental staff could assist students without significantly adding to their own workload. Some very common difficulties experienced by dyslexic students relate to difficulties in combining non-automatized tasks (such as reading or writing) with other tasks. This is especially the case where one or both tasks may involve subskills or functions which are themselves affected by dyslexia, such as the sound and word discrimination or sequencing involved in listening. Any tasks which require a student to listen (as in lectures, seminars, tutorials) and to note simultaneously, may create difficulties for dyslexic students. If this must be done in bulk or at speed, the difficulties can be exacerbated. The student may become lost in a word when writing, become distracted by the loss of sound or visual recognition of the word they are writing, and 'not hear' the word stream of the next portion of the lecture. As it may take time to reorientate into a word stream; even when the student stops writing, they may miss the next portion of the lecture. The fragments they note or hear may not amount to a coherent picture and the student may not be able to tell whether vital information has been missed.

However, it is not only dyslexic students who have difficulties copying from overheads in the time permitted, who copy inaccurately, or whose note-making strategies leave them confused about the information given in lectures. Many students lack the knowledge base which is necessary to distinguish the 'gist' or the key points of a lecture or text. This affects their ability to select salient details; they may jot everything down or write any words they catch in the hope they can make some sense of it later. Bored or tired students may drift off – especially those supplementing their dwindling or vanished grants with long hours of low-paid work, or being kept awake by crying babies, sick children or other needy dependants, as is so often the case with mature students. Students often do not have the time to put in the background reading and may arrive in lectures less able to understand specialist vocabulary or less knowledgeable about the subject.

What helps a dyslexic student in such circumstances tends also to serve a wide range of students who have not been identified as having a particular need. Often the help required is little more than good practice in teaching. For example, it includes considerations such as giving an overview of a topic at the beginning, drawing attention to the main points, summarizing main points on handouts along with references or definitions of specialist terms, and summing up main points at the end of the lecture. Anticipating where difficulties might lie and monitoring learning should be a main task of any good lecturer or teacher. Inclusion of 'white space' on handouts and overheads is also general good practice. The Open University provides glossaries, as well as study books which clarify key concepts, theories, and methodologies for all students as a matter of good practice; these are generally of help to dyslexic students. Some dyslexic students benefit from reading from tinted paper, or reading enlarged or double-spaced copy. This may be an additional service which some departments may offer to students. However, the important point is that students are given a good, clear copy; they may then be able to scan and alter texts using ICT, or photocopy onto tinted paper themselves. The needs of the dyslexic students can serve to highlight where good practice or provision of good materials is lacking. Perhaps this is one reason why highlighting the needs of dyslexic students can raise such animosity in some quarters.

Positive learning environments for all

The preceding section illustrates that although dyslexic students may have different reasons for requiring certain provisions, that provision in itself need not, in many instances, be regarded as more than good practice. The needs of any particular group of students are likely to throw light upon the quality of, rationale for, ethics of or theory underlying any existing practice. Not surprisingly many lecturers may find this extremely challenging. This is especially the case for 'traditional' university teaching. It is not uncommon for lecturers to read out complete papers because they are too anxious and lacking in confidence to take any other approach. Some fear student questions in case they cannot answer them and would lose authority. Moves have already been taken in many universities to encourage lecturers to undertake some teacher training, a development which has gained impetus since the establishment of the Institute for Learning and Teaching. An outline of some initatives undertaken to alter concepts of student support is offered in *Opening Doors* (Wolfendale and Corbett 1996).

Similar issues arise around assessment. Requests by students with disabilities for 'amended' procedures raise many questions which are difficult to answer. Some students have recommendations from psychologists or support tutors that their work be marked on 'content' rather than on technical aspects of writing, such as spelling or grammar. This may work very well when students' technical errors are minor. However, when spelling makes words unrecognizable, sentences become convoluted, key words are omitted or the sense is hard to fathom, markers may reasonably conclude that they cannot 'see' the content. The student may think the content is obvious. Alternatively, students may argue that they were accepted onto the course and it was up to the institution to find a method whereby their understanding can be tested. Moreover, students may assume that their being accepted means that they have the requisite skills for the course, whereas this is not always the case.

This raises a number of issues in relation to assessment and the fostering of a 'positive environment' for all students. First, it is important that all courses, whether in further or higher education, are more specific in their guidance on what knowledge base, performance levels or skills are necessary from the point of entry, as well as on what will be developed on-course, how this will be achieved and how skills and knowledge will be assessed. Courses should make clear what alternatives in assessment are or are not feasible, and have good reasons, from an educational and disability perspective, why restrictive assessment practices cannot be modified. There may appear to be some validity in the notion that some courses, such as modern languages, need to mark grammar or engineering mathematical calculations very closely. However, the relationship between modes of assessment and the overall aims of the course needs to be examined. For example, if the course is designed to produce a graduate who can perform in business negotiations with French counterparts, is that reflected in the assessment procedure or does the assessment focus unnecessarily on minutiae of grammar and spelling? If a student makes errors in calculations, have the reasons for the errors and alternative ways of arranging data been explored? One student found that her mathematical errors were reduced once she was given enlarged numbers on a computer screen; another found numbers 'stayed in place' when she was offered number displays with heavy lines drawn between columns.

There is a pressing case for many courses to think through what they are really assessing. It is highly probable that many university lecturers are allocating far more marks for good writing style than they are aware. A good stylist can also infer and hint in ways that suggest additional subject knowledge when there has been insufficient research: they know how not to give their ignorance away. This not only disadvantages dyslexic students, but also mature students - those who speak English as a foreign or additional language and any students whose writing style is weak. Courses need to draw up clear criteria for marking, including specific indications on the percentage of marks allocated to use of English (if any). The marking criteria should be stated in such as way as to enable any student to be able to see what is required for each grade.

It follows from what has been said that a change in university ethos may be essential to many institutions. Universities and funding bodies need to prioritize teaching as a goal and recognize that ongoing development of learning must be facilitated in higher education. This would involve recognition of how teaching both structures and facilitates learning, and how different types of teaching can help or hinder differ categories of student. In many cases dyslexic students cannot receive the support they need because the attitude and support available to all students is inappropriate and the demands made on the ordinary lecturer are far too high. In some cases, many students require additional help because the course is aimed at an antiquated notion of what a prototypical student should be like rather than at the actual students recruited. If the curriculum content and teaching methods matched the overall standard of achievement of the students recruited, many students, including dyslexic students would require less additional support.

The same is true regarding the standard of teaching materials offered, the physical environments, or clarity about course aims, curriculum content, and assessment criteria. What may be passed off as 'poor study skills' is often poor orientation to the course and its hidden curriculum. Recognition of the importance of good higher education teaching needs to be reflected in both university recruitment and promotion of lecturers with interest, training and experience in teaching rather than solely in research. It should also be reflected in higher education quality assessment and funding mechanisms.

Conclusions

The university experience of dyslexic students will be strongly influenced by their degree of preparedness for higher education. Schools and further education have a part to play in adequately informing and preparing students for higher education. Bridging courses, provided by either further or higher education, and longer access courses could play an important role in this respect. There are also many ways in which current practice within higher education could be altered in order to create a more positive learning experience for dyslexic students. In many respects, the presence of dyslexic students who are aware of what they need highlights where the learning environment could be improved for all students. Improvements in course delivery and clarity in assessment procedures affect all students. A whole institution approach is required to ensure that policy, funding, awareness, training and expertise cover all areas of the university, and all aspects of the student experience. A learning development approach which integrates support into the teaching and assessment procedures, and which is multi-tiered to provide the additional support required by particular groups of students, offers a model for maximizing support for all students.

CHAPTER 18

Staff development in higher education: a student-centred approach

ELLEN MORGAN

Introduction

This chapter addresses the following issues:

- The learning needs of dyslexic students.
- Providing students with a voice.
- Encouraging staff attendance at training sessions.
- Effective presentation of teaching and learning issues.

The issues explored

Dyslexic students in higher education often find themselves on the horns of a dilemma: on the one hand, they want to be considered as intellectual equals with their non-dyslexic peers and do not wish to be singled out for any 'special' treatment; on the other, they recognize that they may need to be taught in a way that conforms to their individual learning styles. To accommodate differences in learning styles, academics must first understand the needs of their students and then adjust their teaching styles accordingly.

However, the experience of dyslexic students within higher education institutions has frequently been one of frustration, resulting from lack of understanding by academic staff. One student summoned up the courage to discuss her reading difficulties with her lecturer, only to be asked why the university had accepted her if she could not read. The student explained that she could read, but that the process was extremely slow and laborious. She was, therefore, asking the lecturer to identify the essential reading so that she could structure her workload accordingly. At the end of a lengthy meeting, the lecturer wished the student well and told her she hoped her condition would soon be cured! The student left feeling as if she had a contagious disease and vowed that this was the last time she would put herself in such a vulnerable position.

Hence, some students report that they feel marginalized and isolated. Others drop out of higher education because they lack the confidence to explain their difficulties to their subject tutors. Still others feel angry when disclosure of their difficulties results in insensitive treatment or dismissive comments. Even well-intentioned lecturers often fail to appreciate that public comments highlighting a student's dyslexic difficulties can be embarrassing and damaging.

The obvious way of altering these attitudes is to heighten awareness of staff about the nature of dyslexia and about the support dyslexic students need. Unfortunately, staff development sessions are generally poorly attended. This is understandable at a time when teaching loads are being increased. Lecturers may feel that it simply is not possible to devote their limited discretionary time to understanding the needs of individual students. Moreover, there tends to be a misconception that bright students are not dyslexic. Many academics feel inclined to encourage those students whom they believe show the greatest promise and are, as a result, less supportive of those they perceive as being less able. The lecturers who do attend staff development sessions are often those who are already sensitized, resulting in a model of 'preaching to the converted'.

Challenges and solutions

Any challenge to the above required consideration of three questions. First, how could staff be encouraged to attend staff development sessions? Second, how could the teaching and learning issues be effectively presented? Third, how could students have their voice and so feel that their needs were both understood and taken into account. The following case study shows how these questions were addressed and how major progress was achieved in one university.

Case study

The University of North London

The University of North London prides itself on being an institution with a large proportion of mature students, many of whom gain entrance to university through non-traditional routes, such as Access courses. In recognition of the fact that an increasing number of non-traditional entrants may be people whose needs were not addressed at school, the university first made some provision for dyslexia support during the late 1980s. Initially, the dyslexia support service catered for the needs of a handful of students, but numbers have risen exponentially in line with a heightened awareness of dyslexia resulting from external and internal publicity.

In response to the frustration and alienation expressed by a number of students, a dyslexia support group was established in 1991 to introduce dyslexic students to others with similar experiences. This group formed the basis of a student network within which problems could be aired and effective learning strategies shared. One recurring theme was the common feeling that academic lecturers lacked knowledge about dyslexia and therefore did not understand the teaching and learning needs of dyslexic students. From this communal sense of frustration emerged a positive outcome: the students themselves agreed to offer a workshop to explain how their dyslexia affected their academic work. The goal would be to give lecturers insights into some of the problems of dyslexic learners by creating exercises to simulate the experience of being dyslexic.

Considerable time was spent identifying the issues which the students wanted to explain. This required careful analysis of the nature of the problems; it was insufficient to say '*My lecturer doesn't understand*'. Rather, it became necessary to identify exactly what the students wanted their lecturers to appreciate. As areas were selected, each student devised an exercise to demonstrate to the audience exactly how that problem was manifested. Group workshops became highly focused; students shared ideas with each other and jointly worked on developing materials and practising the simulation activities to test their effectiveness. The experience of frustration and isolation was dramatically reversed; the group had a purpose and individual members developed strength and confidence.

Attracting an audience

Given increased pressures of teaching and research, many academic staff are inclined to limit their professional development activities to areas directly related to their subject specialisms and to avoid workshops which are perceived as catering for a small group with 'special needs'. Occasionally, lecturers will attend a workshop on dyslexia if they are familiar with an individual student whose difficulties are of particular interest to them.

Although dyslexic students may have specific needs, many of the teaching strategies recommended might benefit other, non-dyslexic students. Therefore, it is useful to portray the difficulties experienced by dyslexic students as at one end of a continuum of problems faced by all students, and hence to see the issues in the broader context of teaching and learning.

Traditional approaches to publicizing events had resulted in very low attendance; those who did come tended to be tutors who had previous knowledge of dyslexia. The group decided to limit the time and energy devoted to ordinary recruitment techniques. A flyer was designed and distribution was targeted by the students. Each student hand-delivered a leaflet to those members of academic staff known to the students. The leaflets were often accompanied by an individual note or a personal touch (for example, '*I'm part of a staff development workshop and would be very grateful if you could come so that you can better understand the nature of the academic difficulties I face.*'). Perhaps this was a 'hard sell', but it did ensure that the people who mattered were individually targeted. Staff had to come up with a legitimate excuse, or else enter the date into their diaries! The results were positive; although numbers were not great (workshops have varied between 12 and 35 people in attendance), the students were satisfied that they had encouraged several sceptics to attend.

The publicity itself acknowledged the existence of doubters. The title, 'Fact or Fiction: Does Dyslexia Exist?' advertised a student-facilitated workshop exploring the experience of being dyslexic. The leaflet was designed to attract the attention of precisely those people who ordinarily either overtly or covertly treat dyslexic students as less able than their non-dyslexic peers.

Preparation

Once the time and place were established, and publicity undertaken, all that remained was to co-ordinate the activities. This required work with the specialist dyslexia tutor to ensure that the proposed activity made sense and that the method of enactment demonstrated the desired outcome. It was then necessary to have a dress rehearsal with the entire group, to iron out any last-minute wrinkles and to give presenters the opportunity to practise their exercises.

Structuring the event

Several experiential workshops facilitated by dyslexic students have been offered at the university; in each case the composition of the student group differed, although some members participated in more than one event. One workshop was 'commissioned' by the School of Architecture and Interior Design and was intended to give students from that department the opportunity to address teaching and learning issues specific to their course. Another workshop, aimed at a more general audience, was offered through equal opportunity lunchtime workshops sponsored by the Personnel Department. A third event was promoted by a small group of learning development tutors, designed as part of a series of workshops on learning issues.

In each case, the time allowed for the workshop was approximately one and a half hours, the last half hour of which was devoted to questions and answers. The specialist dyslexia tutor chaired the session and offered introductory comments which lasted approximately ten minutes. In the remaining time, each student was allocated approximately five minutes to present a brief explanation of the nature of the difficulty followed by an exercise chosen to offer an experiential insight into the effect of the problem on the learner.

The number of students involved in each workshop varied from eight to ten. Students sat at individual desks or at long tables at the front of the room. Each student had a folded sign printed with the 'problem area' the student was addressing (e.g. 'reading', 'sentence structure', etc.). This was placed on the table at the beginning of the individual's presentation. When the last speaker had finished, approximately ten signs remained facing the audience, depicting a range of difficulties associated with dyslexic learners (see Figure 18.1).

The audience was asked to save questions until the end, although if a pressing question arose, it was dealt with at the time. The discussion session at the end proved lively and informative, with students generally demonstrating great confidence in their ability to articulate both their weaknesses and their strengths. Audience participants showed tangible signs of the impact of the workshop, such as comments reflecting changes in their attitudes and preconceptions about dyslexic students.

The content

Perhaps the best way of providing a flavour of the workshops is to offer a summary of some of the exercises which students developed and illustrated.

Reading

Several aspects of reading difficulties were addressed by different students. A design student explained that her visual processing difficulties resulted in print moving on the page, creating a 'rivers' effect. She demonstrated this by

Figure 18.1.

taking a piece of 12" × 15" card and cutting grooves at one inch intervals. She then reproduced a passage from a book typed in a large font on the computer. Each word was cut out and mounted so that it could be inserted into the groove. The sentences were carefully arranged and the card was made rigid so that it 'stood' on the desk, with the words facing outwards. The student then moved the words by manipulating the handles at the back of each word. These moving words created the sensation of 'rivers' appearing as a result of the developing spaces (see Figure 18.2). The time and effort devoted to creating this model was in itself testimony to the desire to demonstrate the frustration caused by this reading difficulty.

Another student began his discussion by stating that reading was an extremely slow and painstaking process for him. He commented that, although he could decode the words, the actual process of gaining understanding from print was so slow that he became physically exhausted. He asked for a friendly volunteer from the audience and asked his unsuspecting tutor to read aloud a page of print that was placed on the floor. However, to demonstrate the physical strain which this caused, the tutor was requested to read the passage whilst doing press-ups!

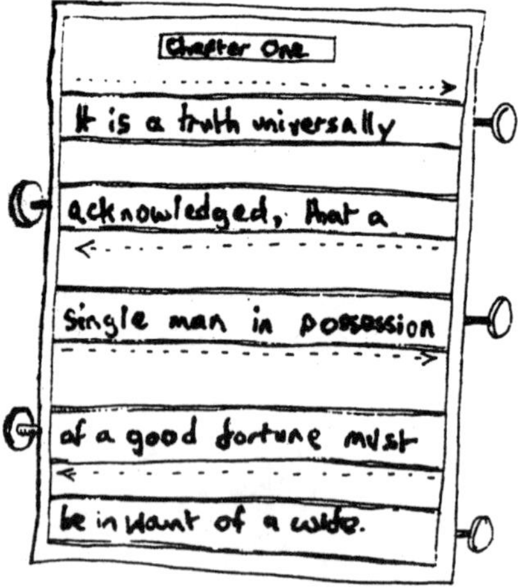

Figure 18.2.

Word retrieval

Jane explained that her frequent difficulty in retrieving the words she wanted often created an impression of having an immature vocabulary. This problem affected her both in written work and oral presentations. She felt embarrassed and was reluctant to speak in group situations. Often the pressure to substitute a different word for the one she wanted resulted in the intended meaning being altered or lost.

Jane devised an exercise to give workshop participants a sense of the frustration she experienced. She selected a paragraph from a topical newspaper article and highlighted several key words. She then asked the audience to work in pairs and asked one person to read aloud the paragraph to their partner, but with the stipulation that any highlighted words must be replaced by a similar word (or words). The communication problem was manifested by the halting nature of the reading and the difficulty the receiver had in understanding the content of the article.

Sentence structure

Ruth explained that her ideas often tumbled onto the paper in the same order as they appeared in her thoughts. With the help of her support tutor, she was able to identify a pattern which was common in many of her jumbled sentences. Ruth then demonstrated the strategy she had developed with her support tutor to help correct the word order in her sentences. She displayed a sentence which had been physically cut up into three sections and explained that by moving the sections around, she was able to improve the word order. This kinaesthetic strategy enabled her to improve her sentence structuring problems.

Handwriting

Issues of directionality and difficulties in motor co-ordination often cause dyslexic people to have poorly constructed, messy handwriting. An unsympathetic tutor may view this as the student's lack of concern for presentation. Simon described how embarrassed he felt about his handwriting; he particularly hated examinations where it was impossible to conceal his barely legible scrawl and he feared that the difficulty which tutors found in reading his script would work against him.

Simon asked his audience to write a short paragraph about what motivated them to come to this workshop. After a minute or so elapsed and he was confident that everyone was engaged in the flow of writing, he interrupted the group, apologizing for forgetting something. He asked them to put their pens down and then to pick them up again in the opposite hand – and continue writing. This activity usually elicits considerable discussion about how it feels to have to concentrate on aspects of letter formation, including directionality, being able to stay on the line, etc. and the consequent loss of attention to the content of what is being written.

Copying

Lucy explained that her difficulties with spelling coupled with her poor short-term memory resulted in a need to devote considerable concentration to copying from an overhead 'slide'. In addition to the load on short-term memory, she had to cope with finding her place on the overhead as well as maintaining the sequence of the letters and the words. The energy she expended because of the constant need to check meant that she was unable simultaneously to take in new information, so her ability to take notes in lectures was severely hampered.

To demonstrate the degree to which this slowed her down, she asked the audience to try to concentrate on her 'lecture' on dyslexia (she read aloud an abstract from a journal article, appropriately dealing with automaticity deficits) whilst copying some information from an overhead. The overhead which Lucy prepared said '*Dyslexia is not just a problem of reading and writing*' – but the sentence was written in Hebrew! (See Figure 18.3.)

Halfway through reading the abstract aloud, Lucy stopped and asked the audience what they had understood. The responses indicated that it was her own struggle which had been clearly communicated.

דיסלקסיה אינה רק בעיה של קריאה וכתיבה.

Figure 18.3.

Left/right confusion

Dyslexic difficulties are not confined to the academic sphere. David described how his difficulty in distinguishing between left and right had almost resulted in a divorce. He and his wife decided to take a class in ballroom dancing, as she was a keen dancer. Unfortunately, every time the instructor gave a direction to move the left foot, David moved his right – and stepped on his wife's toes! She was less than sympathetic, until his subsequent diagnosis of dyslexia provided an explanation for his difficulties in learning how to dance (see Figure 18.4).

David designed a simulation activity in which the audience was divided into two groups facing each other in a line. The dance instructor (David) gave directions for the step he was planning to teach. However, the opposing lines were given different instructions; one side was told to follow his call while the other group were told to do the opposite of what they heard. The resulting confusion was both amusing and illustrative of David's own experience. This exercise encouraged the lecturers to be active and to approach a task in a non-cerebral, kinaesthetic way.

Responses and results

Several positive outcomes for both students and staff have resulted from these workshops. Perhaps most significant of all is the fact that, by conveying

Figure 18.4.

their experiences in a meaningful way, the student participants were able to dissipate the frustration they felt at being misunderstood. Many students who participated in one workshop, volunteered to replicate it for another group of tutors. An exciting group dynamic emerged which resulted in individuals gaining confidence in their ability to communicate with academic staff. Group members have formed friendships and have supported one another in a variety of academic tasks.

The staff who attended these workshops have been overwhelmingly positive in their evaluations. The question 'What implications for your teaching has the workshop raised?' elicited responses such as:

> Awareness must lead to action.
>
> I shall reassess my teaching technique.
>
> There is a need for clarity in description – oral and written – without being overly prosaic.

Other, general comments, included:

> Excellent workshop – it must have taken courage for the students to expose their problems so openly.

> Fun but educational exercises.

> Interesting, lively presentation. Dyslexic students should be encouraged to stage more of these workshops. There is a need to reach more teaching staff.

The question and answer sessions at the end of each workshop generated lively discussion and exchange of ideas about teaching and learning. How often do students, dyslexic or not, gain a forum to talk to their tutors about approaches to improve the learning experience? This workshop format provided a unique opportunity for an often under-represented group to establish themselves as a significant voice. The composure and, in some cases, eloquence, which the students demonstrated in their presentations had a visible effect on the audience. It would have been difficult to come away from any of the presentations without feeling admiration for the courage and honesty demonstrated by all the presenters.

Another benefit, on a more global scale, was the 'cascade effect' resulting from the workshop. In one case, two lecturers from one academic department were so enthused by the insights gained during the workshop that they asked their head of department to make a similar workshop a compulsory part of a full day's staff development. This ensured that all members of that department had some awareness of the issues facing their dyslexic students. Of course, the inevitable consequence of ensuring that a wide number of staff have exposure to these issues is that all students will benefit if the teaching needs of dyslexic students are put on the agenda. Lecturers will be forced to re-assess their teaching approach and may be encouraged to adopt more multisensory teaching techniques.

Perhaps the most moving response I have had to these workshops is the reaction of a tutor from the School of Education. Martha spoke at the end of one workshop and explained that she had originally trained as a teacher of deaf and hearing-impaired children. She described how, as part of her training, she had been asked to listen to some tapes which were muffled and indistinct. The level of audibility – or inaudibility – made it extremely frustrating for a person of normal hearing to listen to. This experience had provided a sense of what it is like to be hearing impaired and how it feels to be constantly on the outside of whatever is going on.

Martha described this as one of the most illuminating and important parts of her training; however, the second time she'd experienced anything similar was in this workshop – and she wanted to thank the students for their willingness to share their insights into how they learn and what obstacles create barriers to their success. I, too, applaud those students and admire their strength and courage to open the eyes and minds of academics to a range of learning styles which demand a creative approach from teaching staff.

Acknowledgements

Thanks are due to Lindsay Peer for her assistance with Figure 18.3.

References

Abbs P (1974) Autobiography in Education: An Introduction to the Subjective Discipline of Autobiography and its Central Place in the Education of Teachers. London: Heinemann Educational Books.

Ainscow M (1998) Reaching Out to Everyone. TES (2.1.98).

Alston J (1992) Spelling Helpline. Manchester: Dextral Books.

Alston J (1995) Assessing and Promoting Writing Skills (new edition). Tamworth: NASEN.

Alston J, Taylor J (1990) Handwriting: Theory, Research and Practice. London: Routledge.

Augur J, Briggs S (eds) (1992) The Hickey Multi-Sensory Language Course (second edition). London: Whurr Publishers.

Balshaw M (1991) Help in the Classroom. London: Fulton.

Barbe WB, Swassing RH, Milone MN (1979) Teaching through Modality Strengths: Concepts and Practices. Columbus, Ohio: Zaner-Bloser.

Barnes C, Mercer G (1996) Exploring the Divide. Illness and Disability. Leeds: The Disability Press.

Barton D (1994) Literacy: An Introduction to the Ecology of Written Language. Oxford: Blackwell.

Barton RS, Fuhrmann BS (1994) Counselling and Psychotherapy for adults with learning disabilities. In: PJ Gerber, HB Reiff (eds). Learning Disabilities in Adulthood. Austin, TX: Pro-Ed; 82-92.

Barton D, Padmore S (1991) Roles, networks and values in everyday writing. In: D Barton, R Ivanic (eds). Writing in the Community. London: Sage; 58–77.

Bell N (1991) Visualizing and Verbalizing. Paso Robles, CA: Academy of Reading Publications.

Benson N, Gurney S, Harrison J, Rimmershaw R (1991) The Place of Academic Writing in Whole Life Writing: A case study. Department of Educational Research, University of Lancaster; 14.

Bentley T (1998) Learning Beyond the Classroom. London: Routledge.

Bialystock E (1988) Levels of bilingualism and levels of linguistic awareness. Developmental Psychology 24: 560–567.

Bigler ED (1992) The neurobiology and neuropsychology of adult learning disorders. Journal of Learning Disabilities 25: 448–506.

Binns RHF (1978) From Speech to Writing. Centre for Information on the Teaching of English. Scottish Curriculum Development Centre, Moray House College of Education, Edinburgh.

Binns RHF (1980) A technique for developing written language. In: MM Clark, T Glynn (eds). Reading and Writing for the Child with Difficulties. Ed Review, Occasional Paper No 8, University of Birmingham; 44–54.

Binns RHF (1984) Some issues in the teaching of spelling. In: D Dennis (ed.). Reading: Meeting Children's Special Needs. London: Heinemann; 144.

Binns RHF (1989) Re-creation through writing. In: M Hunter-Carsch (1989) The Art of Reading. Oxford: Blackwell; 100–110.

Binns RHF (1990) Monitoring the development of writing. In: M Hunter-Carsch, S Beverton, D Dennis (eds). Primary English in the National Curriculum. Oxford: Blackwell; 168–176.

Binns R, Sobey J, Hunter-Carsch M (1991) Creating young writers. Language and Learning 5: 9–12.

Bishop DVM (1989) Test for the Reception of Grammar (TROG). Oxford: Medical Research Council.

Bishop DVM, Edmundson A (1987) Specific language impairment as a maturational lag: evidence from longitudinal data on language and motor development. Developmental Medicine and Child Neurology 29.

Blagg N, Ballinger M, Gardner R (1993) Handbook, Somerset Thinking Skills (revised edition). Taunton: Nigel Blagg Associates.

Bloom BS et al. (1956). Taxonomy of Educational Goals: Handbook 1: Cognitive Domain. New York: David McKay.

Bloome D, Theodorou E (1985) Reading, writing and learning in the classroom. Peabody Journal of Education 62: 20–43.

Booth T, Ainscow M, Black-Hawkins K, Vaughan M, Shaw L (2000) Index for Inclusion: Developing Learning and Participation in Schools. Bristol: Centre for Studies on Inclusive Education (CSIE) (website: http://inclusion@uwe.ac.uk).

Bowering-Carr C, West-Burnham J (1997) Effective Learning in Schools. London: Pitman.

Bradley L (1985) Spelling SOS: Poor Spellers, Poor Readers: Understanding the Problems. Reading: The Centre for the Teaching of Reading.

Brand V (1984) Spelling Made Easy. Baldock: Egon Publishers.

Briggs Myers I (1980) Gifts Differing. California: Consulting Psychologists' Press Inc.

British Psychological Society DECP Working Party Report (1999) Dyslexia, Literacy and Psychological Assessment. Leicester: BPS.

Brookfield S (1989) Myths and realities in adult education. RAPAL Bulletin 10, University of Lancaster, RAPAL.

Brooks P, Weeks S (1999) Individual styles in learning to spell: improving spelling in children with literacy difficulties and all children in mainstream schools. London: DfEE.

Brown DA, Ellis NC (1994) Handbook of Spelling: Theory, Process and Intervention. Chichester: John Wiley & Sons.

Brown GDA, Watson F (1991) Reading development in dyslexia: a connectionist approach. In: M Snowling, M Thomson (eds). Dyslexia: Integrating Theory and Practice. London: Whurr Publishers; 165–183.

Bruck M (1990) Word-recognition skills of adults with childhood diagnoses of dyslexia. Developmental Psychology 26: 439–454.

Bruck M (1993) Word recognition and component phonological processing skills of adults with childhood diagnosis of dyslexia. Developmental Review 13: 258–268.

Bruck M, Genesee F (1995) Phonological awareness in young second language learners. Journal of Child Language 22: 307–324.

Bryant P, Nunes T, Bindman M (1999) Children's understanding of the connection between grammar and spelling. In: B Blatchman (ed.). Linguistic Underpinnings of Language. Hillsdale, NJ: Lawrence Erlbaum.

Buber M (1958) Ich und Du (second edition). Translated by RG Smith. Edinburgh: T&T Clark.

Butt RL, Raymond D (1989) Supporting the nature and development of teachers' knowledge using collaborative autobiography. International Journal of Educational Research 13: 403–419.

Buzan T (1993) The Mind Map Book. London: BBC.

Campbell R, Sais E (1995) Accelerated metalinguistic (phonological) awareness in bilingual children. British Journal of Developmental Psychology 13: 61–68.

Caravolas M, Bruck M (1993) The effect of oral and written language input on children's phonological awareness: a cross-linguistic study. Journal of Experimental Child Psychology 55: 1–30.

Carrell PL (1988) Some causes of text-boundedness and schema interference in ESL reading. In: PL Carrell, J Devine, DE Eskey (eds). Interactive Approaches to Second Language Reading. Cambridge: Cambridge University Press; 101–113.

Chapman V (1998) Praxis makes perfect too: dyspraxia: an essential guide for parents and teachers. In P Hunt (ed.). The Voice of Experience: Parental Perceptions of Dyspraxia. Hitchin: Dyspraxia Foundation; 55–67.

Charnley AH, Jones HA (1979) The Concept of Success. London: Huntington Publishers.

Chasty H (1987) Adult Dyslexia Checklist. Available from the BDA (British Dyslexia Association), 98 London Road, Reading, Berkshire, RG1 5AU. Also available from ADO (Adult Dyslexia Organisation) 336 Brixton Road, London, SW9 7AA.

Chasty HT, Friel J (1991) Children with Special Needs. London: Jessica Kingsley.

Christenson S, Ysseldyke J, Algozzine B (1982) Instructional constraints and external pressures influencing referral decisions. Psychology in Schools 19: 341–345.

Clarke R (1994) Learning Support for Dyslexic Students in Higher Education. Workshop Paper at the 1st 'Writing Development in Higher Education' Conference. University of Northumbria, Newcastle upon Tyne: Communication Unit and Writing and Numeracy Development Centre.

Cline T, Reason R (1993) Specific learning difficulties (dyslexia): equal opportunities issues. British Journal of Special Education 20: 1.

Cline T, Shamsi T (2000) Language Needs or Special Needs: The Assessment of Learning Difficulties in Literacy among Children Learning English as an Additional Language: A Literature Review. London: DfEE Publications.

Clough P, Corbett J (2000) Theories of Inclusive Education: A Student's Guide. London: Chapman.

Comber B (1985) Towards independence in spelling. British Journal of Special Education: 12(2).

Cooke A (1997) Learning to spell difficult words: why look, cover, write and check is not enough. Dyslexia 3: 240–243.

Cooke S (1998) Collaborative Learning in the Classroom. Resource Centre for Multicultural Education, Forest Lodge Education Centre, Charnor Road, Leicester, LE3 6LH.

Cortazzi M, Hunter-Carsch M (2000) Multilingualism and literacy difficulties. Reading 34: 39–45.

Cortazzi M, Jin L (1997) Communication for learning across cultures. In: D McNamara, R Harris (eds). Overseas Students in Higher Education: Issues in Teaching and Learning. London: Routledge; 76–90.

Costello PJM, Mitchell S (1995). Competing and Consensual Voices. The Theory and Practice of Argument. Clevedon: Multilingual Matters.

Cottrell, SnG (1996) Lexically proficient dyslexic students in higher education. In: Dyslexia in Higher Education, Learning Along the Continuum. 2nd International Conference. Conference Proceedings. University of Plymouth; 17–24.

Cowdery L, Montgomery D, Morse P, Prince M (1988) Teaching Reading Through Spelling (The Kingston Programme). Clwyd: Frondeg Hall Technical Publishing.

Cripps C (1992) A Hand for Spelling. Cambridge: Cambridge University Press.

Crombie A, Crombie M (2001) ICT-based interactive learning. In: M Hunter-Carsch (ed.). Dyslexia: A Psycho-social Perspective. London: Whurr Publishers; 219–231.

Crombie M (1994) Specific Learning Difficulties (Dyslexia) A Teacher's Guide. Glasgow: Jordanhill College Press.

Crombie M (1996) Specific Learning Difficulties (Dyslexia) A Teacher's Guide (second edition). Michigan: Ann Arbor Publications.

Cruickshank W (1963) Handbook for Teaching Hyperactive Brain-injured Children. Syracuse, NY: Syracuse University Press.

Cummins J (1979) Linguistic interdependence and the educational development of bilingual children. Review of Educational Research 49: 222–251.

Cummins J (1984) Bilingualism and Special Education: Issues in Assessment and Pedagogy. Clevedon: Multilingual Matters.

Curnyn JC, Wallace I, Kistan P, McLaren M (1991) Special Educational Need and Ethnic Minority Pupils. Edinburgh: Scottish Office Education Department.

Czerniewska P (1989) National writing project. In: M Hunter-Carsch (ed.). The Art of Reading. Oxford: Blackwell; 57–66.

Daniels J, Diack H (1960) The Standard Reading Tests. London: Chatto & Windus.

Davidson B, Moore J (1996) Across the primary–secondary divide. In: S Hart (ed.). Differentiation and the Secondary Curriculum. London: Routledge; 26–38.

Davies A (1988) The Handwriting, Reading and Spelling System. Chester: THRASS UK Ltd.

Davies A, Ritchie D (1988) THRASS Resource File. Chester: THRASS UK Ltd.

Davis RD (1994) The Gift of Dyslexia. California: Souvenir Press.

De Bono E (1986) CORT Thinking. Oxford: Pergamon Press.

De Luynes M, Zdzienski D (1992) The Hornsby Neurolinguistic Course Handbook. London: Hornsby Publications.

Department for Education and Employment (1988) Meeting Special Needs.

Department for Education and Employment and the Welsh Office (1994) Code of Practice on the Identification and Assessment of Special Educational Needs. London: Central Office of Information.

Department for Education and Employment (1995) English in the National Curriculum. Department for Education and the Welsh Office. London: HMSO.

Department for Education and Employment (1997) Excellence for All Children. London: HMSO.

Department for Education and Employment (1998) National Literacy Strategy Framework for Teaching. London: HMSO.

Department for Education and Employment (2000a) Draft Revision of the Code of Practice on the Identification and Assessment of Children with Special Educational Needs. London: DfEE.

Department for Education and Employment (2000b) Removing the Barriers. Raising Achievement Levels for Minority Ethnic Pupils. Sudbury: DfEE Publications.

Department for Education and Employment (2000c) (DfEE/OISE/UT) Watching and Learning - Evaluation of the Implementation of the National Literacy and Numeracy Strategies. Earl L, Fullan M, Leithwood K, Watson N, Gantzi D, Levin B, Torrance N. London: DfEE. DfEE website: http://inclusion.ngfl.gov.uk.

Department of Education and Science (1978) The Warnock Report, Special Educational Needs. London: HMSO.

Deponio P, Landon J, Mullen K, Reid G (1999) An Audit of the Processes Involved in Identifying and Assessing Bilingual Learners Suspected of Being Dyslexic: A Scottish Study. Paper presented at the British Dyslexia Association's first International Conference on Dyslexia and Multilingualism at Manchester University in June 1999.

Dunn LM, Dunn LM, Whetton D (1982) British Picture Vocabulary Scale. Windsor: NFER-Nelson.

Durgunoglu AY, Nagy WE, Hancin-Bhatt BJ (1993) Cross-language transfer of phonological awareness. Journal of Educational Psychology 85: 453–465.

Edwards J (1994) The Scars of Dyslexia. London: Cassell.

Ehri L (1980) The influence of orthography on readers' conceptualisation of the phonemic structure of words. Applied Psycholinguistics 1: 371–385.

Ehri L (1995) The emergence of word reading in beginning reading. In: P Owen, P Pumfrey (eds). Emergent and Developing Reading: Messages for Teachers. London: The Falmer Press; 9–31.

Ellis AW (1989) Reading, Writing and Dyslexia: A Cognitive Analysis. Exeter: A Wheaton & Co.

Ellis AW, McDougall SJP, Monk AF (1996) Are dyslexics different? II Individual differences among dyslexics. Dyslexia: Journal of the British Dyslexia Association 2(1): 59-68.

Elsey B, Gibb M (1981) Voluntary tutors in adult literacy. A survey of adult literacy volunteers in the Nottingham area. Nottingham Working Papers in the Education of Adults, University of Nottingham, Department of Adult Education.

Ezard J (1998) Guardian 20th January report quoting B Richards from The Oxford Magazine for Students.

Felton RH, Naylor CE, Wood FB (1990) Neuropsychological profile of adult dyslexics. Brain and Language 39: 485–497.

Fenton M, Hughes P (1989) Passivity to Empowerment. London: Radar.

Fernald G (1943) Remedial Techniques in Basic School Subjects (second edition). New York: MacGraw-Hill.

Feuerstein R, Rand Y, Hoffman MB (1979) The Dynamic Assessment of Retarded Performers. Baltimore, MD: University Park Press.

Feuerstein R, Rand Y, Hoffman MB, Muller R (1980) Instrumental Enrichment. Baltimore, MD: University Press.

Fink R (1995) Successful dyslexics: a constructivist study of passionate interest reading. Journal of Adolescent and Adult Literacy 39(4): 268–280.

Finucci JM, Gottfredson L, Childs B (1985) A follow up study of dyslexic boys. Annals of Dyslexia 35: 117–136.

Fisher R (1990) Teaching Children to Think. Oxford: Blackwell.

Fisher-Marriott R, Hughes M (1999) Starspell 2001. Woodbridge, Suffolk: Fisher-Marriott Software.

Flavell JH (1976) Metacognitive aspects of problem solving. In LB Resnick (ed.). The Nature of Intelligence. Hillsdale, NJ: Erlbaum.

Francis H (1994) Teachers Listening to Learners' Voices. Thirteenth Vernon Wall Lecture. British Psychological Society Education Section.

Frederickson N, Frith U (1998) Identifying dyslexia in bilingual children: a phonological approach with Inner London Sylheti speakers. Dyslexia 4: 119-131.

Frederickson N, Frith U, Reason R (1997) The Phonological Assessment Battery (standardization edition). Windsor: NFER-Nelson.

Freire P (1972) Pedagogy of the Oppressed. London: Penguin.

Freire P, Macedo D (1987) Literacy: Reading the Word and the World. South Hadley, MA: Bergin & Garvey.

Frisby CL, Braden JP (1992) Feuerstein's dynamic assessment approach: a semantic, logical and empirical critique. Journal of Special Education 26: 3.

Frith U (1980) Cognitive Processes in Spelling. London: Academic Press.

Frith U, Landerl K, Frith C (1995) Dyslexia and verbal fluency: more evidence for a phonological deficit. Dyslexia 1: 2-11.

Gains C (1995) Reading: issues and directions. In C Gains, D Wray (eds). Reading: Issues and Directions. Stafford: UKRA, NASEN, Nasen Enterprises.

Galaburda AM (ed.) (1993) Dyslexia and Development: Neurological Aspects of Extra-Ordinary Brains. Cambridge, MA: Harvard University Press.

Galton M, Ruddick J, Gray J (in press) The Transfer and Transition Project. A DfEE-supported project at Homerton College, Cambridge and the University of Leicester.

Gardener S (1999/2000) Student writing in the 1970s and 1980s. RAPAL Bulletin 40: 8-11.

Gardner H (1984) Frames of Mind. The Theory of Multiple Intelligences. Guernsey: Guernsey Press Co Ltd.

Gardner H (1995) Leading Minds. New York: Basic Books.

Gee JP (1988) The legacies of literacy: from Plato to Freire through Harvey Graff. A review article of Graff HG (1987) The Legacy of Literacy. Continuities and Contradictions in Western Culture and Society. Bloomington: Indiana University Press. Harvard Educational Review 58: 195-212.

Gerber PJ, Ginsberg R, Reiff HB (1992) Identifying alterable patterns in employment success for highly successful adults with learning disabilities. Journal of Learning Disabilities 25: 475-487.

Gilroy DE (1996) Dyslexia and Higher Education (revised edition). Bangor University; Dyslexia Unit.

Gilroy DE, Miles TR (1983) Dyslexia at College. London: Routledge.

Gilroy DE, Miles TR (1996) Dyslexia at College (second edition). London: Routledge.

Given B, Reid G (1999) Learning Styles: St. Anne's-on-Sea: Red Rose Publications.

Goleman D (1996) Emotional Intelligence. London: Bloomsbury.

Goodwin V (1996a) Counselling of dyslexic students in higher education. In C Stephens (ed.). Dyslexic Students in Higher Education. Practical Responses to Student and Institutional Needs. Conference Proceedings, SKILL/University of Huddersfield; 55-56.

Goodwin V (1996b) Person-centred counselling for the dyslexic student. In: Dyslexia in Higher Education, Learning along the Continuum. Second International Conference, Conference Proceedings, University of Plymouth; 28-29.

Gordon N, McKinlay I (1980) Helping Clumsy Children. London: Churchill Livingstone.

Goswami U (1993) Orthographic analogies and reading development. The Psychologist 6: 312-316.

Goswami U, Bryant PE (1990) Phonological Skills and Learning to Read. Hove: Lawrence Erlbaum.

Graham RJ (1991) Reading and Writing the Self. Autobiography in Education and the Curriculum. New York and London: Teacher's College Press, Columbia University.

Gregory E (1994) Cultural assumptions and early years pedagogy: the effect of the home culture on minority children's interpretation of reading at school. Language, Culture and Curriculum 7: 1-14.

Gregory E (1996) Making Sense of a New World: Learning to Read in a Second Language. London: Paul Chapman.

Guppy P, Hughes M (1999) The Development of Independent Reading: Buckingham: Open University Press.

Haase P (ed.) (2000) Schreiben und Lesen sicher lehren und lernen. Dortmund: Borgmann.

Haase P, Hunter-Carsch M (2001) A 'Dyslexic Friendly' Approach to Individualised Learning of Initial Literacy in Mainstream Schools. Paper presented at the fifth BDA International Conference at York University, April 2001.

Hales G (1994) The human aspects of dyslexia. In: G Hales (ed.). Dyslexia Matters. London: Whurr Publishers.

Hall D (1995) Assessing the Needs of Bilingual Pupils: Living in Two Languages. London: David Fulton.

Hampshire S (1990) Every Letter Counts: Winning in Life Despite Dyslexia. London: Transworld Publishers.

Hanley JR (1997) Reading and spelling impairments in undergraduate students with developmental dyslexia. Journal of Research in Reading 20: 22–30.

Hanley JR, Gard F (1995) A dissociation between developmental surface and phonological dyslexia in two undergraduate students. Neuropsychologia 33: 909–914.

Harste JC (1994) Literacy as curricular conversations about knowledge, inquiry and morality. In: RB Ruddell, MR Ruddell, H Singer (eds). Theoretical Models and Processes of Reading. Newark, NJ: International Reading Association; 1220–1242.

Hart S (1996a) Differentiation and the Secondary Curriculum: Debates and Dilemmas. London: Routledge.

Hart S (1996b) Beyond Special Needs: Encouraging Children's Learning Through Thinking. London: Paul Chapman.

Hart S, Travers P (1999) Bilingual Learners and the Code of Practice; Multicultural Teaching. Stoke-on-Trent: Trentham Books.

Hayward K, Brooks P, Burns S (1992) Bright Start: Cognitive Curriculum for Young Children. USA: Charles Bridge.

Henderson A (2001) Mathematically thinking. In: M Hunter-Carsch (ed.). Dyslexia: A Psycho-social Perspective. London: Whurr Publishers; 205–218.

Henderson EH, Beers JW (eds) (1980) Developmental and Cognitive Aspects of Learning to Spell: A Reflection of Word Knowledge. Newarks, DE: International Reading Association.

Herrington M (1983) Final Report on the ALBSU Special Development Project: Distance Learning in Rural Areas in Leicestershire. London: ALBSU.

Herrington M (1986) Student and Tutor Drop out in the Adult Literacy Scheme 1978-80. MEd Thesis. University of Leicester.

Herrington M (1994) Learning at home. Distance learning in adult basic education. In M Hamilton, D Barton, R Ivanic (eds). Worlds of Literacy. Clevedon: Multilingual Matters; 182–187.

Herrington M (1995) New policies: old dilemmas. RAPAL bulletin 27. University of Lancaster: RAPAL; 3–99.

Herrington M (1996) RAPAL 1996: a turning point. In: S Fitzpatrick, J Mace (eds). Lifelong Literacies. Conference proceedings from RAPAL 1996 Conference; 71–73.

Herrington M (1997) Workshop paper on 'Dyslexia and Time' at Annual RAPAL Conference, Goldsmiths College, University of London.

Herrington M (ed.) (1998) Exploring dyslexia. Report of a student/tutor research group 1987–1989. Unpublished, available from editor.

Herrington M, Hunter-Carsch M (2001) A social interactive model. In: M Hunter-Carsch (ed.). Dyslexia: A Psycho-social Perspective. London: Whurr Publishers; 107–134.

Hetherington J (1996) Approaches to the development of self-esteem in dyslexic students. In: Conference Proceedings: Dyslexic Students in Higher Education, Practical Responses to Student and Institutional Needs. SKILL/University of Huddersfield; 57–61.

Hinton R (1993) Dyslexia and the University Student – A Guide for Staff. Loughborough University, Loughborough.

HM Inspectors of Schools (1996) The Education of Pupils with Language and Communication Difficulties. Edinburgh: HMSO.

Hornsby B, Shear F (1974) Alpha to Omega. London: Heinemann.

Houghton G (1995/96) Who says so ... Who? RAPAL Bulletin 28/29. University of Lancaster: RAPAL; 9–15.

Hunter M (1982) Reading and learning difficulties: relationship and responsibilities. In: A Hendry (ed.). Teaching Reading: The Keys Issues. London: Heinemann Educational Books; 85, 141–152.

Hunter-Carsch M (1989) The Art of Reading. Oxford: Blackwell; 5.

Hunter-Carsch M (1990) Learning strategies for pupils with literacy difficulties: motivation, meaning and imagery. In P Pumfrey, C Elliot (eds). Children's Difficulties in Reading, Spelling and Writing. London: The Falmer Press; 222–236.

Hunter-Carsch M (1991) Celebrating oracy as well as literacy in in-service education in specific learning difficulties. In C Harrison, E Ashton (eds). Celebrating and Defending Literacy. Oxford: Blackwell; 141–154.

Hunter-Carsch M (1993) Reason, rhythm, relaxation and the new literacy: implications for curricular differentiation to meet the special needs of pupils with specific learning difficulties. In SF Wright, R Groner (eds). Facets of Dyslexia and Its Remediation. Amsterdam: Elsevier Science Publishers; 513–539.

Hunter-Carsch M (1996) Access to independent learning through curricular differentiation. In G Reid (ed.). Dimensions of Dyslexia, Volume 2, Literacy, Language and Learning. Edinburgh: Moray House Publications; 359–375.

Hunter-Carsch M (1998) Developing literacy at 11: evaluation of the Leicester Summer Literacy Schools. Leicester City LEA and the School of Education, University of Leicester.

Hunter-Carsch M (2001a) Seeing the wood for the trees. In: M Hunter-Carsch (ed.). Dyslexia: A Psycho-social Perspective. London: Whurr Publishers; 3–31.

Hunter-Carsch M (2001b) Restructuring the standard approach. In: M Hunter-Carsch (ed.). Dyslexia: A Psycho-social Perspective. London: Whurr Publishers; 49–84.

Hunter-Carsch M (2001c) Beyond meta-cognition. In: M Hunter-Carsch (ed.). Dyslexia: A Psycho-social Perspective. London: Whurr Publishers; 85–106.

Idrisano R (1987) Testimony to the inter-agency committee on learning disabilities of the National Institutes of Health. Reading Today 4.

ILEA (1985) Educational Opportunities for All? Research Studies. Fish Report Vol. 2. London: ILEA.

Ivanic R (1996) Linguistics and the logic of non-standard punctuation. In N Hall, A Robinson (eds). Learning About Punctuation. Bristol: Multilingual Matters; 148–169.

Ivanic R (1998) Writing and Identity. The Discoursal Construction of Identity in Academic Writing. Amsterdam/Philadelphia: John Benjamin.

Ivanic R, Simpson J (1988) Clearing away the debris: learning and researching academic writing. RAPAL Bulletin 6, Lancaster University: RAPAL; 6–7.

Jeffrey J, Maginn C (1979) Who Needs Literacy Provision. London: Macmillan.

Jensen J (1993) Universal Shapes. John Jensen.

Johnson M, Phillips S, Peer L (1999) A Multisensory Teaching System for Reading. Based on MTS by Margaret Taylor-Smith. Manchester Metropolitan University.

Jorm AF, Share DL, Matthews R, Mackon (1986) Behaviour problems in specific reading retarded and general reading backward children: a longitudinal study. Journal of Child Psychology and Psychiatry 27: 33–43.

Joyce B, Calhoun E, Hopkins D (1997) Models of Learning – Tools for Teaching. Buckingham: Open University Press.

Katz L, Goldstein G, Rushden S, Bailey D (1993) A neuropsychological approach to the Bannatyne recategorisation of the Wechsler Intelligence Scales in adults with learning disabilities. Journal of Learning Disabilities 26: 65–72.

Kimura Y, Bryant PE (1983) Reading and writing in English and Japanese. British Journal of Developmental Psychology 1: 129–144.

Klein C (1989) Specific learning difficulties. ALBSU Newsletter No 32. (A summary of the ALBSU Project); 1–4.

Klein C (1994) Diagnosing Dyslexia. London: Adult Literacy and Basic Skills Unit.

Klein C, Miller R (1990) Unscrambling Spelling. London: Hodder & Stoughton.

Knowles M (1985) Andragogy in Action. San Francisco, CA: Jossey Bass.

Kohl H (1971) 36 Children. Harmondsworth: Penguin.

Krupska M, Klein C (1995) Demystifying Dyslexia. London: Language and Literacy Unit. (Now based at the South Bank University, London.)

Labuda MC, Defries JC (1989) Differential prognosis of reading disabled children as a function of gender, socio-economic status, IQ and severity: a longitudinal study. Reading and Writing 1: 25–36.

Lake M, Needham M (undated) Top Ten Thinking Tactics. Birmingham: Questions Publishing Company.

Landon J (1996) Reading between the languages: bilingual learners and specific learning difficulties. In: G Reid (ed.). Dimensions of Dyslexia: Vol. 2, Literacy, Language and Learning. Edinburgh: Moray House Institute of Education; 217–228.

Landon J (1998) Early Intervention with Bilingual Learners: Evaluation. Report on a Research Project funded by the City of Edinburgh Education Department. Edinburgh: Moray House Institute of Education.

Lannen S, Lannen D, Reid G (1997) Specific Learning Difficulties: Resources. St Anne's-on-Sea: Red Rose Publishers.

Larsen D (1999) Yak-Yak – The Language Processor. Copenhagen, Denmark. Paper presented at the BDA's first international conference on Multilingualism and Dyslexia. Manchester University, June 1999.

Lawrence G (1983) People Types and Tiger Stripes. Oxford: Oxford Psychologists' Press.

Lazo MG, Pumfrey PD, Peers I (1997) Metalinguistic awareness, reading and spelling: roots and branches of literacy. Journal of Research in Reading 20: 85–104.

Lefly D, Pennington B (1991) Spelling errors and reading fluency in compensated adult dyslexia. Annals of Dyslexia 41: 143–162.

Leong CK (1997) Effects of Children's Phonologic-Orthographic Processing on Spelling - A Developmental Study. Paper presented at the 4th World Congress on Dyslexia. Thessaloniki, Macedonia, Greece, September 1997.

Levine K (1985) The Social Context of Literacy. London: Routledge & Kegan Paul.

Lidz CS (ed.) (1987) Dynamic Assessment: An Interactional Approach to Evaluating Learning Potential. London: The Guilford Press.

Lummis T (1987) Listening to History: The Authenticity of Oral Evidence. London: Hutchinson Education.

Lunzer E, Gardner K (1979) The Effective Use of Reading. London: Heinemann (for Schools Council).

Mace J (1979) Working with Words. Literacy Beyond School. London: Writers and Readers Publishing Co-operative in association with Chameleon.

Mace J (1992) Talking about Literacy: Principles and Practice of Adult Literacy Education. London and New York: Routledge.

MacKay N (1999) Building a dyslexic friendly school. Dyslexia Contact 18: 26.

Maeland AF (1992) Identification of Dyslexia Subtypes based on Deficient Reading and Spelling Strategies. Skrifters 5, Norwegian Society of Sciences and Letters, University of Trondheim, Norway.

Mailley S (2001) Visual difficulties with print. In: M Hunter-Carsch (ed.). Dyslexia: A Psycho-social Perspective. London: Whurr Publishers; 39–48.

Manis FR, Custodio R, Szesuiski PA (1993) Development of phonological and orthographic skill: a 2-year longitudinal study of dyslexic children. Journal of Experimental Child Psychology 56: 64–86.

Markee A (1995) A Hand for Handwriting.

Martin-Jones M, Bhatt A (1998) Literacies in the lives of young Gujarati speakers in Leicester. In AY Durgunoglu, L Verhoeven (eds). Literacy Development in a Multilingual Context. Mahwah, NJ: Lawrence Erlbaum; 37–50.

McCarthy D (1972) McCarthy Scales of Children's Abilities. San Antonio, TX: Psychological Corporation.

McClelland N (1997) Building a Literate Nation: The Strategic Agenda for Literacy over the Next Five Years. Stoke-on-Trent: Trentham Press.

McLaren PL (1988) Culture or canon? Critical pedagogy and the politics of literacy. Harvard Educational Review 58: 213–234.

McLoughlin D, Fitzgibbon G, Young V (1994) Adult Dyslexia: Assessment, Counselling and Training. London: Whurr Publishers.

McMillan G, Leslie M (1998) The Early Intervention Handbook: Intervention in Literacy. Edinburgh: City of Edinburgh Council Education Department.

McNamara S, Moreton H (1995) Changing Behaviour: Teaching Children with Emotional and Behavioural Difficulties in Primary and Secondary Schools. London: David Fulton.

McNeil C (1995) Peer Tutoring. Centre for Citizenship. University of Leicester. Northampton: University of Leicester and Kingfisher Press.

Michelson C (1995) Out of the Frying Pan into the Fire. Some Observations on Supporting Dyslexic Students Who Have Progressed to University. RAPAL Bulletin 27. Lancaster University: RAPAL; 22–24.

Miles E (2001) Aspects of Spelling: Historical Influences; Paper presented at a day conference on Aspects of Grammar for Writing, at the University of Leicester, March 2001.

Miles T (2001) Reflections and research. In: M Hunter-Carsch (ed.). Dyslexia: A Psychosocial Perspective. London: Whurr Publishers; 32–38.

Miles TR (1982) The Bangor Dyslexia Test. Cambridge: Learning Development Aids.
Miles T, Varma V (eds) (1995) Dyslexia and Stress. London: Whurr Publishers.
Miller I (1984) Problem solving, hypothesis testing and language disorders. In: GP Wallach, KG Butler (eds). Language Learning Disabilities in School-age Children. Baltimore, MD: Williams & Wilkins.
Mirkin P, Potter M (1982) A Survey of Program Planning and Implementation Practices of LD Teachers. Research Report No 80, University of Minnesota, Institute for Research on Learning Disabilities.
Montessori M (1967a) The Montessori Method. New York: Shocken Books.
Montessori M (1967b) The Absorbent Mind. New York: Dell.
Montgomery D (1997) Spelling Remedial Strategies. London: Cassell.
Moore M-S (1994) The emotional impact of dyslexia on the adult learner professional: 'Truth, Believing and Reality Testing'. In: Dyslexia in Higher Education: Learning Along the Continuum. International Conference Papers, Dartington Hall, Devon, UK, 31 Oct. to 2 Nov. 1994.
Moorhouse C (1977) Helping Adults to Spell. London: Adult Literacy Resource Agency. (Now the Basic Skills Agency, BSA),
Morgan E (1995) Releasing potential in the dyslexic writer. RAPAL Bulletin 27. Lancaster University: RAPAL; 27–33.
Morgan E, Klein C (2000) The Dyslexic Adult in a Non-dyslexic World. London: Whurr Publishers.
Morris J (1984) Phonics 44 for initial literacy in English. Reading 8: 13–22.
Morris J (1993) Phonicsphobia. In: B Hornsby (ed.). Literacy 2000. London: Hornsby International Centre; 29–38.
Moseley D, Nicol C (1989) Aurally Coded Spelling Dictionary. Wisbech: LDA.
Moss W, Cairns T (1995) Students with Specific Learning Difficulties. A Research Report. London: Goldsmiths College, University of London.
Moyles J (1997) Jills of All Trades. London: ATL.
Murphy R, Burke P, Gillespie J, Rainbow R, Wilmut J (1997) The Key Skills of Students Entering Higher Education. Report of a Project Commissioned by the Department for Education and Employment. Nottingham: University of Nottingham School of Education.
Norwich B (1996) Special Needs Education, Inclusive Education or Just Education for All? Inaugural lecture, London University Institute of Education.
Nunes T, Bryant P, Bindman M (1997) Morphological spelling strategies: developmental stages and processes. Developmental Psychology 33: 637–649.
OFSTED (1999) Pupils with Specific Learning Difficulties in Mainstream Schools. London: Office for Standards in Education.
O'Malley JM, Chamot AU (1990) Learning Strategies in Second Language Acquisition. Cambridge: Cambridge University Press.
O'Neill JO (1974) The failures of literacy schemes. Adult Education 47: 356–363.
Orton ST (1932) Special Disability in Spelling, Word-Blindness in School Children and Other Papers on Strephosymbolia 1966. Baltimore, MD: Orton Dyslexia Association.
O'Shea J, Dalton J (1994) Dyslexia: How Do We Learn? Melbourne, Australia: Hill of Content Publishing Company.
Ott P (1997) How to Detect and Manage Dyslexia. Oxford: Heinemann.
Otto W (1986) Ysseldyke and Algozzine – these two guys are friends of mine. Journal of Reading 29: 572–575.

Otto W, McMenemy RA, Smith RJ (1973) Corrective and Remedial Teaching. Boston, MA: Houghton Mifflin.

Patton JR, Polloway EA (1996) Learning Disabilities: The Challenges of Adulthood. Austin, TX: Pro-Ed.

Peer L (1996) Winning with Dyslexia. Reading: British Dyslexia Association.

Peer L (2001) Dyslexia and multilingual matters. In: M Hunter-Carsch (ed.). Dyslexia: A Psycho-social Perspective. London: Whurr Publishers; 187–204.

Peer L, Reid G (2000) Multilingualism, Literacy and Dyslexia. London: David Fulton.

Pennington BF, Van Orden GC, Smith SD, Green PA, Haith MM (1990) Phonological processing skills and deficits in adult dyslexics. Child Development 61: 1753–1778.

Peters M (1967) Spelling Caught or Taught? London: Routledge & Kegan Paul.

Peters M (1983) Teaching Spelling, guest lecture to teachers at Elmbank Teachers' Centre, Coventry 17/9/83.

Peters M (1985) Spelling Caught or Taught: A New Look. London: Routledge.

Peters M, Smith B (1993) Spelling in Context. Slough: NFER-Nelson.

Pollak D (1996) Learning life histories of higher education students who are dyslexic. In: Dyslexia in Higher Education, Learning Along the Continuum. 2nd International Conference. Conference Proceedings, University of Plymouth; 46–52.

Pool (1993) On the video of the Literacy Conference at the Hornsby International Centre.

Poussu-Olli H-S (2001) Adult dyslexia: research and practice. In: M Hunter-Carsch (ed.). Dyslexia: A Psycho-social Perspective. London: Whurr Publishers; 160–173.

Preston M, Gorbold J (1996) The special needs of mature dyslexic students. In: Dyslexia in Higher Education, Learning Along the Continuum. 2nd International Conference. Conference Proceedings. University of Plymouth; 24–27.

Pumfrey P (2001) Specific developmental dyslexia. In: M Hunter-Carsch (ed.). Dyslexia: A Psycho-social Perspective. London: Whurr Publishers; 137–159.

Rack J (1997) Issues in the assessment of developmental dyslexia in adults: theoretical and applied perspectives. Journal of Research in Reading (Special issue: Dyslexia in Literate Adults) 20: 66–76.

Ramsden M (1993) Rescuing Spelling. Crediton: Southgate Spelling; 2.

Raven JC (1993) Progressive Matrices A, Ab, B. Oxford: Psychologists' Press.

Read C, Zhang Y-F, Nie H, Ding B (1986) The ability to manipulate speech sounds depends on knowing alphabetic spelling. Cognition 24: 31–44.

Reid G (1996a) Dimensions of Dyslexia, Volume 1, Assessment, Teaching and the Curriculum. Edinburgh: Moray House Publications.

Reid G (1996b) Dimensions of Dyslexia, Volume 2, Literacy, Language and Learning. Edinburgh: Moray House Publications.

Reid G (1998) A Practitioner's Handbook (second edition). Chichester: John Wiley & Sons.

Reid G (2001) Specialist teacher training in the UK. In: M Hunter-Carsch (ed.). Dyslexia: A Psycho-social Perspective. London: Whurr Publishers; 254–264.

Riddick B, Farmer M, Sterling C (1997) Students and Dyslexia. Growing Up With a Specific Learning Difficulty. London: Whurr Publishers.

Riding R, Rayner S (1998) Cognitive Styles and Learning Strategies. London: David Fulton.

Rivis V (1994) Learning from Audit. London: Higher Education Quality Council.

Rivis V, Herrington M (1994) Guidance and Counselling in Higher Education.. London: Higher Education Quality Council.

Roth FP (1987) Discourse Abilities of Learning Disabled Students: Patterns and Intervention Strategies, Workshop presented at the Language Learning Disabilities Institute. Emerson College, Boston, MA.

Sage R (1986) A Question of Language Disorder. Trent Region Medical Council Project.

Sage R (1990) Information Processing in Normally Functioning Primary School Children Compared with Those with Language Impairment. MPhil thesis. Milton Keynes: Open University.

Sage R (1998) The Sage Assessment of Language and Thinking. Trial copies available from HCI, 47 West End, West Haddon, Northampton, NN6 7AY.

Salmon P (1995) Psychology in the Classroom. London: Cassell Educational.

Salter R, Smythe I (1997) The International Book of Dyslexia. London: World Dyslexic Network Foundation.

Sassoon R (1995) The Acquisition of a Second Writing System. Oxford: Intellect Ltd.

Schwab I, Stone J (1986) Language, Writing and Publishing. London: Inner London Education Authority.

Scribner S, Cole M (1981) The Psychology of Literacy. Cambridge, MA: Harvard University Press.

Semel E, Wiig E, Secord W (1987) The Clinical Evaluation of Language Fundamentals (CELF). San Antonio, TX: The Psychological Corporation.

Share DL, Silva PA (1986) The stability and classification of specific reading retardation; a longitudinal study from age 7 to 11. British Journal of Educational Psychology 56: 32–39.

Sharp P (2000) Nurturing Emotional Literacy: A Practical Guide for Teachers, Parents and those in the Caring Professions. London: David Fulton.

Siegel LS (1992) An evaluation of the discrepancy definition of dyslexia. Journal of Learning Disabilities 25: 618–629.

Siegler RS (1991) Strategy choice and strategy discovery. Learning & Instruction 1: 89–102.

Singleton C (1994) Computers and Dyslexia. Hull: University of Hull.

Singleton C (1996) Dyslexia in higher education: policy, provision and practice. In: Dyslexia in Higher Education, Learning Along the Continuum. 2nd International Conference. Conference Proceedings. University of Plymouth; 9–17.

Singleton C (1999a) Dyslexia in Higher Education: Policy, Provision and Practice. Hull: University of Hull.

Singleton C (1999b) Dyslexia in Higher Education. Report of the National Working Party on Dyslexia in Higher Education. Hull: Department of Psychology, University of Hull.

Smith B (1994) Teaching Spelling. Widnes: United Kingdom Reading Association Minibook 5.

Smith D (1996a) Special Educational Needs Co-ordinators. Stoke-on-Trent: NASEN.

Smith D (1996b) Spotlight on Special Educational Needs: Specific Learning Difficulties. Stoke-on-Trent: NASEN.

Smith T (1991) Communicating Quality: Professional Standards for Speech and Language Therapists. Canterbury: The College of Speech and Language Therapists.

Snowling M (1990) Dyslexia. A Cognitive Developmental Perspective. Worcester: Billing & Son Ltd.

Snowling M (1995) Phonological processing and developmental dyslexia. Journal of Research in Reading. 18: 32–38.

Snowling MJ (2000) Dyslexia (second edition). Oxford, Blackwell.

Snowling M, Stackhouse J (1996) Dyslexia, Speech and Language: A Practitioner's Handbook. London: Whurr Publishers.

Snowling MJ, Goulandris N, Defty N (1996) A longitudinal study of reading development in dyslexic children. Journal of Educational Psychology 88: 653–669.

Snowling M, Nation K, Moxham P, Gallagher A, Frith U (1997). Phonological processing skills of dyslexic students in higher education: a preliminary report. Journal of Research in Reading 20: 31–41.

Somerfield S (c.1993) Dyslexia from the Student's Point of View. Extracts from 'A Personal View of Dyslexia'. Loughborough University Dyslexia Workshop paper, circulated to UK midlands universities during 1993–1994.

Sovik N, Frostag P, Lia A (1994) Discrepancies between IQ and basic skills. British Journal of Educational Psychology 64: 389–405.

Speckman NJ, Goldberg RJ, Herman KL (1992) Learning disabled children grow up: a search for factors related to success in the young adult years. Learning Disabilities Research and Practice 7: 161–170.

Springer SP, Deutsch G (1993) Left Brain, Right Brain. New York: Freeman and Co.

Stacey G (1996). Organising thoughts to improve study skills. In: C Stephens (ed.). Dyslexic Students in Higher Education. Practical Responses to Student and Institutional Needs. Conference Proceedings. SKILL/University of Huddersfield; 51–54.

Stacey G (1997) A dyslexic mind a-thinking. Dyslexia, Journal of the British Dyslexia Association 3: 112–119.

Stackhouse J, Wells B (1997) Children's Speech and Literacy Difficulties: Psycholinguistic Framework. London: Whurr Publishers.

Stanovich KE (1989) Explaining the differences between the dyslexic and the garden-variety poor reader: the phonological-core variable-difference model. Journal of Learning Disabilities 21: 590–612.

Stanovich KE (1991) Discrepancy definitions of reading disability: has intelligence led us astray? Reading Research Quarterly 26: 7–29.

Stanovich KE (1996) Towards a more inclusive definition of dyslexia. Dyslexia 2: 179–189.

Stanovich KE, West RF (1989) Exposure to print and orthographic processing. Reading Research Quarterly 24: 402–433.

Stanovich KE, Nathan RG, Zolman JE (1989) The developmental lag hypothesis in reading: longitudinal and matched reading-level comparisons. Child Development 59: 71–86.

Steffert B (1996) Sign minds and design minds: the trade-off between visual spatial skills and linguistic skills. In: Dyslexia in Higher Education, Learning Along the Continuum. 2nd International Conference. Conference Proceedings. University of Plymouth; 53–69.

Stephens C (1996) Developing awareness of learning with individual students. In C Stephens (ed.). Dyslexic Students in Higher Education. Practical Responses to Student and Individual Needs. Conference Proceedings. SKILL/University of Huddersfield; 46–50.

Street BV (1984) Literacy in Theory and Practice. Cambridge: Cambridge University Press.

Street BV (1997) Adult literacy in the United Kingdom. A history of research and practice. University of Lancaster: RAPAL; 180.

Swanson HL (1994) The role of working memory and dynamic assessment in classification of children with learning disabilities. Learning Disabilities Research and Practice 9: 190–202.

Teacher Training Agency (1997) Career Entry Profile for Newly Qualified Teachers: Standards for the Award of Qualified Teacher Status. London: TTA.

Teacher Training Agency (1999) National Special Educational Needs Specialist Standards. London: TTA.

Thomas G (1992) Effective Classroom Teamwork: Support or Intrusion? London: Routledge.

Thomas J (1996) Dyslexic-linearlexic. In: P Thomson, P Gilchrist (eds). Dyslexia in Higher Education, Learning Along the Continuum. 2nd International Conference. Conference Proceedings. University of Plymouth; 42–45.

Thomas WP, Collier V (1997) School Effectiveness for Language Minority Students. Washington DC: National Clearinghouse for Bilingual Education.

Topping K (1987) Peer-tutored paired reading: outcome data from ten projects. Education Psychology 7: 133–135.

Topping K (1992) Cued Spelling Training Tape. Kirklees Metropolitan Council.

Topping K (1995) Peer-assisted learning: mentoring and tutoring. Reading 3: 30–38.

Topping K (1996) Parents and peers as tutors for dyslexic children. In: G Reid (ed.). Dimensions of Dyslexia Vol. 2. Literacy, Language and Learning. Edinburgh: Moray House Publications; 63–76.

Tuckett A (1979) Literacy in the community. Adult Literacy Unit Newsletter 7.

Turner M (1997) Psychological Assessment of Dyslexia. London: Whurr Publishers.

Tzuriel D (undated) Children's Inferential Thinking Cognitive Modifiability Test. Israel: Bar Ilan University.

Verhoeven LT (1990) Acquisition of reading in a second language. Reading Research Quarterly 25: 90–114.

Vincent D, Claydon J (1992) Diagnostic Spelling Test. Slough: NFER-Nelson.

Vincent D, Crumpler M (1997) British Spelling Tests. Slough: NFER-Nelson.

Vinegrad M (1994) Dyslexia at College: A Practical Study. Educare. London: SKILL.

Visser J (1995) Differentiation: Making it Work: Ideas for Staff Development. Stafford: National Association for Special Education Needs (NASEN).

Vogler GP, De Frees JC, Decker SN (1985) Family history as an indicator of risk for reading disability. Journal of Learning Disabilities 18: 419–421.

Vygotsky LS (1978) Interaction between learning and development. In M Cole, V John-Steiner, S Scribner, E Souberman (eds). Mind in Society: The Development of Higher Psychological Processes. Cambridge, MA: Harvard University Press; 79–91.

Walker ME (1994) Tuition for Adults with Specific Learning Difficulties. Unpublished thesis, Leicester University.

Walker ME (2000) A Resource Pack for Tutors of Students with Specific Learning Difficulties (fifth edition). Details from (01564) 779092.

Wallach GP, Liebergott JW (1984) Who shall be called 'learning disabled'?: some new directions. In GP Wallach, KG Butler (eds). Language Learning Disabilities in School-age Children. Baltimore, MD: Williams & Wilkins.

Wallach GP, Miller L (1989) Language Intervention and Academic Success. Boston: College Hill Press.

Walmsley J (1995) Life history interviews with people with learning disabilities, Oral History, Health and Welfare: 71.

Warin S (1995) Implementing the Code of Practice: Individual Educational Plans. Tamworth: NASEN.

Warwick C (1999) A partnership approach. Dyslexia Contact 18: 8–10.

Watkins G (1996) A Teacher's Guide to Prompt Spelling: Using the Franklin Electronic Spellmaster. Sunbury: Franklin Electronics.

Watkins G (1997) Prompt Spelling: An Approach to Teaching and Learning Spelling at Secondary School Level. Unpublished PhD thesis. University of Leicester.

Watkins G, Hunter-Carsch M (1995) Prompt spelling: a practical approach to paired spelling. NASEN Support for Learning 10: 133–138.

Webster W (1996) Some keys to understanding stuttering management. The British Stammering Association 17.

Wechsler D (1992) Wechsler Intelligence Scale for Children. Third Edition UK. New York: Psychological Corporation.

Wechsler D (1993) Objective Reading Dimensions. London: Psychological Corporation.

Wechsler D (1996) Wechsler Intelligence Scale for Children. Third Edition UK (WISC-III UK). London: The Psychological Corporation.

Wedell K (1982) Children with Perceptuo-Motor Difficulties. Cambridge: Cambridge University Press.

Weizenbaum J (1984) Computer Power and Human Reason. London: Pelican.

West T (1991) In the Mind's Eye. Visual Thinkers. Gifted People with Learning Difficulties. Computer Images and the Ironies of Creativity. New York: Prometheus.

Williams LV (1986) Teaching for the Two-Sided Mind. New York: Simon and Schuster.

Wilsher C (1986) Characteristics of successful dyslexics. In T Miles, D Gilroy (eds). Dyslexia at College. London: Methuen; 109–112.

Wolfendale S, Corbett J (eds) (1996) Opening Doors. Learning Support in Higher Education. London: Cassell.

Wray D (1995) The Excell Project. Exeter University.

Wright A (1991) The assessment of bilingual pupils with reported learning difficulties. In T Cline, N Frederickson (eds). Bilingual Pupils and the National Curriculum. London: University College.

Wright J, Jacobs M (1995) Unpublished paper presented at the School of Education, University of Leicester at a 'Sharing Good Practice' day conference for teachers.

Wright SF, Field H, Newman SP (1996) Dyslexia: stability of definition over a five-year period. Journal of Research in Reading 19: 46–60.

Wydell TN, Butterworth B (1997) The case of AS: Dyslexia in an English–Japanese Bilingual. Paper delivered at the International Symposium on Bilingualism, Newcastle upon Tyne, 9–12 April.

Zdzienski D (1994) The interaction between SpLD and NLP techniques. An evaluation of the role of neuro-linguistic programming in the field of specific learning difficulties and education. NLP World 1: 45–66.

Zdzienski D (1997) QuickScan and StudyScan: Diagnostic Computer Assessments for Students in Higher and Further Education. Dublin: Interactive Services Ltd.

Zdzienski D (1998) Dyslexia and Higher Education: An Exploratory Study of Learning Support, Screening and Diagnostic Assessment. Unpublished PhD Thesis, Leicester University.

Zdzienski D (in press) Dyslexia in Higher Education: A Tutor's Handbook. London: Whurr Publishers.

Index